AA TOW PLANS

D1649866

Cover photographs reproduced by courtesy of the British Tourist Authority, Bath City Council (Department of Leisure and Tourist Services) and K S Reynolds, Sally Lunn's House, Bath.

Editor: *Gail Harada*   Designer: *Gill Hiley*   Assisted by: *Susan Davies*

Compiled by the Publications Research Unit

Town Plans produced by the Cartographic Unit of the Automobile Association and based upon Ordnance Survey maps with the sanction of the controller of HM Stationery Office. Crown copyright reserved.

Every effort has been made to ensure that the plans, including one-way systems, were up to date at the time of going to press. Recent changes may not have been included however: keep a careful watch for signs.

Printed by: *Chorley & Pickersgill Ltd*

ISBN 0 09 128191 1   55288

WHEREVER YOU WIND UP, THERES'S A CREST HOTEL TO WIND YOU DOWN!

It's reassuring to know that whichever strange town you wind up in, chances are there's the friendly, familiar atmosphere of a Crest Hotel, Motel or Esso* Hotel nearby. A place where you can unwind after a tiring journey. Well stocked bars where you can relax before a well-earned meal in a good restaurant. A room with private bath, TV and comfortable bed where you can re-charge your batteries, during a long uninterrupted night's sleep.

Then we'll wake you up, give you an English breakfast and send you on your way refreshed next morning.

Crest Hotels, Motels and Esso Hotels. Great places to unwind.

Aberystwyth	Belle Vue Royal Hotel
Birmingham	Plough and Harrow Hotel
Blackpool	Carlton Hotel
Bristol	Bristol Esso Hotel
Coventry	Coventry Crest Motel
Coventry	Coventry Esso Hotel
Durham	Durham Crest Motel
Edinburgh	Edinburgh Esso Hotel
Exeter	Buckerell Lodge Hotel
Exeter	Exeter Crest Motel
Glasgow (Erskine)	Glasgow Esso Hotel
Hull	Hull Crest Motel
Leeds	Leeds Crest Motel
Liverpool	Liverpool Crest Motel
London (Wembley)	London Esso Hotel
Middlesbrough	Middlesbrough Crest Motel
Newcastle upon Tyne (Tynemouth)	Grand Hotel
Swansea (Mumbles)	Mermaid Hotel

But let us know before you arrive. Phone one of our Reservations Centres.

RESERVATIONS:

MIDLANDS (0203) 613261 LONDON (01) 903 6422

Crest Hotels Europe

Hotels and Motels across Austria, Belgium, France, Germany, Holland, Italy & United Kingdom.

* Crest Hotels are the authorised licensee of Esso Hotel marks and names.

CONTENTS

LEGEND

Plans

AA Recommended route	
Other roads	
Restricted roads (Access only/ Buses only)	
Traffic roundabout	
One-way street	
Parking zone	
Official car park (open air)	P
Parking available on payment (open air)	P
Multi-storey car park	G
Convenience	C
Convenience with facilities for the disabled	C
Tourist Information Centre	i
Pedestrians only	
Shopping area	
Parks and open spaces	
AA Service Centre	AA
AA Road Service Centre	AA 83
Church/Cathedral	+ ✝
City Walls	
Post Office	HPO/GPO/PO
Public buildings and places of interest	
Grid square letter	L
Map continuation	

The following symbols relate to advertisers:

Text

Reference to the grid square and public buildings and places of interest is shown as a letter and number respectively. The letter comes first with the number following, in brackets.

Ancient Monument	(AM)
National Trust	(NT)
National Trust for Scotland	(NTS)

Trust Houses Forte says welcome all over England

In most parts of England you are within 20 miles of a Trust Houses Forte Hotel. In fact, wherever you go you are never more than 60 miles away from one.

Trust Houses Forte says Welcome at nearly 200 hotels in England — quiet country inns, city centre hotels, modern Post Houses and TraveLodges, famous London hotels and hotels in seaside resorts. Wherever you go you will find a Trust Houses Forte Hotel.

Each is different in character but all offer excellent value and ensure that you are well looked after from the moment you arrive. Take your holiday in England at a Trust Houses Forte hotel — you are very welcome.

QUEEN'S HOTEL CHELTENHAM

GEORGE HOTEL CRAWLEY

SWAN HOTEL GRASMERE

Free Map
To help you choose the hotel that's just right for your holiday ask for the Trust Houses Forte Map and Tariff. It is available free from any Trust Houses Forte Hotel or Reservations Office.

Hotel Reservations:
For Hotel Reservations and any further information contact :—

Trust Houses Forte Reservations Office (A.A.T.G.),
71/75 Uxbridge Road, London, W5 5SL.

Trust Houses Forte Reservations Office (A.A.T.G.),
Nelson House, Park Road, Timperley, Cheshire.

LONDON 01-567 3444	**LEEDS** (STD 0532) 31261
MANCHESTER 061-969 6111	**LIVERPOOL** 051-236 0841
BIRMINGHAM 021-236 3951	**EDINBURGH** 031-226 4346
GLASGOW 041-221 6164	**DURHAM** (STD 0385) 62561

thf Hotels

Save money
with an AA members
personal loan

Specially arranged terms mean that, as an AA Member you can obtain a personal loan at a reduced rate of interest. And that means lower monthly instalments to pay. For full details fill in this coupon, cut out the complete page, then fold and post as shown overleaf. You don't need to find an envelope or a stamp.

P.T.O. for posting instructions

Please send AA Members Personal Loan details, current rate card, and application form to:-

Name_____

Address_____

_____

County_____ Postcode _____

IVI Mercantile Credit

AA

Post now for the best route to a personal loan

(Remember to fill in the coupon overleaf first)

3. Fold here and tuck in.

NO
STAMP
REQUIRED

Mercantile Credit Co. Ltd.,
Marketing Administration,
FREEPOST,
London WC2B 5XA.

2. Fold here.

No stamp needed to get details of AA members loans

The only loan plan approved by the AA.

How to post

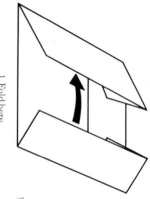

1. Fold here.

1. For full details of AA Members Loans complete coupon overleaf.

2. Detach complete page.

3. Fold and tuck in as indicated, and post. No stamp needed.

CENTRE HOTELS

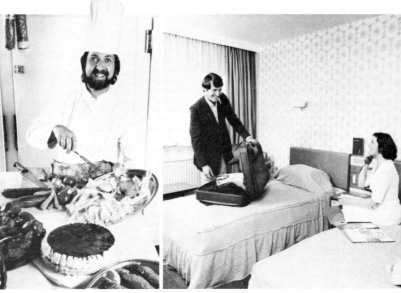

Where you get more comfort for less money

When you go to an hotel you want to be comfortable—but you don't want to spend a fortune. Step into a Centre Hotel, and you can <u>feel</u> the comfort.

Now look at the price! For as little as

£8.25 a night, plus VAT

you can have a single room with bath/shower, continental breakfast and service. **No hidden extras!** Drinks in the Bars and Meals in the Restaurant are at equally comfortable prices—and in most Centre Hotel bedrooms you will find radio, TV, electric alarm clock, dial heating, auto-dial telephone—and out of London—a Tea and Coffee Maker; and the Centre Staff are trained to make your stay a delight! All Centre Hotels are run to the same high standard of comfort, and all offer really execptional value for money. See your Travel Agent, or contact the address below.
You know where you are at a Centre Hotel.

CENTRE HOTELS, Centre Supranational Reservations, 101 Great Russell Street, London WC1B 3LH. Tel: 01-637 1661. Telex: 2636561.

Hotels in London (7), Heathrow, Basildon, Birmingham, Cardiff, Dundee (2), Edinburgh, Glasgow, Hull, Leicester, Liverpool, Newcastle, Portsmouth, York. Amsterdam, Netherlands (4). Centrelink Hotels in Birmingham, Bournemouth, Brighton, Cambridge, Carlisle, Newtown, Peebles, Torquay, plus Supranational and Hotel Management International Hotels throughout the world.

ABERDEEN

CENTRAL PLAN

F   **AA Service Centre** — Fanum House, 19 Golden Square *tel 51231*

G [*i*]   **Tourist Information Centre** — City Tourist Bureau, St Nicholas House, Broad Street *tel 23456* Monday to Friday; *24890/ 21814/21810* Saturdays and Bank Holidays

Public buildings and places of interest

G(1)   **Art Gallery and Museum, John Dun's House, War Memorial and Cowdray Hall** The Art Gallery contains works of art of the Scottish school from the 16thC to the present day, the French Impressionists and post-Impressionists and the Modern English school; sculpture; lithography; and the decorative arts. The Museum covers the maritime history of the Aberdeen region. John Dun's House is an 18th-C building now used as a museum for children.

H(2)   **Civic Arts Centre**

G(3)   **East and West Churches of St Nicholas** These churches were divided into their separate parts at the Reformation. Notable features include the tapestries by Mary Jamesone, daughter of the Scottish artist George Jamesone, St Mary's Chapel (15th-C) and the fine Gothic roof.

L(4)   **Fish Market** Guided tours are available.

G(5)   **Gordon's College** Founded in 1739 by Robert Gordon.

F(6)   **Grampian Regional Offices**

L(7)   **Harbour Offices**

F(8)   **Library**

G(9)   **Marischal College** Founded in 1593 and since 1860 part of the University of Aberdeen. The building has an impressive frontage of white Kemnay granite of 1906, and houses the University's Anthropological Museum.

H(10)   **Mercat Cross** Dating from 1668, with relief portraits of Scottish kings.

G(11)   **Municipal Buildings** City of Aberdeen District Council.

J(12)   **Music Hall** Two adjoining halls built in the 19thC in Classic style.

H(13)   **Provost Ross's House (NTS)** Built in 1593, it is Aberdeen's third oldest house.

G(14)   **Provost Skene's House** A 17th-C house restored as a museum of local history and social life.

E(15)   **Rubislaw Academy (Grammar School) and Byron Statue**

H(16)   **St Andrew's Episcopal Cathedral** Built in 1816 and elevated to Cathedral status in 1914, it is the mother church of the Episcopal Communion in America.

J(17)   **St Mary of the Assumption Cathedral (RC)** Built in 1860 and raised to Cathedral status in 1878.

H(18)   **Tolbooth** The tower and spire remain of the 14th-C tolbooth, outside which public executions took place until 1857.

H(19)   **Town House** A medieval Gothic building of 1868-74 with a fine collection of portraits in the Council Chamber.

G(20)   **Union Bridge** One of the widest single-span granite arches in Britain.

Hospitals

F   **Aberdeen Royal Infirmary** (Out-patients Department), Woolmahill *tel 23423*

M   **Fonthill Maternity Home,** 62 Fonthill Road *tel 23423*

E   **Queen's Cross Maternity Home,** 70 Carden Place *tel 23423*

Sport and Recreation

C   **ABC Tenpin Bowling Alley,** George Street

I   **Bon Accord Swimming Pool,** Justice Mill Lane

C   **Ice Rink,** Spring Garden

Theatres and Cinemas

H   **ABC Cinema,** Shiprow *tel 51477*

J   **Capitol Cinema,** 431 Union Street *tel 23141*

F   **Cosmo 2,** Diamond Street *tel 24620*

C   **Grand Central Picture House,** 286 George Street *tel 22826*

F   **His Majesty's Theatre,** Rosemount Viaduct *tel 28080*

I   **Odeon Cinema,** Justice Mill Lane *tel 26050*

G   **Queen's Cinema,** 120 Union Street *tel 23688*

Department Stores

Arnotts, 143 George Street
Co-operative (Northern), 88-154 George Street
Esslemont and MacIntosh Ltd, 30 Union Street
Falconers, 65 Union Street
Lawson's Ltd, 190 George Street
Marks and Spencer Ltd, 68 Netherkirkgate
Talbots Ltd, 32 Market Street
Early closing day Wednesday or Saturday

Markets

L(4)   **Fish Market** (see also public buildings and places of interest)

G   **Green Market,** Market Street (Open-air) (Friday)

H   **Justice Market,** Castle Street (Open-air) (Friday)

Advertisers

M   **Mercantile Credit**

J   **Godfrey Davis**

Provost Ross's House

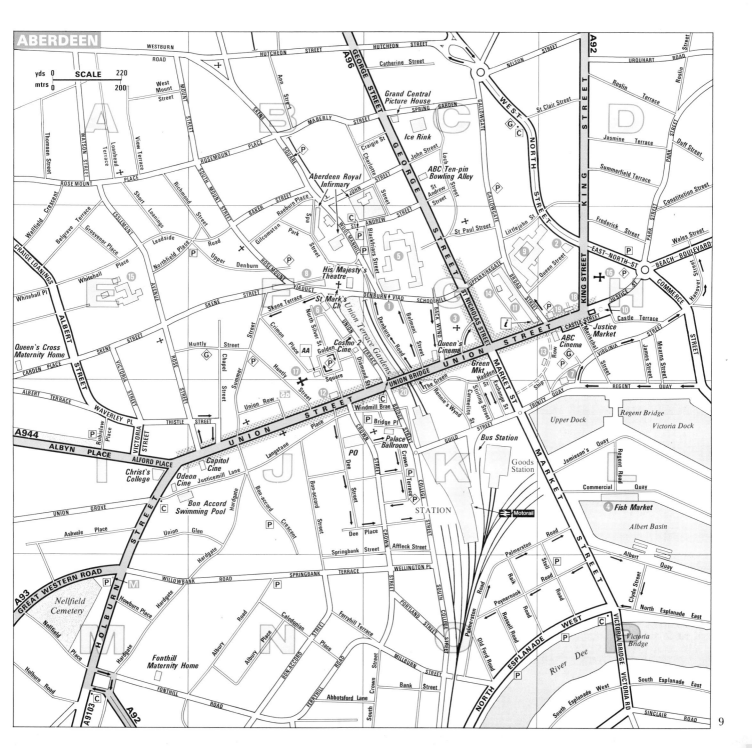

DISTRICT PLAN
Public buildings and places of interest

B(21) **Auld Brig o'Don** Also known as the Bridge of Balgownie, this single-span Gothic bridge, with great buttresses and pointed arch, dates back to the 14thC.

H(22) **Bridge of Dee** A notable seven-arched structure of 1520-27.

B(23) **Cruikshank Botanical Gardens**

F(24) **Girdleness Lighthouse** Dating from 1833, this lighthouse is approximately 150ft high

D(25) **Gordon Highlanders Regimental Museum** Medals, uniforms etc.

B(26) **King's College** Founded in 1494, and part of the University since it was created in 1860. It is the oldest school of medicine in Great Britain. The chapel, with a rare 'crown' spire, and the library of 1885 are particularly notable.

B(27) **St Machar's Cathedral** The present structure, which dates from 1357, is a fine example of a fortified church. Features include a beautiful 16th-C heraldic ceiling, ancient records, 15th-C effigies and modern stained glass.

B(28) **Wallace Tower** A fine example of a Scottish Z-plan tower, built in 1616, and resited following a city centre redevelopment scheme.

Hazlehead Park Contains zoo with large collection of British indigenous animals; free-flying aviary and walk-through parrot house; maze and three golf courses. (D)

Hospitals

D **Aberdeen Royal Infirmary,** Forresterhill *tel 23423*

F **City Hospital,** Urquhart Road *tel 22242*

D **Morningfield Hospital,** King's Gate *tel 23423*

D **Royal Aberdeen Children's Hospital,** Cornhill Road *tel 23423*

E **Royal Cornhill Hospital,** 26 Cornhill Road *tel 52411*

D **Summerfield Maternity Hospital,***tel 23423*

Auld Brig o'Don

Sport and Recreation

B	**Aberdeen Football Club,** Pittodrie Park	C	**Royal Balgownie Golf Course,** Bridge of Don
G	**Aberdeenshire Cricket Club,** Mannofield		
F	**Balnagask Golf Course**	B	**Sports Stadium,** Linksfield Road
D	**Hazlehead Park Golf Courses**	C	**The Links Golf Course**

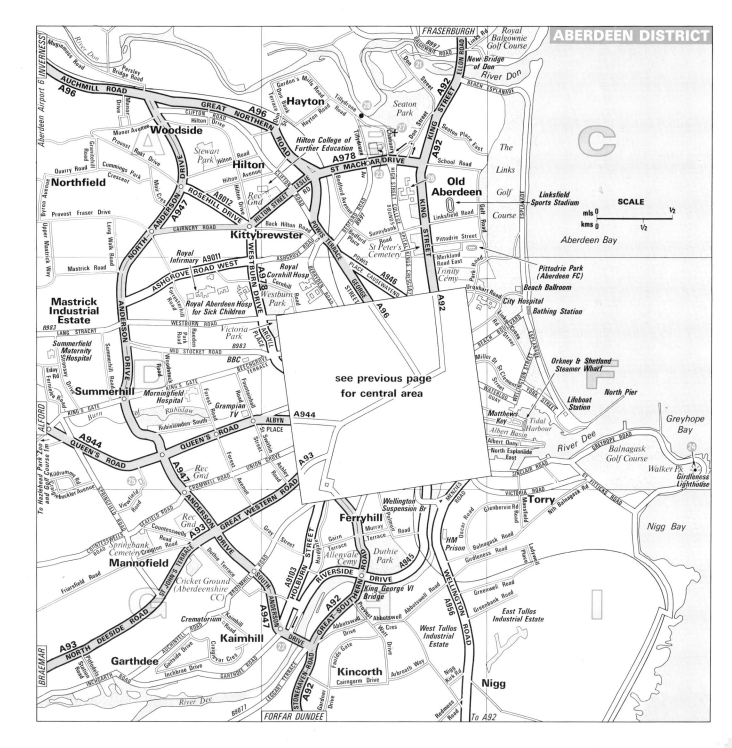

ABERDEEN DISTRICT

ABERYSTWYTH

J   **AA Road Service Centre** (2) Park Avenue *tel 4801*

F   **Tourist Information Centre** — Promenade *tel 7111 (Whitsun to September)*

J(3)   **Information Bureau** — Ceredigion District *i*   Council Entertainment and Tourism Department, Park Avenue *tel 7911* (open all year except weekends)

Public buildings and places of interest

I(1)   **Castle** Remains of 12th- to 13th-C Castle on the promontory.

I(2)   **Ceredigion Museum** A museum illustrating aspects of life and history in the district of Ceredigion (formerly the county of Cardigan).

J(3)   **Information Bureau**

L(4)   **National Library of Wales** Founded by Royal Charter in 1907, the Library is a national storehouse of printed, manuscript and graphic material relating to Wales. It is one of Britain's six copyright libraries. The library is open to any responsible person who obtains a reader's ticket.

F(5)   **Town Hall**

I(6)   **University College of Wales** Established in 1872, the original building is scheduled as a building of historic and architectural interest and is open to members of the public. The new campus is located on the south side of the A487 Machynlleth Road adjacent to the National Library. The campus also houses the Arts Centre which consists of the Great Hall, an art gallery and the Theatre y Werin. The complex is open to the public for most of the year and presents a wide range of concerts, exhibitions and theatrical performances.

J(7)   **Vale of Rheidol Railway** This famous narrow-gauge railway, British Rail's only steam-operated line, climbs to 680ft in the course of its 12-mile route to Devil's Bridge along the very attractive Rheidol Valley.

Hospitals

H   **Bronglais General Hospital** *tel 3131*

Sport and Recreation

I   **Castle Grounds** — crazy golf and putting green

F   **Queens Road Recreation Ground** — putting green, bowling green and tennis courts

C   **Aberystwyth Golf Club,** Bryn-y-mor Road

N   **Aberystwyth Football Ground,** off Park Avenue

P   **Plas Crug Avenue** — indoor swimming pool

Theatres and Cinemas

F   **Commodore Cinema and Conference Centre** *tel 2421*

F   **Coliseum Theatre,** Terrace Road *tel 2226*

F   **Kings Hall,** Marine Terrace *tel 7911*

H   **Theatre y Werin,** University Campus, Penglais *tel 4277*

Shopping

Early closing day Wednesday

Markets

J   **Cattle Market,** Park Avenue (Monday)

Advertisers

F   **Crest** Belle Vue Royal Hotel

Castle ruins

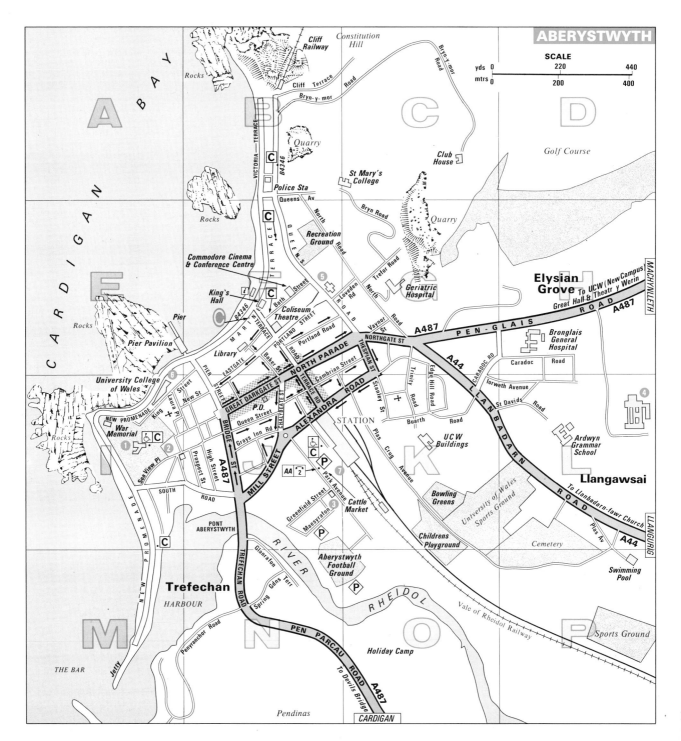

ABERYSTWYTH

SCALE
yds 0 ... 220 ... 440
mtrs 0 ... 200 ... 400

CARDIGAN BAY

Constitution Hill

Cliff Railway

Cliff Terrace

Bryn-y-mor Road

Rocks

Quarry

Golf Course

Club House

St Mary's College

Bryn Road

Quarry

VICTORIA TERRACE

B4346

Police Sta

Queens Av

North Road

Recreation Ground

Trefor Road

Elysian Grove

To UCW (New Campus) Great Hall & Theatr y Werin

MACHYNLLETH

A487

Commodore Cinema & Conference Centre

King's Hall

Loveden Rd

Geriatric Hospital

PEN-GLAIS ROAD

A487

Bronglais General Hospital

Caradoc Road

CARADOC RD

Coliseum Theatre

Bath Street

PORTLAND STREET

Portland Road

Vaynor St

NORTHGATE ST

A44

Torweth Avenue

St Davids Road

Edge Hill Road

Pier

Library

EASTGATE

Baker St

Road

NORTH PARADE

TERRACE RD

Cambrian Street

THESPIAN ST

Stanley St

Trinity Road

Buarth Road

Pier Pavilion

PIER STREET

GREAT DARKGATE ST

P.O.

Queen Street

CHALYBEATE ST

Grays Inn Rd

ALEXANDRA ROAD

STATION

Plas Crug Avenue

University College of Wales

Street

New St

King Street

Laura Pl

NEW PROMENADE

War Memorial

Sea View Pl

High Street

Prospect St

MILL STREET

BRIDGE ST

A487

Park Avenue

AA 2

Cattle Market

UCW Buildings

Rocks

SOUTH ROAD

PONT ABERYSTWYTH

Greenfield Street

Maesyrafon

Bowling Greens

University of Wales Sports Ground

Ardwyn Grammar School

Llangawsai

To Llanbadarn-fawr Church

LLANBADARN ROAD

A44

LLANGURIG

Aberystwyth Football Ground

Childrens Playground

Cemetery

Plas Av

Swimming Pool

Trefechan

HARBOUR

RIVER RHEIDOL

Glanrafon Terr

Spring Gdns Terr

TREFECHAN ROAD

Penyranchor Road

Jetty

THE BAR

PEN PARCAU ROAD

A487

To Devils Bridge

Holiday Camp

Vale of Rheidol Railway

Sports Ground

Pendinas

CARDIGAN

13

AYR

CENTRAL PLAN

J **i**   **Tourist Information Centre** — 30 Miller Road *tel 68077*

Public buildings and places of interest

F(1)   **Academy** Founded in the 13thC, and now occupying a striking building.

F(2)   **Auld Brig** Probably 13th-C, and for 500 years the only bridge over the river at Ayr, it was renovated in 1910. Burns' poem *The Twa Brigs* refers to it.

J(3)   **Auld Kirk** Erected in 1655 after Cromwell despoiled the Kirk of St John. The churchyard contains a tombstone commemorating the Covenanting Martyrs.

N(4)   **Burns Statue** By Lawson in 1891.

F(5)   **Carnegie Library, Museum and Art Gallery** Local history and monthly changing art exhibitions.

I(6)   **Strathclyde Regional Offices, Ayr Division** On the site of the old county prison.

F(7)   **Loudoun Hall** Restored house of c1500, now the oldest building in the town.

J(8)   **McAdam's Monument** Erected 1936 in memory of the inventor of the 'Macadam' road-making process, who was born nearby.

F(9)   **St John's Tower** This 13th-C tower, a splendid viewpoint, was part of the 12th-C Kirk of St John absorbed by Cromwell's Citadel, of which remains of the walls can be seen nearby.

J(10)   **Tam o'Shanter Inn** This thatched inn associated with Burns' poem, is now a museum of Burns' relics.

K(11)   **Technical College**

F(12)   **Town Buildings** Including the Town Hall and featuring a fine steeple.

J(13)   **Wallace Tower** 113ft-high, built in 1832 with a small statue of Sir William Wallace in a niche halfway up.

Hospitals

O   **Ayr County Hospital,** Holmston Road *tel 66991*

Sport and Recreation

E   **Ayr Baths,** South Beach Road

H   **Ayr Racecourse**

C   **Ayr United Football and Athletic Club,** Somerset Park

P   **Indoor Bowling Green,** off Holmston Road

Theatres and Cinemas

K   **Civic Theatre,** Craigie Road *tel 63755*

J   **Gaiety Theatre,** Carrick Street *tel 64639*

N   **Odeon Cinema,** Burns Statue Square *tel 64049*

F   **Orient Cinema,** Main Street *tel 63419*

Department Stores

Arnotts, 39 Alloway Street

Marks and Spencer Ltd, High Street

Wilsons of Ayr, 62 Alloway Street

Early closing day Wednesday

Markets

O   **Cattle Market** (Tuesday)

Advertisers

F   **Mercantile Credit**

Auld Brig

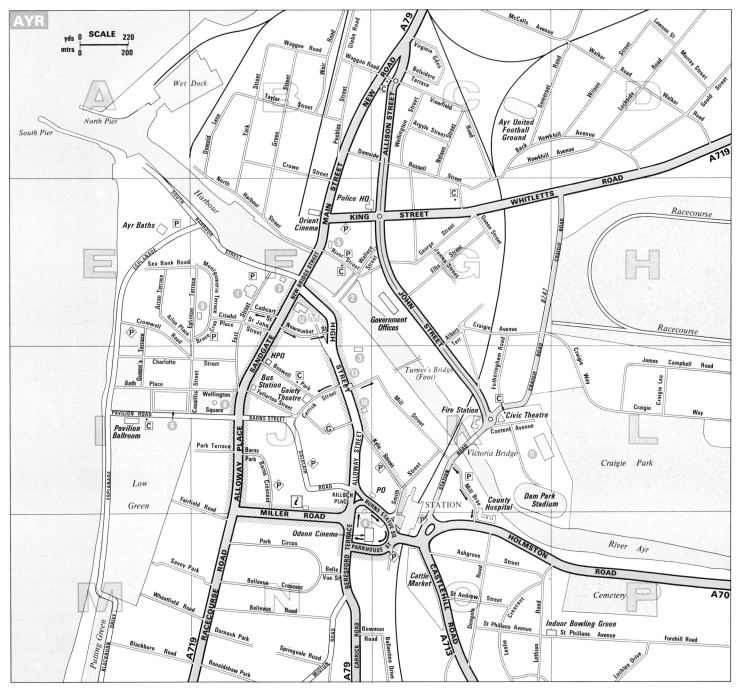

AYR

SCALE
yds 0   220
mtrs 0   200

Wet Dock

North Pier

South Pier

Harbour

McCalls   Avenue

Lawson St

Waggon   Road

Glebe Road

Waggon Road

Walker   Street

Murray Street

Gould   Street

Virginia Gdns

Belvidere
Terrace

Viewfield

Wilson   Street

Lochside   Road

Walker   Road

Somerset   Road

Argyle Street

Ayr United
Football
Ground

Back   Hawkhill   Avenue

Hawkhill   Avenue

A719

Wellington

Russell

Nelson   Street

Street

A719

Oswald   Lane

York   Street

Taylor   Street

Green   Street

Peebles   Street

Crown   Street

North   Harbour   Street

Damside

Police HQ

King   Street

Whitletts   Road

Racecourse

Racecourse

Ayr Baths

P

Esplanade

Sea Bank Road

Montgomerie Terrace

Arran Terrace

Eglinton   Terrace

Citadel   Place

Orient
Cinema

River   Street

Wallace   Street

George   Street

Queen   Street

James   Street

Elba   Street

B7471

Craigie   Road

H

1

7

9

Cathcart   St

St John   Street

Bruce   Cres

Furt   Street

2

Government
Offices

Craigie

Albert
Terr

Avenve

Fotheringham Road

Craigie   Way

James   Campbell   Road

Craigie Lea

Craigie

Craigie   Way

Cromwell   Terrace

Queen's   Terrace

Charlotte   Street

Bath   Place

P

12

M

Newmarket   St

HPO

Boswell   Park

Bus
Station

Gaiety
Theatre

Fullarton Street

Cassillis

Wellington   Square

8

High   Street

3

13

Carrick   Street

10

Turner's Bridge
(Foot)

Mill   Street

John   Street

Fire Station

Civic Theatre

Content   Avenue

Craigie   Park

Pavilion Road

C

6

Pavilion
Ballroom

Barns   Street

Park Terrace

Low
Green

Esplanade

Park   Barns

Barns   Crescent

Dalblair   Road

G

P

P

Alloway   Street

Kyle   Street

Mill   Street

Victoria Bridge

11

Fairfield Road

Miller   Road

i

Killoch
Place

PO

Burns Statue Sq

Smith   Street

Station   Road

STATION

Mill Brae

P

County
Hospital

Dam Park
Stadium

Racecourse   Road

Savoy Park

Wheatfield   Road

Blackburn   Road

Dornoch Park

Ronaldshaw Park

A79

Park   Circus

Belle   Vue   Crescent

Bellevue   Crescent

Bellevue   Road

Springvale   Road

Beresford   Terrace

Parkhouse   St

4

Odeon Cinema

Bowman   Road

Ballantine Drive

Carrick   Road

Midton   Road

A79

A713

Castlehill   Road

Cattle
Market

St Andrew   Street

Ashgrove   Street

Dongola   Road

St Phillans Avenue

Leslie   Crescent

Lothian

Holmston   Road

River Ayr

Cemetery

A70

Indoor Bowling Green

St Phillans Avenue

Forehill Road

Lochlea Drive

Putting Green

Blackburn   Drive

DISTRICT PLAN

D **AA Road Service Centre (78)** — On the Ayr bypass, ½m S of junction A77/A719 *tel 77789*

Public buildings and places of interest

E(14) **Alloway Auld Kirk (Ruins)** It was here that Tam o'Shanter was reputed to have witnessed the witches' orgy described so vividly by Burns in his poem, *Tam o'Shanter.* In the churchyard is the grave of Burns' father.

E(15) **Auld Brig o'Doon** A single-arched bridge, dating probably from the 13thC, which is referred to in Burns' poem *Tam o'Shanter.*

E(16) **Burns' Cottage** Birthplace of the poet in 1759, with a museum of Burns' relics adjoining.

E(17) **Burns Monument** Built 1823 to a design of Thomas Hamilton Junior, it contains a number of Burns' relics including bibles belonging to Burns and his 'Highland Mary'.

E **Belleisle Estate** 220 acres of parkland, with beautiful gardens, an aviary and a deer park.

E **Rozelle Estate and Nature Trail** 96 acres, given to the town in 1968, of woodland, ponds and gardens.

Hospitals

F Ailsa Hospital *tel 65136*
B Biggart Hospital *tel Prestwick 70611*
C Heathfield Hospital *tel 68621*
E Seafield Sick Children's Hospital *tel 65161*

Sport and Recreation

E **Ayr Cricket Club**, Cambusdoon
C **Ayr Ice Rink**, 9 Limekiln Road
E **Ayr Rugby Football Club** , Cambusdoon
E **Belleisle Golf Course**
D **Dalmilling Golf Course**
A **Old Prestwick Golf Course**
A **Prestwick Indoor Bowling Club**
A **Prestwick St Nicholas Golf Course**
E **Seafield Golf Course**
A **Troon Golf Club**

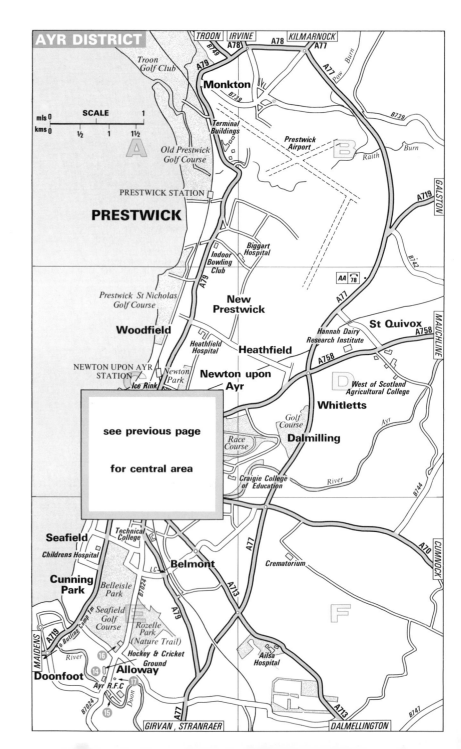

see previous page

for central area

N   **AA Road Service Centre** — Avon Street Car Park *tel 24731*

J i   **Tourist Information Centre** — 8 Abbey Churchyard *tel 62831*

Public buildings and places of interest

K(1)   **Abbey Church** A splendid example of Perpendicular Gothic, notable for its fine tower, with façade portraying the ladder dream of Bishop Oliver King, which led to his rebuilding of the abbey 1495-1503. It was again restored in the late 16th to early 17thC after suffering much damage after its dissolution in 1539. Also of interest are the fan-vaulted chancel, the Prior Bird's chantry and the enormous clerestory windows.

F(2)   **Assembly Rooms** Built c1771 to a design by John Wood the younger. Now fully restored (NT) after severe Second World War damage. They contain the Museum of Costume with displays illustrating fashion through the ages.

N(3)   **Beechen Cliff** Affords a fine view over the city.

F(4)   **Costume and Fashion Research Centre** An extension of the museum of costume, with a library and study collection. It is housed in No.10 The Circus. The Circus is considered to be John Wood the elder's greatest work.

J(5)   **Grand Pump Room and Roman Baths** The Grand Pump Room was designed by Baldwin and Palmer and built 1798-99. The Roman Baths of Aquae Sulis are England's most impressive survival from the Roman period. Excavations have taken place over the past two centuries. The impressive Great Bath was re-discovered in 1880. There is also a museum.

K(6)   **Guildhall and Municipal Buildings** The Guildhall, built 1766-75, is the work of Baldwin and contains a notable banqueting room, a masterpiece of late 18th-C interior decoration.

H(7)   **Holburne of Menstrie Museum** A collection of paintings, silver, porcelain, glass, and furniture housed in a building of 1796.

J(8)   **New Royal Baths and Treatment Centre** The mineral water springs which feed the baths and treatment centre are Britain's only natural hot water springs.

G(9)   **Pulteney Bridge** An Adam design, built in 1770 by Sir William Pulteney. It is lined on both sides by shops.

F(10)   **Reference Library and Exhibition Rooms** These house the Charles Moore Geological collection and a varied programme of temporary exhibitions.

A(11)   **Royal Crescent** Perhaps Bath's most imposing 18th-C crescent, designed in 1767-74 by John Wood the younger. No.1 Royal Crescent has been restored with furniture and fittings of this period.

J(12)   **Theatre Royal**

K(13)   **Victoria Art Gallery and Library** Contains a permanent collection of paintings and applied arts including English and Bohemian glass, coins of Bath mint, ceramics and watches.

American Museum in Britain, Claverton Manor. A museum of American decorative arts, and domestic life of the late 17th to mid 19thC, housed in a building of 1820 by Sir Jeffry Wyatville. 1¾m E via George Street (L)

Botanical Gardens, Victoria Park. Over 5,000 species of plants from all over the world. ¼m W via Weston Road (A)

Hospitals

J   **Royal National Hospital for Rheumatic Diseases,** Upper Borough Walls *tel 27341*

Sport and Recreation

A   **Approach Golf Course,** Victoria Park

K   **Bath Cricket Club,** North Parade Cricket Ground

K   **County Cricket and Rugby Football Ground**

K   **Sport and Leisure Centre** — varied facilities including a swimming pool

Bath City Association Football Club, Twerton Park. 1m W via Lower Bristol Road, A36 (I)

Bath Racecourse, Lansdown. 2m N via Lansdown Road (B)

Theatres and Cinemas

J   **ABC Beau Nash Cinema,** 22 Westgate Street *tel 4330*

J   **Little Theatre (Cinema),** St Michael's Place *tel 66822*

J(12)   **Theatre Royal,** Sawclose *tel 66700*

Department Stores

Best Clothing Store, 34 Southgate Street

Maggs B and Co, 3 Marchants Passage

Marks and Spencer Ltd, 16 Stall Street

Owen Owen Ltd, Union Street

Early closing day Thursday, but most stores are open six days a week.

Markets

Market day Wednesday

K   **Market,** Guinea Lane

G   **Cattle Market,** Walcot Street

Advertisers

J   **Mercantile Credit**

K   **Godfrey Davis**

J   **THF** Francis Hotel

Sally Lunn's House

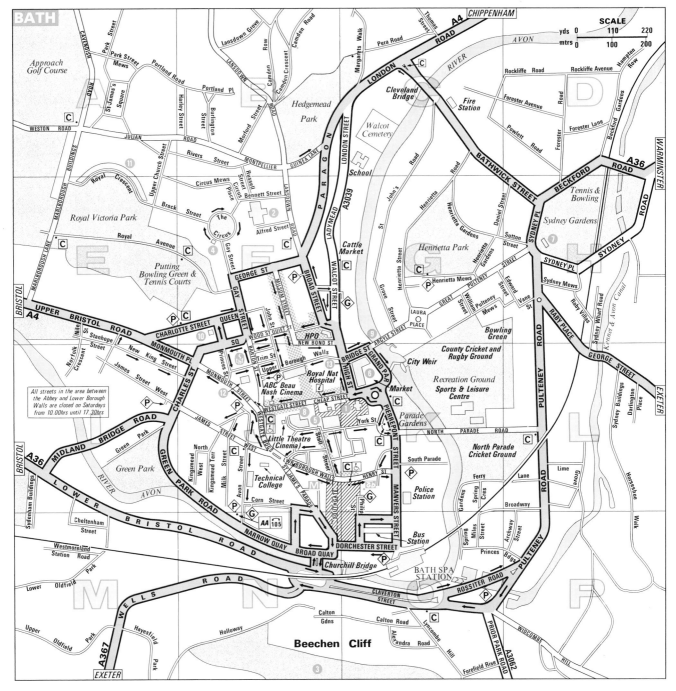

BATH

CENTRAL PLAN

M   **AA Service Centre** — 134 New Street *tel 021-550 4858*

M(5) **Tourist Information Centres** — Council
[i] House, Victoria Square *tel 021-235 3411* (Regional) (see also public buildings and places of interest)

M[i] **Birmingham Art Shop**, City Arcade *tel 021-643 2514* (Specialised)

Public buildings and places of interest

L(1) **British Waterways Information Centre**

L(2) **Central Public Library and School of Music** Includes Shakespeare Memorial Library.

L(3) **Civic Centre** (Baskerville House)

L(4) **College of Food and Domestic Arts**

M(5) **Council House, City Museum, Art Gallery and Tourist Information Centre**
The Council House is a 19th-C building in Italian Renaissance style. The museum contains important archaeological, ethnographical, natural and local history collections. The art gallery is noted for its fine collection of pre-Raphaelite paintings, and its collections of Old Masters and 17th-C Italian paintings.

L(6) **Engineering and Building Centre**

L(7) **Hall of Memory (War Memorial)** Contains illuminated Roll of Honour of Citizens of Birmingham who died in the two world wars.

L(8) **Midland Institute and Birmingham Library**

L(9) **Museum of Science and Industry** An interesting museum with exhibits including machinery, veteran cars and motor bikes and the *City of Birmingham* locomotive.

S(10) **Old Crown House** This inn, the oldest building in the city centre, is a splendid timber-framed structure of 1368, partially rebuilt in 1830.

L(11) **Repertory Theatre** A magnificent building of 1972.

H(12) **St Chad's Cathedral (RC)** Built 1839-41 to a design by A W Pugin. Of particular interest are the 15th-C Flemish pulpit, throne, canon's stalls and statue of Our Lady.

M(13) **St Martin's Church** Rebuilt in Gothic style in 1873 and contains De Bermingham tombs and a Burne-Jones window.

M(14) **St Philip's Cathedral** The 18th-C baroque-style church of St Philip, begun in 1711 to a design by Thomas Archer and raised to Cathedral status in 1905. Notable features are four magnificent Burne-Jones stained-glass windows, a fine organ case of 1715 and a wrought iron screen.

M(15) **School of Art**

X(16) **Stratford House** An old house dating from 1601.

L(17) **Town Hall** A building of 1834-50 designed by Joseph Hansom, best known for 'hansom cabs'. There is a notable organ in the large hall.

I(18) **University of Aston in Birmingham and College of Art and Commerce**

H(19) **West Midlands County Hall**

Hospitals

A   **All Saints Hospital**, Lodge Road *tel 021-523 5151*

Q   **Birmingham Accident Hospital**, Bath Row *tel 021-643 7041*

M   **Birmingham and Midland Ear, Nose and Throat Hospital**, Edmund Street *tel 021-236 6576*

M   **Birmingham and Midland Eye Hospital**, Church Street *tel 021-236 4911*

L   **Chest Clinic**, 151 Great Charles Street *tel 021-236 8781*

P   **Children's Hospital**, Ladywood Road *tel 021-454 4851*

H   **Dental Hospital**, St Chad's Queensway *tel 021-236 8611*

H   **General Hospital**, Steelhouse Lane *tel 021-236 8611*

V   **Midland Nerve Hospital**, Elvetham Road *tel 021-440 3206*

Q   **Royal Orthopaedic Hospital**, 80 Broad Street *tel 021-643 3804*

M   **Skin Hospital**, 35 George Road *tel 021-455 7444*

Sport and Recreation

C   **Aston Swimming Baths**, Newtown Shopping Centre

T   **Birmingham City Football Club**, St Andrew's Ground

R   **Kent Street Swimming Pool**

K   **Monument Road Swimming Baths**, Ladywood Middleway

R   **Silver Blades Ice Rink**, Pershore Street

I   **Woodcock Street Baths**

Theatres and Cinemas

M   **ABC Cinemas**, New Street *tel 021-643 4549*

W   **ABC Cinemas 1, 2 & 3**, Bristol Road *tel 021-440 1904*

R   **Alexandra Theatre**, Suffolk Street Queensway *tel 021-236 1231*

L(11) **Birmingham Repertory Theatre**, Broad Street *tel 021-236 4455* (see also public buildings and places of interest)

R   **Cinephone**, Bristol Street *tel 021-692 1761*

L   **Crescent Theatre**, Cumberland Street *tel 021-643 5858*

M   **Futurist Cinema**, John Bright Street *tel 021-643 0292*

M   **Gaumont Cinerama**, Colmore Circus, Queensway *tel 021-236 1488*

R   **Hippodrome Theatre**, Hurst Street *tel 021-622 2576*

M   **Jacey News Cinema**, Station Street *tel 021-643 1556*

M   **Odeon Cinema**, New Street *tel 021-643 6101*

R   **Odeon Queensway Cinema**, Holloway Circus Queensway *tel 021-643 2418*

W   **Pakistani Film Theatre**, 125 Balsall Heath Road *tel 021-440 2008*

L(17) **Town Hall Concert Hall** *tel 021-236 2392* (see also public buildings and places of interest)

Department Stores

Bini Beca, 120 Corporation Street
Debenhams, Bull Street
Lewis's Ltd, Bull Street
Marks and Spencer Ltd, High Street
Rackhams (Harrods) Ltd, 35 Temple Row
Early closing day Wednesday

Markets

M   **Open Market,** Bull Ring Centre (Monday to Saturday)

M   **Covered Market,** Bull Ring Centre (Monday to Saturday except Wednesday afternoon)

Advertisers

P   **Mercantile Credit**

M   **Crest** Market Hotel

P   **Crest** Plough and Harrow Hotel

R   **Godfrey Davis**

M   **Centre** Birmingham Centre Hotel

DISTRICT PLAN

M   **AA Service Centre and Midland Region Headquarters** — Fanum House, Dogkennel Lane, Halesowen tel 021-550 4858

B   **AA Vehicle Inspection Centre,** West Bromwich

Public buildings and places of interest

J(20)   **Aston Hall** A magnificent Jacobean mansion of 1618-35, with fine oak staircase, panelled long gallery, marble chimney pieces and intricate plaster ceilings. It is now a museum.

O(21)   **Barber Institute of Fine Arts** Superb art collection including masterpieces by Degas, Botticelli, Rembrandt, Goya and Rubens.

Q(22)   **Birmingham Railway Museum** Tyseley steam locomotive preservation centre covering 125 years of railway history, with exhibits including locomotives, reproductions of historic coaches and former working machinery.

Q(23)   **Blakesley Hall,** Yardley. A half-timbered 16th-C yeoman's house, furnished in 17th-C style and now a museum of local history and rural crafts.

O(24)   **Botanical Gardens,** Edgbaston. Founded over 140 years ago these gardens contain a wide variety of trees, flowering shrubs and other plants.

O(25)   **Canon Hill Nature Reserve and Museum** This centre is concerned with the appreciation and preservation of nature. Animals, birds, freshwater fish and insects are shown in their natural surroundings.

O(26)   **King Edward VI School** Founded originally in 1552.

O(27)   **Midland Arts Centre**

B(28)   **Oak House,** West Bromwich. A 16th-C house furnished in the Jacobean style.

O(29)   **Oratory** Home of the Congregation of the Oratory established by Cardinal Newman in 1847.

O(30)   **Queen Elizabeth Hospital, Medical School, and Birmingham Maternity Hospital**

V(31)   **Sarehole Mill,** Hall Green. A restored 18th-C watermill containing exhibits on agricultural history and rural crafts.

U(32)   **Selly Manor House and Minworth Greaves,** Bournville. Two 13th- and 14th-C timbered houses (rebuilt), now museums containing old furniture and domestic equipment.

O(33)   **University of Birmingham**

N(34)   **Weoley Castle,** Selly Oak. Remains of a 13th-C fortified manor house, with small site museum displaying finds from excavations.

Hospitals

O(30)   **Birmingham Maternity Hospital,** Edgbaston tel 021-472 1377 (see also public buildings and places of interest)

P   **Birmingham and Midland Hospital for Women,** Showell Green Lane tel 021-772 1101

I   **Dudley Road Hospital** tel 021-554 3801

K   **East Birmingham Hospital,** Bordesley Green Road tel 021-772 4311

B   **Hallam Hospital,** Hallam Street, West Bromwich tel 021-553 1831

E   **Jaffrey Hospital,** Erdington tel 021-373 1428

H   **Midland Neurosurgical Hospital,** Smethwick tel 021-558 2311

P   **Moseley Hall Hospital,** Alcester Road tel 021-449 5201

V   **Monyhull Hospital,** Monyhull Hall Road tel 021-444 2271

O   **St Chad's Hospital,** 213 Hagley Road tel 021-454 4151

U   **Selly Oak Hospital,** Raddlebarn Road tel 021-472 5313

X   **Solihull Hospital,** Lode Lane tel 021-705 6741

P   **Sorrento Maternity Hospital,** 15 Wake Green Road tel 021-449 4011

I   **Summerfield Hospital,** Western Road tel 021-554 3801

Continued on page 28

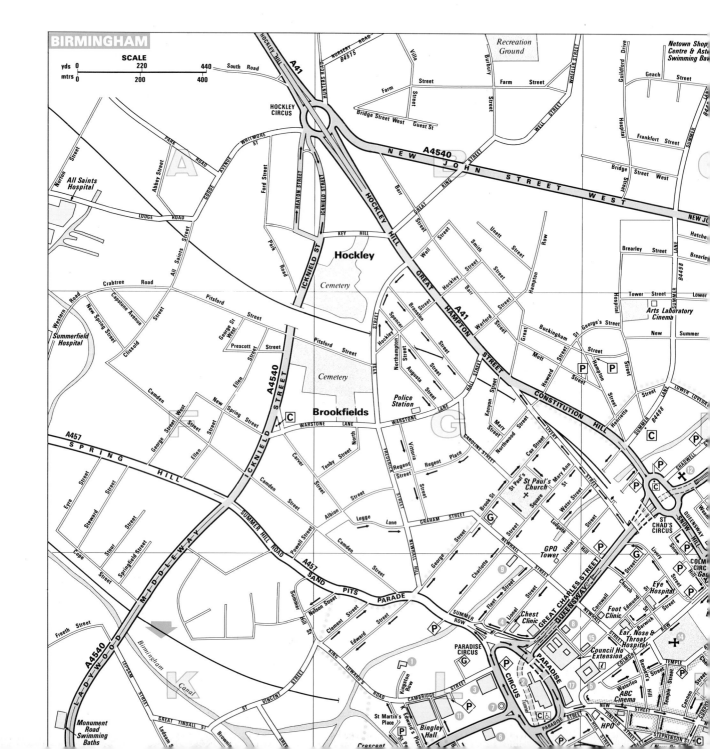

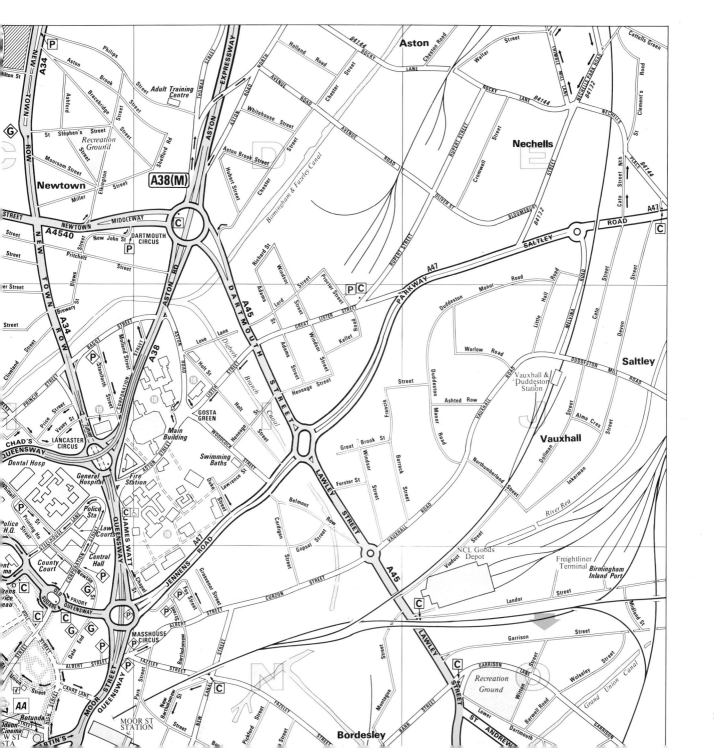

23

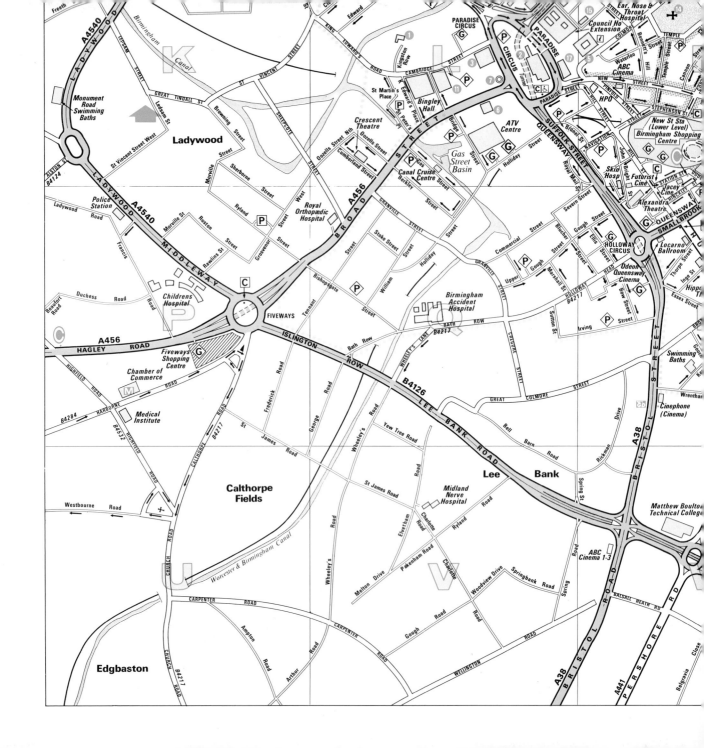

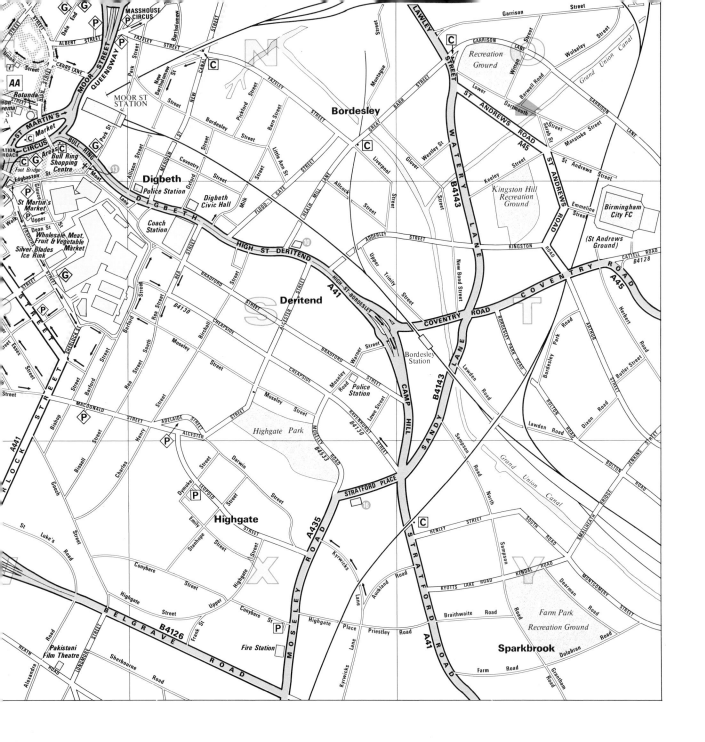

25

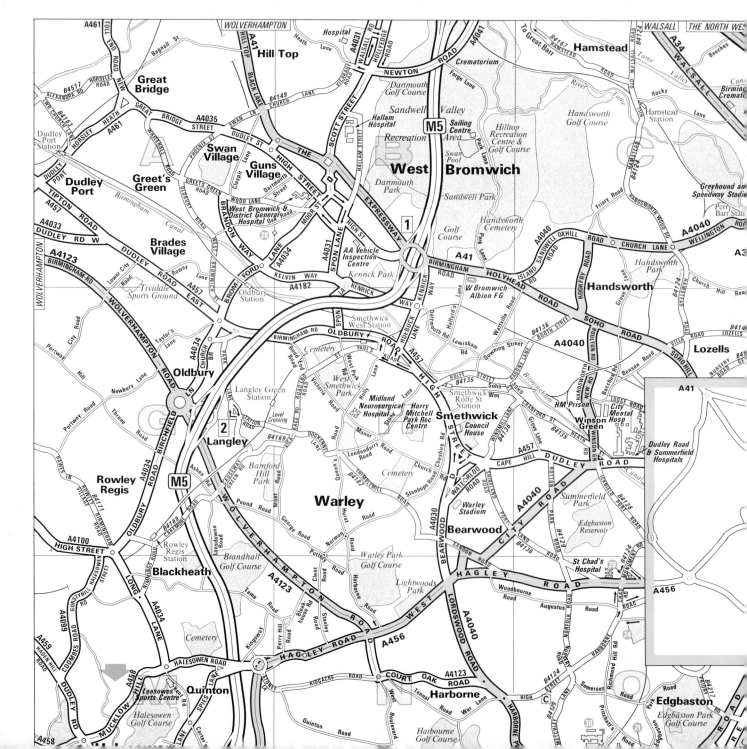

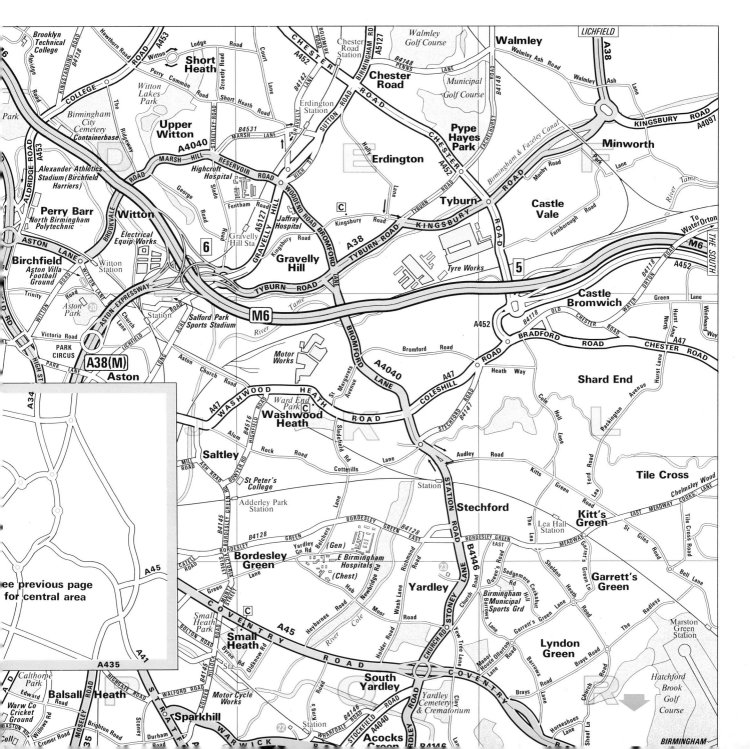

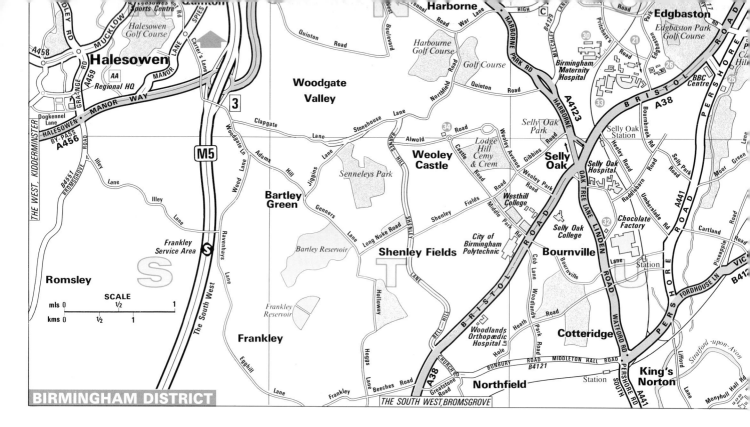

| V | Uffculme Hospital, Queensbridge Road tel 021-449 4011 |
| B | West Bromwich and District General Hospital, Edward Street tel 021-553 3021 |

Sport and Recreation

D	Aston Villa Football Club, Villa Park
R	Birmingham Municipal Sports Ground, Queens Road
M	Brandhall Golf Course, Heron Road, Oldbury
V	Cocks Moors Woods Golf Course
B	Dartmouth Golf Club, Churchfields, Stonecross
O	Edgbaston Golf Club
M	Halesowen Golf Club, The Leasowes, Leasowes Lane, Halesowen
W	Hall Green Stadium, York Road — greyhound racing
N	Harborne Golf Club, Tennal Road
H	Harry Mitchell Recreational Centre

R	Ice Rink, Hobs Moat Road, Solihull
V	Moseley Golf Club, Springfield Road
P	Moseley Rugby Football Club, The Reddings, Reddings Road
W	Old Edwardians Rugby Football Club, Streetsbrook Road
X	Olton Golf Club, Solihull
C	Perry Barr Stadium, Walsall Road — greyhound racing and speedway
E	Pype Hayes Golf Course
W	Robin Hood Golf Club, St Bernards Road, Solihull
B	Sandwell Park Golf Club, Birmingham Road, West Bromwich
X	Solihull Rugby Club, Sharmans Cross Road
A	Tividale Sports Ground, Lower City Road
H	Warley Stadium, Waterloo Road, Smethwick
P	Warwickshire County Cricket Club, County Ground, Edgbaston
B	West Bromwich Albion Football Club, Hawthorns, Birmingham Road, West Bromwich

Department Stores

Barretts of Feckenham, 146 High Street, Solihull
Beattie James Ltd, 700 Warwick Road, Solihull
Owen Owen (Erdington) Ltd, 224 High Street

Advertisers

| R | THF Excelsior Hotel |

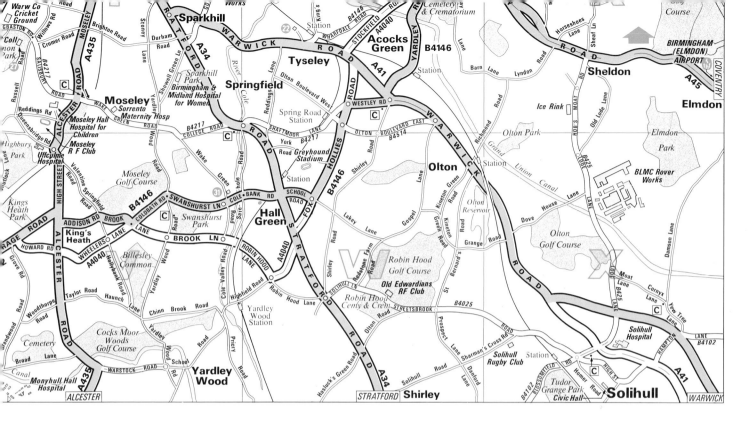

NATIONAL EXHIBITION CENTRE

See plan on page 30

The new exhibition centre was opened by HM the Queen in February 1976. It is situated some 8 miles east of Birmingham City Centre on the main A45 road to Coventry, and adjacent to the junction of the M6 and newly-constructed M42 Motorways. A network of road, rail and air services provide the centre with excellent transport facilities. It is located at the hub of Britain's Motorway system and alongside the complex is Birmingham International Station which is on the main railway line between London and Birmingham. In close proximity is Birmingham Airport (1 mile to west).

The six exhibition halls yield a gross interior area of 962,510 square feet and when the centre is fully developed it will cover 310 acres including the man-made Pendigo Lake. The central feature of the complex — the Piazza — houses shops, banks, medical and visitor services. There is also a Tourist Information Centre and Hotel Accommodation Bureau, and special provisions have been made to serve the disabled visitor. Catering services range from snack kiosks to an international restaurant with full a la carte menu. Two new hotels, the Warwick and Metropole, have been built within the complex; the latter providing conference and banqueting facilities.

Parking

Extensive parking facilities have been provided for 15,000 cars in the form of three main parking areas. In addition there is parking space for 200 coaches. The charge per session is £1 per car (£2 for coaches) and payment is made by purchasing a ticket from special kiosks located inside the Piazza. A vehicle cannot be removed from a car park until this payment ticket is produced at the exit barriers.

A free shuttle bus service operates between the car parks and the main entrance of the exhibition buildings.

Public Transport

By rail — to Birmingham International Station which is adjacent to the centre, and connected to the main building by a covered walkway.

By air — to Birmingham Airport then by taxi or bus to the centre (2½ miles).

By bus — the West Midlands Passenger Transport Executive operate regular services from Birmingham and Coventry City centres to either the National Exhibition Centre or Birmingham International Station.

By taxi — a taxi rank is provided outside the Piazza canopy and also the forecourt of Birmingham International Station.

Exhibitions

Details of shows and exhibitions can be obtained from the National Exhibition Centre Ltd, Birmingham B40 1NT. Tel 021-780-4141

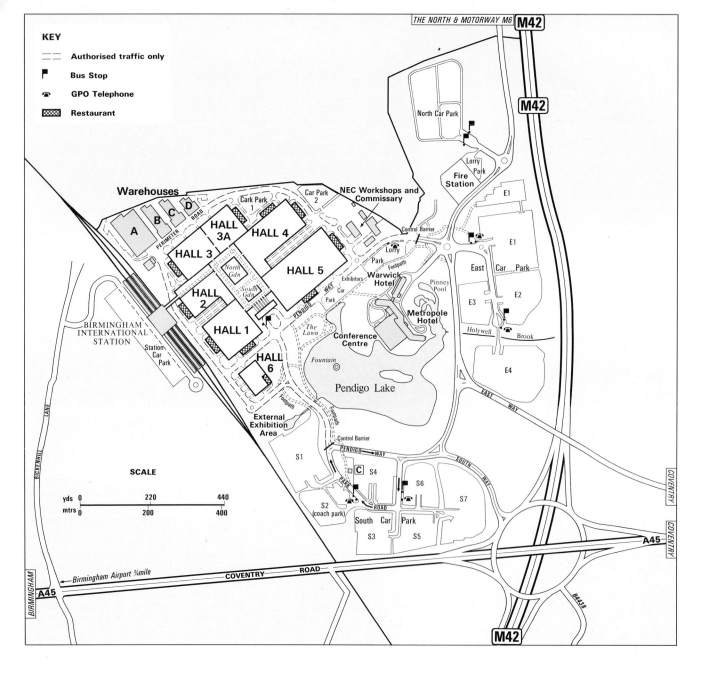

KEY

── ── Authorised traffic only

⚑ Bus Stop

☎ GPO Telephone

▨ Restaurant

THE NORTH & MOTORWAY M6

M42

M42

North Car Park

Lorry Park

Fire Station

E1

E1

Warehouses

Cark Park 1

Car Park 2

NEC Workshops and Commissary

Control Barrier

PERIMETER ROAD

A B C D

HALL 3A

HALL 4

HALL 3

Car Park

North Gdn

South Gdn

HALL 5

Lorry Park

Footpath

Exhibitors Car Park

Warwick Hotel

East Car Park

E3

E2

PENDIGO WAY

HALL 2

Pinney Pool

Metropole Hotel

Holywell

Brook

BIRMINGHAM INTERNATIONAL STATION

Station Car Park

HALL 1

The Lawn

Conference Centre

E4

HALL 6

Fountain

Pendigo Lake

EAST WAY

External Exhibition Area

Footpath

Control Barrier

PENDIGO WAY

SOUTH WAY

COVENTRY

S1

PENDIGO PARK

C S4

S6

S7

COVENTRY

S2 (coach park)

ROAD

SCALE

yds 0   220   440
mtrs 0   200   400

South Car Park

S3

S5

A45

B4438

Birmingham Airport ¾ mile

COVENTRY ROAD

BIRMINGHAM

A45

M42

Easily reached by road, rail and air Birmingham is the ideal base for visitors touring the Heart of England. The visitor to Birmingham will find that it has much to offer.

Top quality night clubs, theatres and cinemas . . . world renowned City of Birmingham Symphony Orchestra . . . splendid pubs and restaurants . . . superb shopping centres, museums, art galleries . . . sports facilities to suit all tastes.

To find out more about Birmingham call in at the City's Information Office in the heart of the city centre or ring 021-235 3411. Map leaflets and guides are available on request.

**City of Birmingham Information Office
The Council House, Birmingham, B1 1BB**

city at the centre
BIRMINGHAM

AA Road Service Centre (6) — Squires Gate
tel 44947 3m S via Promenade A584 (G)
A 🛈   Tourist Information Centre — Central
Promenade *tel 21623*

Public buildings and places of interest

A(1)   **Grundy Art Gallery and Central Library**
Established 1911, this gallery exhibits
a permanent collection of paintings and
drawings by 19th- and 20th-C British
artists. Also temporary exhibitions.

D(2)   **Louis Tussaud's Waxworks** Lifelike
models of famous people; Chamber of
Horrors; many tableaux, including Robin
Hood and his Merry Men and Bernadette
of Lourdes; and educational exhibition
of anatomy.

F(3)   **Model Village, Stanley Park** An accurate
and realistic representation of a real-
life village.

G(4)   **Platform 3 Model Railway,** South Shore
Station. The largest electronically-
controlled 00 Gauge System in Britain.

A(5)   **Royal Lancastrian Pottery** Production
of pottery has recently restarted at
these late 19th-C premises, which
became famous at the beginning of the
present century receiving the Royal
Assent in 1913. Visitors welcome.

C(6)   **Stanley Park** 256 acres of formal gardens
including rose and Italian gardens,
conservatories, lake and recreational
facilities.

A(7)   **Tower Buildings and Circus** The tower
stands 518ft high. The buildings at
its base contain a spacious ballroom,
Ocean room, cabaret lounge, Apollo
playground, zoo and aquarium, and the
Tower Circus.

A(8)   **Town Hall**

C(9)   **Zoopark** Over 400 different species of
animals and birds, in natural landscaped
setting. Also free flight bird hall,
with over 200 tropical and sub-tropical
birds; children's corner; and miniature
railway.

Seafront Tramway Operating along the seafront
between Squires Gate (Blackpool) and Fleetwood
and is Britain's only electric tram service.

Hospitals

C   **Victoria Hospital** *tel 34111*
Devonshire Road Hospital *tel 32121* ¾m N via
Talbot Road A586 (A) or Devonshire Road
A587 (B)

Sport and Recreation

C   **Blackpool Cricket Club,** Stanley Park
D   **Blackpool Football Club,** Bloomfield Road
D   **Blackpool Rugby League Ground and**
Greyhound Stadium, Princess Street
A   **Cocker Street Swimming Baths**
G   **Lido Pool**
G   **Open Air Baths,** South Shore
C   **Stanley Park Golf Course**
Go-Karting and Conoeing, Starr Gate, South
Shore 3m S via Promenade A584 (G)
Ice-Drome, South Shore 1¾m S via Promenade
A584 (G)
North Shore Golf Course 2m N via Talbot
Road A586 (A) then Devonshire Road A587

Theatres and Cinemas

A   **ABC Theatre** (Cinema), Church Street
tel 24233
D   **Central Pier Theatre** *tel 20423*
A   **North Pier Theatre** *tel 20980*
A   **Odeon Cinema,** Dickson Road *tel 23565*
G   **Palladium Cinema,** Waterloo Road *tel
420232*
G   **Rendezvous Cinema,** Bond Street
D   **Royal Pavilion Cinema,** Rigby Road *tel
25313*
G   **South Pier Theatre** *tel 43096*
A   **Studios 1, 2, 3 and 4,** Star Entertainment
Centre, The Promenade *tel 25957*
A   **Tivoli Cinema,** Clifton Street *tel 20508*
A   **Winter Gardens Theatre and Opera House**
tel 25252
Ice Drome, Pleasure Beach *tel 41707* 1¾m
S via Promenade A584 (G)

Department Stores

Hills R H O (Blackpool) Ltd, Bank Hey Street
Hincks D S, 175 Central Drive
Lewis's Ltd, 50 The Promenade
Marks and Spencer Ltd, 78 Bank Hey Street
Marks and Spencer Ltd, 51 Church Street
Early closing day Wednesday

Blackpool Tower

ABERDEEN 56571 ABERDEEN AIRPORT 723404 BATH 5763 BIRMINGHAM 021-622 5311 BIRMINGHAM BIRMINGHAM AIRPORT 021-742 4461 BOURNEMOUTH 764078 BRADFORD 33048 BRIGHTON 29332 BRISTOL 22111 CAMBRIDGE 48198 CARDIFF 45448 COVENTRY 27477 DOVER 204699 DUNDEE 21281 EDINBURGH 031-661 1252 EDINBURGH AIRPORT 031-334 7062 EXETER 75398 GLASGOW 041-423 5667 GLASGOW AIRPORT 041-889 8359 GLOUCESTER 28248 HULL 27253 INVERNESS 34886 INVERNESS INVERNESS AIRPORT 34886 IPSWICH 211067 LEEDS 459438 LEICESTER 709611 LINCOLN 30101 LIVERPOOL 051-709 0028 LONDON 01-834 8484 LONDON AIRPORT 01-897 0811 MANCHESTER 061-834 5842 MANCHESTER AIRPORT 061-437 6161 MIDDLESBROUGH 244744 NEWCASTLE UPON TYNE 32120 NORWICH 45798 NOTTINGHAM 861871 OXFORD 46373 PERTH 31322 PLYMOUTH 69850 PORTSMOUTH PORTSMOUTH 817331 READING 583733 SALISBURY 5625 SHEFFIELD 78802 SHREWSBURY 59623 SOUTHAMPTON 22035 STOKE ON TRENT 262856 SWANSEA 50526 SWINDON 22500 TORQUAY 26992 WOLVERHAMPTON 52173 WORCESTER 354096 YORK 59241

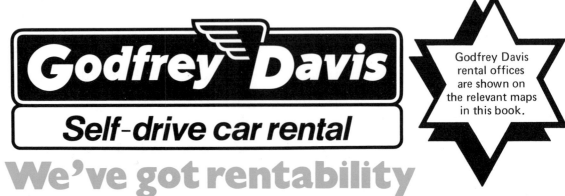

Wherever you go, Godfrey Davis rentability is only a phone call away

Godfrey Davis

Self-drive car rental

Godfrey Davis rental offices are shown on the relevant maps in this book.

We've got rentability

I   **AA Service Centre** — Fanum House, 3 Wimbourne Road *tel 25751*

O(3)   **Tourist Information Centres** — Tourism
🛈   Department, Westover Road, Bournemouth *tel 291715*

L(2)   **Information Bureau,** Royal Arcade,
🛈   Boscombe *tel 35561*

Public buildings and places of interest

O(1)   **Ice Rink**
L(2)   **Information Bureau,** Boscombe
O(3)   **Information Centre,** Bournemouth
O(4)   **Lower Pleasure Gardens**
J(5)   **Municipal College and Library**
O(6)   **Pavilion**
I(7)   **Railway Museum,** Dalkieth Hall. A large collection of railway relics and models. There are also film shows and lectures.
O(8)   **Rothesay Museum** Contains collections including early Italian paintings; pottery; china; 17th-C furniture; an armoury room; a marine room; and butterflies and moths.
P(9)   **Russell-Cotes Art Gallery and Museum** Housed in East Cliff Hall, a building of 1894 and containing 17th- to 20th-C paintings; period rooms; Oriental art; the Henry Irving Theatrical collection; and an aquarium. Outside is a geological terrace of about 200 rocks, building stones and ores covering 2,600 million years of history.
L(10) **St John's Church,** Boscombe. A Victorian church of flint and stone.
O(11) **St Peter's Church** This church by Street, dates from 1879.
I(12) **St Stephen's Church** A late Victorian church by Pearson, perhaps the finest in town.
O(13) **Swimming Pool**
I(14) **Town Hall**
O(15) **Winter Gardens**
Compton Acres Gardens, Canford Cliffs. Seven distinct gardens: Japanese, Italian, Roman, English, Rock, Heather, and Palm Court covering an area of 15 acres. 3¾m SW via the Avenue B3065 (M)

Hospitals

F   **Royal Victoria Hospital,** Shelley Road, Boscombe *tel 35201*

H   **Royal Victoria Hospital** (Eye, Ear, Nose and Throat Unit), Poole Road *tel 761332*

Sport and Recreation

F   **AFC Bournemouth,** Dean Court Ground
J   **County Cricket Ground,** Dean Park
F   **King's Park Athletic Centre**
B   **Meyrick Park Golf Course**
O(13) **Pier Approach Baths** (see also public buildings and places of interest)
O(1)   **Westover Ice Rink,** Westover Road (see also public buildings and places of interest)

Theatres and Cinemas

O   **ABC Film Centre,** Westover Road *tel 28433*
O   **Galaxy Cinema,** Westover Road *tel 23277*
O   **Gaumont Twin Cinema** *tel 26491*
G   **Grand Cinema,** Poole Road *tel 763118*
O(6)   **Pavilion Theatre** *tel 25861* (see also public buildings and places of interest)
O(13) **Pier Approach Baths** (Aqua Show) *tel 24393* (see also public buildings and places of interest)
O   **Pier Theatre,** Bournemouth Pier *tel 20250*
O   **Playhouse Theatre,** Westover Road *tel 23275*
O(1)   **Westover Ice Rink** (Ice Follies) *tel 22611* (see also public buildings and places of interest)
O(15) **Winter Gardens** *tel 26446* (see also public buildings and places of interest)

Department Stores

Beales, Old Christchurch Road
Bealesons, Commercial Road
Debenhams Ltd, The Square
Marks and Spencer Ltd, 23 Commercial Road
Marks and Spencer Ltd, 603 Christchurch Road, Boscombe
Neal Daniel and Sons Ltd, Westover Road
Early closing day Wednesday or Saturday

Advertisers

I   **Mercantile Credit**

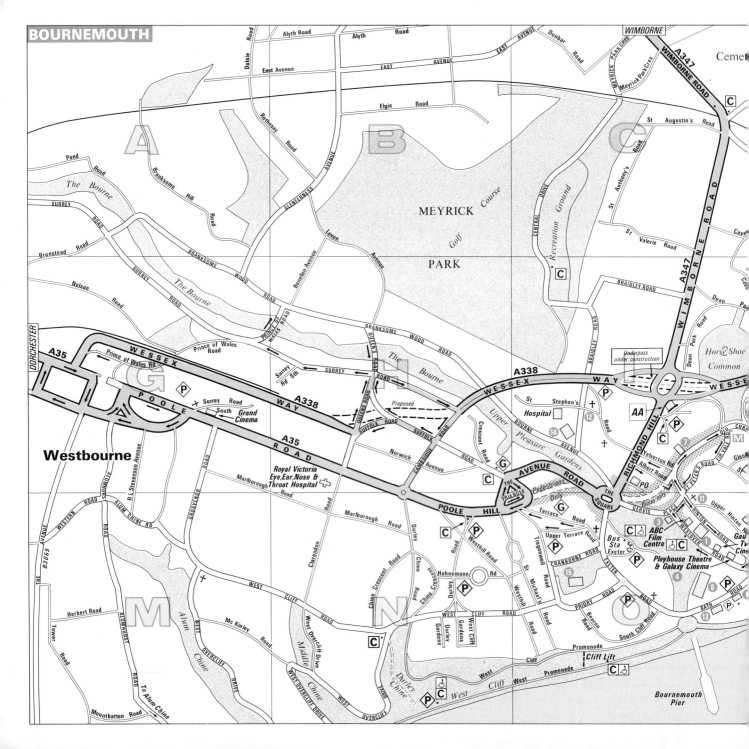

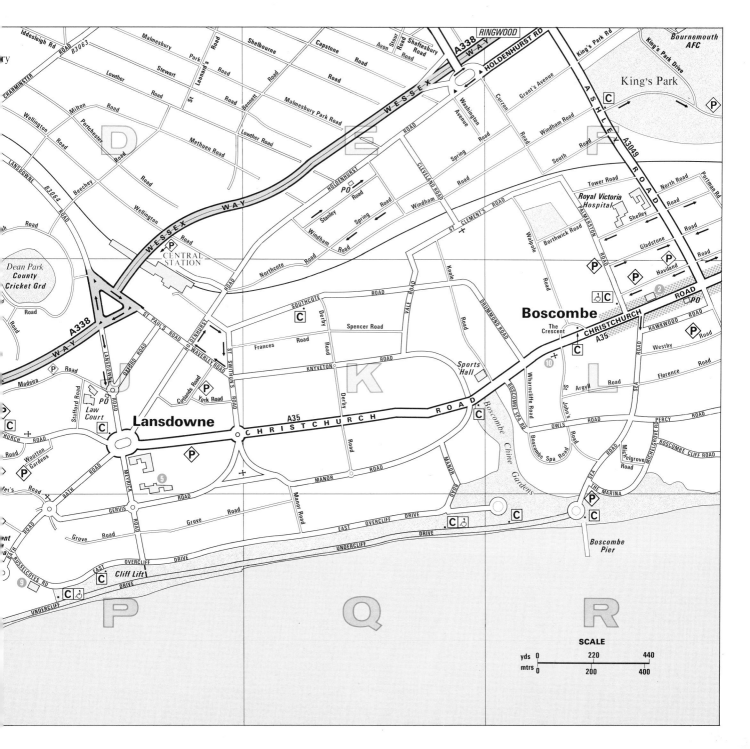

CENTRAL PLAN

G AA Road Service Centre (99) — Hall Ings Car Park *tel 24703*

J(2) Tourist Information Centre — Central
i Library, Princes Way *tel 33081 ext 45* (Regional)

Public buildings and places of interest

G(1) **Cathedral** Formerly the parish church, which was raised to Cathedral status in 1919. It is mainly 15th-C, notably the Bowling Chapel and typical Yorkshire four-square tower, but also includes modern extensions of 1951-63. Features of note are the 15th-C font cover; a stone, probably of Saxon origin, in the north wall, and a sculpture by Flaxman.

J(2) **Central Library, Theatre and Tourist Information Centre** A modern building opened in 1967.

J(3) **City Hall** Dates from 1873. The 220ft tower is styled on the campanile of the Palazzo Vecchio in Florence.

G(4) **Exchange** Opened in 1867, the Wool Exchange is a reminder of Bradford's importance in the wool trade. The clock tower is 150ft high and beneath it are statues of Bishop Blaize and Edward IV.

K(5) **St George's Hall** One of the main centres of northern musical tradition. Today the setting for great orchestral and choral works.

Sport and Recreation

J Wardley Entertainment Centre — Ice Rink and Swimming Pool

J Windsor Swimming Pool, Morley Street

Theatres and Cinemas

G ABC 1, 2 & 3 Cinemas, Broadway *tel 28689*

J Alhambra Theatre, Morley Street *tel 27007*

H Bradford Playhouse and Film Theatre, Chapel Street *tel 20329*

G Cinecenta, 12/16 Cheapside *tel 23177*

B Classic Cinema, Manningham Lane *tel 28183*

J(2) Library Theatre *tel 23975* (see also public buildings and places of interest)

J Majestic Cinema, Morley Street *tel 33943*

J Odeon Twin 1 & 2 Cinemas, Princes Way *tel 267616*

K(5) St George's Hall, Hall Ings (Concerts) *tel 32513* (see also public buildings and places of interest)

Department Stores

Brown Muff and Co Ltd, 26 Market Street
Debenhams Ltd, Manningham Lane
Eleganza, 677 Little Horton Lane
Lingard's (Bradford) Ltd, 29 Westgate
Marks and Spencer Ltd, 16 Darley Street
Early closing day Wednesday

Markets

F James Street Market (Daily)

F John Street Open Market (Thursday, Friday and Saturday)

F Kirkgate Market (Daily)

F Rawson Place Market (Daily)

L St James's Wholesale Market (Daily)

Advertisers

B Mercantile Credit

E Godfrey Davis

K THF Victoria Hotel

DISTRICT PLAN

K(6) **Bolling Hall** A fine 14th- to 18th-C house, now a museum of social history, with well-furnished period rooms.

B(7) **Cartwright Hall, Art Gallery and Museum,** Lister Park. It was built as a memorial to Edward Cartwright, inventor of the power loom. It now houses Bradford's permanent art collection and temporary exhibitions on natural history, geology and archaeology.

D(8) **Moorside Mills Industrial Museum,** Moorside Road. Housed in an old textile mill and illustrating the history and development of the worsted and woollen industry. Also included are sections on dyeing and printing, and a transport section featuring the last trolley bus to run in this country.

Hospitals

O Bierley Hall Hospital, Bierley Lane *tel 682837*

B Bradford Children's Hospital, St Mary's Road *tel 45324*

A Bradford Royal Infirmary, Duckworth Lane *tel 42200*

D Calverley Hospital, Thornbory *tel 662692*

G Leeds Road Hospital *tel 29661*

N Northern View Hospital, Rooley Avenue *tel 29130*

J St Luke's Hospital, Little Horton Lane *tel 34744*

B Waddilove's Hospital, Queen's Road *tel 44397*

Sport and Recreation

B Bradford City Association Football Club

J Bradford Cricket Club, Park Avenue

C Bradford Moor Golf Club

N Bradford Northern Rugby League Football Club, Odsall Stadium

E Bradford Rugby Union Football Club

I Clayton Golf Club

P East Bierley Golf Club

B Lister Park Open-air Swimming Pool

N South Bradford Golf Club, Taylor Road

O West Bowling Golf Club

Cinemas

B Sangeet Cinema, Ambler Street *tel 492626*

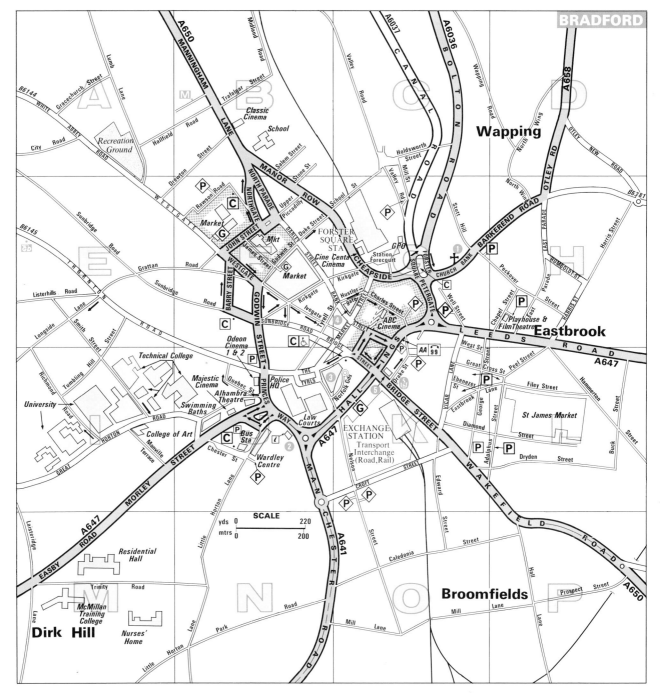

Wapping

Eastbrook

Broomfields

Dirk Hill

University

Technical College

Recreation Ground

Residential Hall

McMillan Training College

Nurses' Home

College of Art

Swimming Baths

Alhambra Theatre

Majestic Cinema

Police HQ

Odeon Cinema 1 & 2

THE TYRLS

Law Courts

Norfolk Gas

EXCHANGE STATION
Transport Interchange (Road, Rail)

Bus Sta

Wardley Centre

St James Market

Playhouse & Film Theatre

ABC Cinema

FORSTER SQUARE STA

Cine Centa Cinema

Station Forecourt

GPO

Market

Mkt

Classic Cinema

School

SCALE
yds 0   220
mtrs 0   200

MANNINGHAM LANE
A650

MANOR ROW

NORTHGATE

JOHN STREET

WESTGATE

GODWIN STREET

BARRY STREET

PRINCES WAY

HALL

BRIDGE STREET

MANCHESTER ROAD
A641

MORLEY ROAD
A647

EASBY ROAD
A647

CHEAPSIDE

FORSTER SQUARE

PETERGATE

CHURCH BANK

BARKEREND ROAD

OTLEY RD
A658

BOLTON ROAD
A6036

A6037

CANAL ROAD

LEEDS ROAD

WAKEFIELD ROAD

A650

A647

B6381

NEW ROAD

St James Market

39

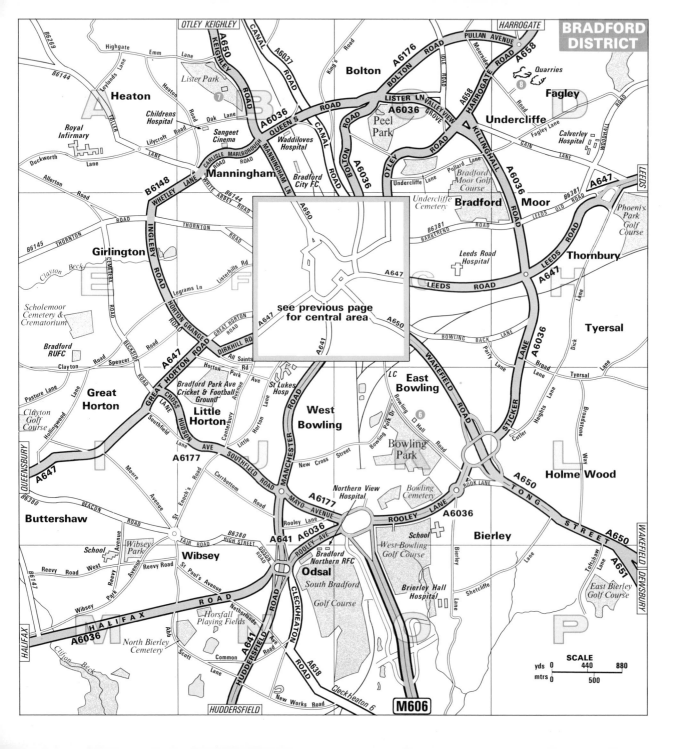

BRIGHTON

CENTRAL PLAN

N   **AA Service Centre** — 10 Churchill Square
tel 24933

O(5)   **Tourist Information Centres** —
ℹ   Marlborough House, 54 Old Steine
tel 23755 (weekends *tel 26450)* (see
also public buildings and places of
interest)

N   Seafront *tel 26450* (summer only)

Public buildings and places of interest

O(1)   **Aquarium and Dolphinarium** Thousands
of tropical and freshwater fish, sea
lions, turtles, seals and performing
dolphins.

N(2)   **Doll's Museum** A unique display of
over 300 dolls displayed in a
wonderland setting.

K(3)   **Dome** A 2,100-seater concert and
conference hall, housed in former
Royal stables of the Royal Pavilion.

O(4)   **Louis Tussaud's Waxworks** Famous and
infamous characters of the past and
present presented in wax.

O(5)   **Marlborough House** Designed by Robert
Adam in 1786, and now housing the
Tourist Information Centre.

K(6)   **Museum, Art Gallery and Library** Housed
in part of former Royal stables.
Collections include Old Master
paintings, watercolours, Sussex
archaeology and folk life,
ethnography, natural history, musical
instruments, the Willet collection of
pottery and porcelain and displays of
20th-C fine and applied art.

K(7)   **Royal Pavilion** A marine residence built
for the Prince Regent, later George IV.
It was begun in 1787 by Henry Holland
and completed in the style of the Moghul
palaces of India by John Nash. The
interior contains some fantastic
Chinoiserie decorations and is
furnished in its original style.

F(8)   **St Bartholomew's Church** Built between
1872 and 1874 and has a nave 135ft-high.

J(9)   **St Nicholas Church** Dates from the
14thC and preserves a Norman font.

G(10)   **St Peter's Church** The parish Church
of Brighton, built in 1824 to a design
by Sir Charles Barry. It has a notable
reredos and fine east window.

O(11)   **The Lanes** These quaint old lanes of
17th-C fishermen's cottages now form
a paradise for seekers of all kinds
of antiques and curios.

O(12)   **Town Hall**

P(13)   **Volks Railway** This delightful relic
of the Victorian era was the first
public electric railway in Great
Britain, opened in 1883.

Hospitals

I   **New Sussex Hospital**, Windlesham Road
tel 736255

I   **Royal Alexandra Children's Hospital**,
Dyke Road *tel 28145*

J   **Sussex Throat and Ear Hospital**, Church
Street *tel 29054*

Sport and Recreation

K   **North Road Swimming Baths**

J   **Sussex Sports Centre**, 11 Queen Square

Theatres and Cinemas

O   **ABC Cinema**, East Street *tel 27010*

K   **Astoria Cinema**, Gloucester Place *tel
683385*

J   **Brighton Film Theatre**, 64 North Street
tel 29563

I   **Classic Cinema**, Western Road *tel 29414*

K(3)   **Dome**, Church Street *tel 682127* (see
also public buildings and places of
interest)

B   **Duke of York's Theatre** (cinema), Preston
Circus *tel 62503*

M   **Embassy Cinema**, 1 Western Road, Hove
tel 735124

N   **Odeon Film Centre**, Kingswest Centre,
West Street *tel 23317*

K   **Pavilion Theatre**, New Road

K   **Theatre Royal**, New Road *tel 28488*

Department Stores

Co-operative, 92 London Road
Debenhams, 95 Western Road
Hannington's Ltd, North Street and East Street
Marks and Spencer Ltd, 195 Western Road
Marks and Spencer Ltd, 5 London Road
Vokins, North Street
Wades of Brighton, 188 Western Road
Early closing day Wednesday — St James' Street;
Thursday — London Road and Western Road;
Saturday — North Street area

Markets

K   **Fruit and Vegetable Market**
G   **Open Market**

Advertisers

K   **Mercantile Credit**
N   **Godfrey Davis**
M   **THF** Hotel Curzon

Royal
Pavilion

DISTRICT PLAN

J (17) Tourist Information Centre — Hove Town
⒤ Hall, Church Road *tel 775400* (see also
public buildings and places of interest)

Public buildings and places of interest

F(14) **Booth Museum of Natural History**
Contains a comprehensive collection of
birds displayed in their natural
habitat, a notable butterfly collection
and an evolution gallery.

G(15) **College of Technology**

J(16) **Hove Museum of Art** Contains paintings
and prints, particularly of the 18th
to 19thCs, a fine collection of
ceramics, period furniture and other
valuable items.

J(17) **Hove Town Hall** A modern building,
opened 1974.

F(18) **Preston Park and Preston Manor** A
Georgian house (with Edwardian
additions) showing a fine collection
of period furniture including the
Maquoid bequest, pictures, china
and silver.

D(19) **University of Sussex**

Hospitals

H **Bevendean Hospital**, Bear Road *tel 67091*

H **Brighton General Hospital**, Elm Grove *tel 66444*

J **Hove General Hospital**, Sackville Road *tel 735244*

I **Lady Chichester Hospital**, Aldrington House, New Church Road, Hove *tel 778383*

L **Royal Sussex County Hospital**, Eastern Road *tel 66611*

L **Sussex Eye Hospital**, Eastern Road *tel 66126*

Sport and Recreation

L **Black Rock Swimming Pool**

J **Brighton and Hove Albion Football Club**, Goldstone Ground, Hove

E **Brighton and Hove Golf Course**, Dyke Road

B **Brighton Rugby Club**, Pavilion, Recreation Ground, Vale Avenue

F **Brighton Sports Arena**, Tongdean Lane

F **Greyhound Stadium**, Nevill Road, Hove

C **Hollingbury Park Golf Course**, Ditchling Road

F **Hove Rugby Football Club**, New Pavilion, Hove Park

J **King Alfred Sports Centre**, Kingsway, Hove — tenpin bowling and swimming baths.

L **Marina** At present under construction, it has been designed to provide moorings for over 2,000 boats. The scheme also includes commercial and leisure facilities

J **Sussex County Cricket Club**, County Ground, Eaton Road, Hove

A **Waterhall Golf Club**, Mill Road

I **West Hove Golf Course**, Old Shoreham Road, Portslade

Theatres and Cinemas

L **Continentale Cinema**, Sudeley Place *tel 681348*

D **Gardner Arts Centre**, Sussex University

Department Stores

Hills of Hove, Western Road, Hove
Stuart Norris, 141 Church Road, Hove
Early closing day Wednesday — Hove

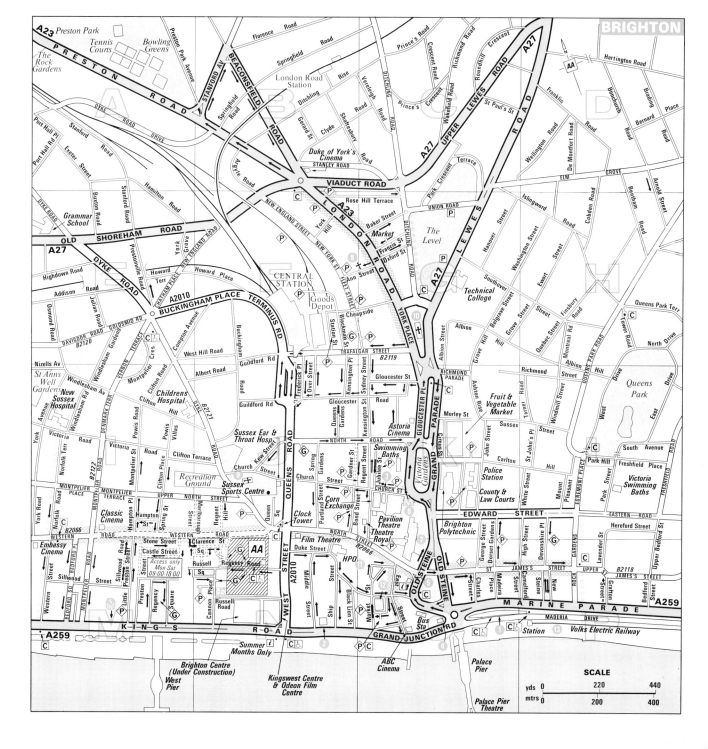

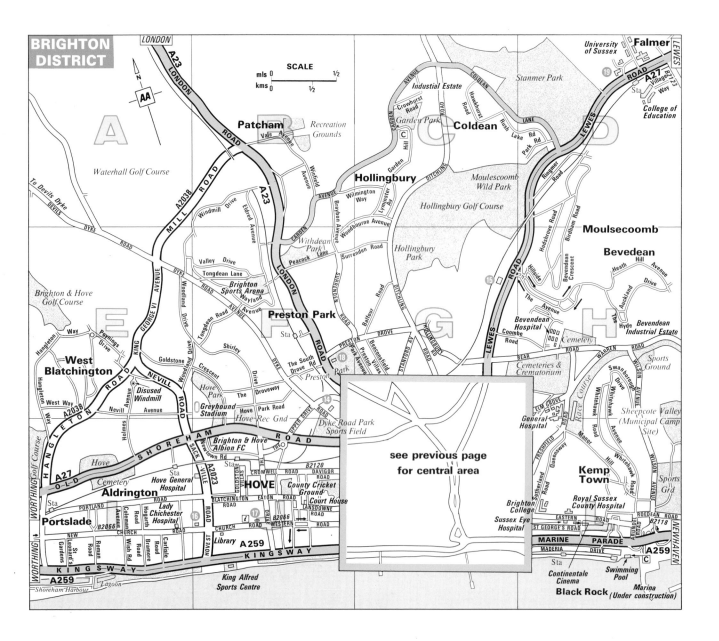

BRIGHTON DISTRICT

LONDON

A23

AA

N

SCALE

mls 0 ½
kms 0 ½

Waterhall Golf Course

To Devils Dyke

DYKE ROAD

DEVILS

Patcham

Vale Avenue

Recreation Grounds

Winfield Avenue

MILL ROAD

A2038

A23

LONDON ROAD

Windmill Drive

Eldred Avenue

Valley Drive

Tongdean Lane

Brighton Sports Arena

Wayland Avenue

Withdean Park

Peacock Lane

Tongdean Road

Brighton & Hove Golf Course

Way

Poynings Drive

KING GEORGE VI AVENUE

Woodland Drive

DYKE ROAD

Shirley Drive

Crescent

Preston Park

Sta

The South Drove Rd

Preston

Goldstone

AVENUE

Industial Estate

Crowhurst Road

Garden Park

GARDEN

AVENUE

COLDEAN

Hawkhurst Road

Rush Lake Rd

Park Rd

LANE

Coldean

University of Sussex

Falmer

LEWES ROAD

A27

Sta

Village Way

B2123

College of Education

19

Stanmer Park

Hollingbury

Wilmington Way

Braybon Avenue

Woodbourne Avenue

Lyminster Av

Garden

DITCHLING

Moulescoomb Wild Park

Hollingbury Golf Course

Hollingbury Park

Hodshrove Road

Birdham Road

Ringmer Road

Moulsecoomb

Bevedean

Heath Hill

Avenue

Auckland Drive

Hillside

The Avenue

Bevendean Crescent

Bevendean Hospital

Coombe Road

Cemetery

The Hyde

Bevendean Industrial Estate

LEWES ROAD

15

BEAR ROAD

Cemeteries & Crematorium

Sports Ground

WARREN ROAD

Sheepcote Valley (Municipal Camp Site)

RACE COURSE

Swanborough Drive

Whitehawk Road

Whitehawk Way

Heath Hill

WILSON AVENUE

Manor Hill

Whitehawk Road

Sports Grd

West Blatchington

A2038

HANGLETON

Hangleton Way

West Way

Nevill Avenue

Holmes Avenue

NEVILL ROAD

Disused Windmill

Hove Park

The Droveway

Hove Park Road

Greyhound Stadium

Hove Rec Gnd

UPPER DRIVE

Dyke Road Park Sports Field

The Drive

Brighton & Hove Albion FC

14

SHOREHAM ROAD

OLD A27

Hove

A259

Cemetery

WORTHING Golf Course

Sta

Aldrington

Portslade

Sta

PORTLAND ROAD

New Leonard's Gardens

St. Leonard's Road

Coleman Road

Roman Road

B2066

CHURCH ROAD

Wish Rd

Bramore Road

Hogarth Road

Carlisle Road

HOVE ST

SACKVILLE ROAD

A2023

Hove General Hospital

Lady Chichester Hospital

BLATCHINGTON ROAD

EATON ROAD

16

CHURCH ROAD

Library

17

HOVE

Newtown Rd

CROMWELL ROAD

B2120

DAVIGOR ROAD

County Cricket Ground

Court House

B2066 ROAD

WESTERN ROAD

LANSDOWNE ROAD

A259 KINGSWAY

King Alfred Sports Centre

A259 KINGSWAY

WORTHING

Shoreham Harbour

Lagoon

see previous page for central area

General Hospital

ELM GROVE

Brighton College

Sussex Eye Hospital

Kemp Town

Royal Sussex County Hospital

ST GEORGE'S ROAD

Queensway

Sutherland Road

Eastern Road

ROEDEAN ROAD

B2118

Sports Grd

MARINE PARADE

MADERIA

Sta

Continentale Cinema

Black Rock

Swimming Pool

Marina (Under construction)

MARINE DRIVE

A259

NEWHAVEN

C

C   **AA Service Centre** — Fanum House, Park Row *tel 298531*

CENTRAL PLAN

D 🛈   **Tourist Information Centre** — City Information Centre, Colston House *tel 293891*

Public buildings and places of interest

C(1)   **Cabot Tower** A 150ft-high tower on the summit of Brandon Hill. Built 1897-98 on the four hundreth anniversary of John Cabot's discovery of the mainland of North America at Labrador.

J(2)   **Cathedral** Founded as an Augustinian monastery in 1140, it has developed continuously over the past 800 years, with examples of Norman, Early English, Gothic and Victorian architecture.

B(3)   **Cathedral (RC)**

K(4)   **Chatterton House** The birthplace of Thomas Chatterton (1752-70), famous boy poet.

C(5)   **City Museum and Art Gallery** Collections of archaeological, geological, natural history, scientific and transport exhibits.

A(6)   **Clifton Observatory** Situated on a hill above the Avon Gorge, with a large camera obscura on the summit of the tower. A passage below the tower leads to Giants Cave.

A(7)   **Clifton Suspension Bridge** Designed by Isambard Kingdom Brunel in 1836, the bridge carries the toll road from Bristol towards Portishead 254ft above the Avon Gorge.

D(8)   **Colston Hall** One of the finest concert halls in the country.

D(9)   **Corn Exchange** In front of the building (1743) are four bronze pillars known as 'Nails' which were at one time used by merchants to complete cash transactions.

I(10)   **Council House**

D(11)   **Foster Almshouses** A 19th-C building on 15th-C foundations. Adjacent is the chapel of the Three Kings of Cologne (1504), and Christmas Steps (1669).

C(12)   **The Georgian House** With 18th-C furniture and fittings.

D(13)   **Guildhall** Now used as the Court House.

E(14)   **Quakers Friars** Once a Dominican Friary, part of the building now houses the Bristol Register Office and the Permanent Planning Exhibition.

D(15)   **Red Lodge** The 16th-C house, altered in the early 18thC with oak carvings and furnishings of both periods.

C(16)   **Royal Fort House** An 18th-C merchant's house with decorated plaster work on both ceilings and walls, now part of the University of Bristol.

C(17)   **Royal West of England Academy**

I(18)   **SS Great Britain** Built in Bristol by Isambard Kingdom Brunel in 1843, it was the largest iron ship of its time. It was shipwrecked in the Falkland Islands and finally raised and towed back to Bristol in 1970.

D(19)   **St John's Church and Old City Gate** The small 14th-C church is built above the gate which has statues of Brennus and Belinus, mythical figures of the founders of Bristol.

Demoiselle Crane, Clifton Zoo

J(20)   **St Marks** The Lord Mayor's Chapel is noted for its monuments and vestry. Founded in 1220 and restored in 1889.

K(21)   **St Mary Redcliffe Church** A magnificent church of the 13th-15thCs, one of the largest in England. It has a large 13th-C tower with a 285-ft spire. The hexagonal north porch dates from 1290.

D(22)   **St Nicholas Church and City Museum** Contains the history of Bristol from its beginnings until the Reformation including Bristol church art. There are also displays of watercolours and drawings.

D(23)   **St Stephen's Church** A 15th-C church with several interesting monuments.

K(24)   **Temple Church** A ruined 15th-C church with a leaning tower.

C(25)   **University**

E(26)   **Wesley's Chapel** Dating from 1739, it is the oldest Methodist Chapel in the world and was built by John Wesley whose statue is outside.

Clifton Zoo Extensive gardens, and varied collection of animals, reptiles and fishes. (B) 1¾m NW via Pembroke Rd B4467

Hospitals

D   **Bristol Eye Hospital,** Lower Maudlin Street *tel 27988*

J   **Bristol General Hospital,** Guinea Street *tel 25001*

D   **Bristol Royal Infirmary,** 2 Marlborough Street *tel 22041*

B   **Chesterfield Hospital,** Clifton *tel 30391*

D   **Dental Hospital,** Lower Maudlin Street *tel 23385*

B   **St Brenda's Maternity Hospital,** Clifton Park *tel 38774*

C   **St Mary's Private Hospital,** Up Byron Place *tel 23186*

B   **Walker Dunbar Maternity Hospital,** Clifton Down Road *tel 39963*

Sport and Recreation

N   **Bristol City Football Club,** Ashton Gate

D   **Bristol Ski School,** Bryant's Outdoor Centre, Colston Street

P   **Bristol South Swimming Baths,** Dean Lane

E   **Broad Weir Baths,** Stratton Street

C   **Clifton Pool,** Southleigh Road, Clifton

I   **Jacob's Wells Baths,** Jacob's Wells Road

D   **Silver Blades Ice Rink,** New Bristol Centre, Frogmore Street

Theatres and Cinemas

D   **ABC Cinema,** New Bristol Centre, Frogmore Street *tel 22848*

E   **Europa Cinemas,** adj Holiday Inn, Lower Castle Street *tel 291810*

D   **Gaumont Cinema,** Baldwin Street *tel 25882*

J   **The Hippodrome,** St Augustines Parade *tel 299444*

E   **Kings Cinema,** Old Market Street *tel 24613*

D(8)   **Little Theatre,** Colston Hall, Colston Street *tel 291182* (see also public buildings and places of interest)

E   **Odeon Film Centre,** Broadmead *tel 26141*

D   **Studios 1, 2, 3** and Pithay Centre, 9 All Saints Street *tel 25069*

J   **Theatre Royal and New Vic Theatre,** King Street *tel 24388*

Department Stores

The Co-operative, Fairfax House, Fairfax Street, Newgate

Debenhams Ltd, 1 St James Barton

Dingles, House of Fraser, Queens Road

Lewis's Ltd, 2 The Haymarket

B Maggs and Co, Queens Road

Marks and Spencer Ltd, 78 Broadmead

Primark Stores, 82 The Horsefair

Terrett Taylor and Sons Ltd, 119 High Street, Staple Hill

Early closing day Wednesday and Saturday (many shops in the main shopping area are open six days a week)

Markets

D   **St Nicholas Market,** (general — Monday to Saturday)

M   **Bristol City Football Club Car Park,** Ashton Gate (Sunday morning)

Advertisers

D   **Mercantile Credit**

E   **Godfrey Davis**

Continued on page 50

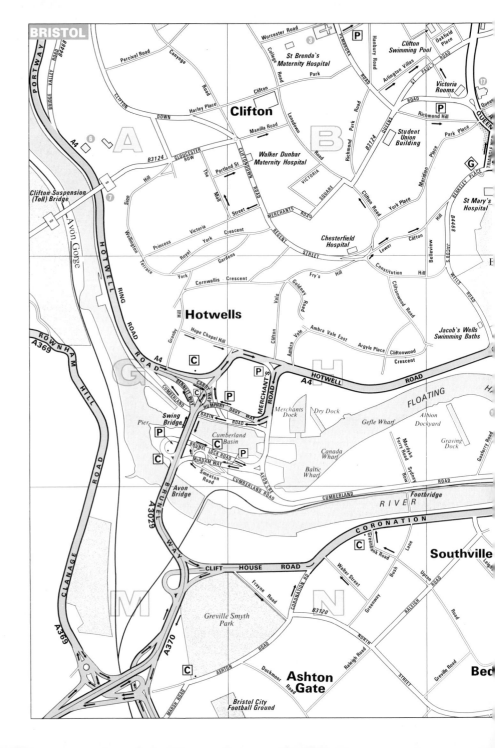

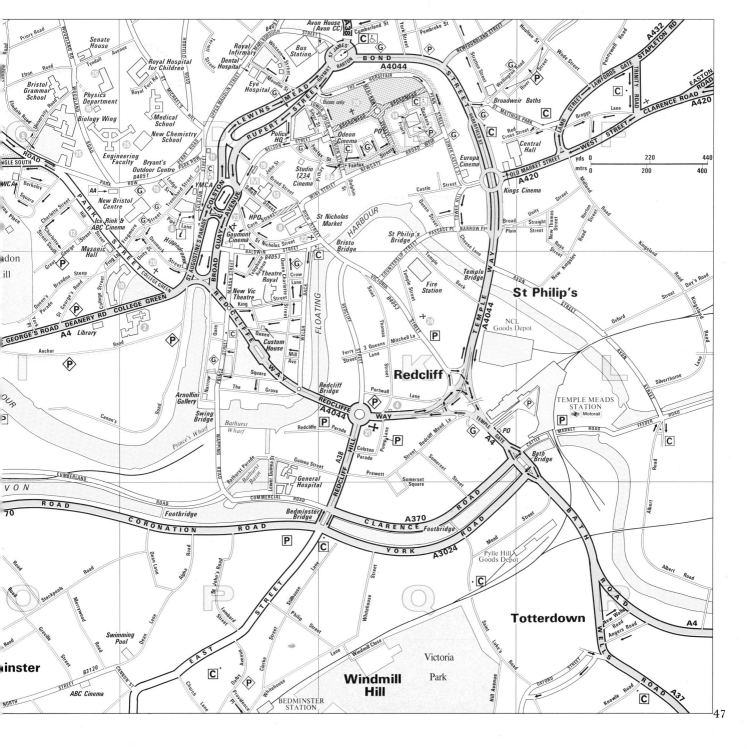

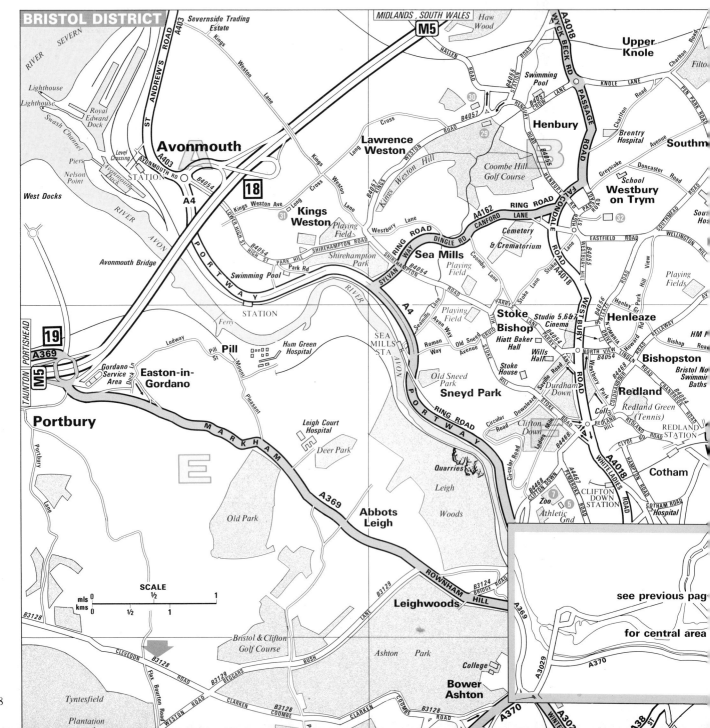

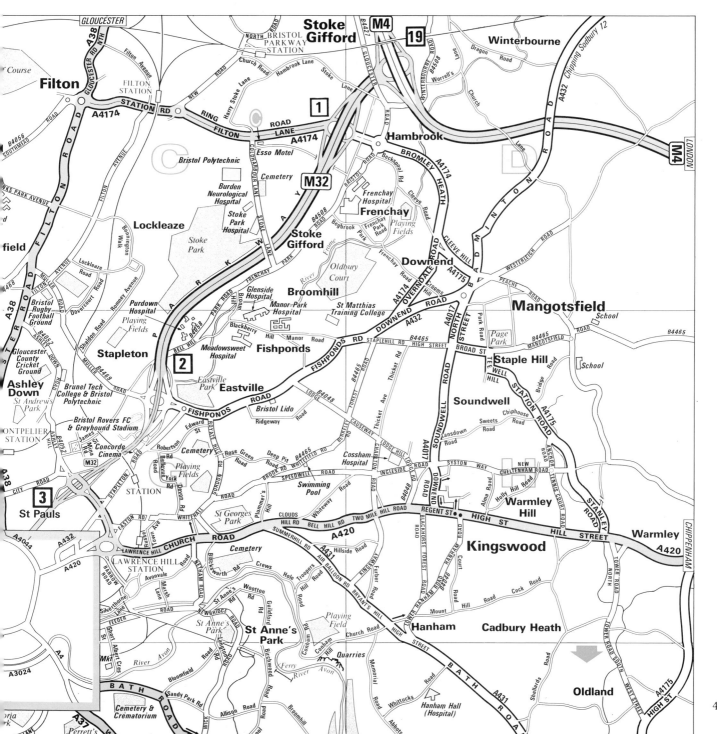

49

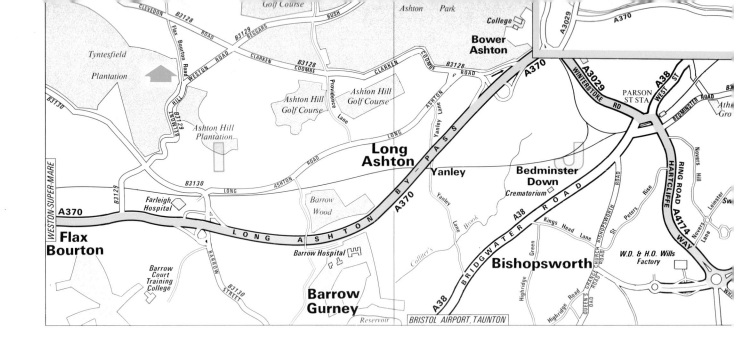

DISTRICT PLAN

Public buildings and places of interest

- **L(28) Bitton Station** Bristol Suburban Railway
- **B(29) Blaise Castle House** An 18th-C mansion, now a folk museum. The extensive grounds contain a thatched dairy and a watermill.
- **B(30) Blaise Castle Hamlet** (NT)
- **A(31) Kings Weston Roman Villa** Mosaics and walls of a Roman villa occupied between AD270 and AD370.
- **B(32) Wild Life Park** Opened in 1967 by Peter Scott, the Park contains wild animals and birds of Britain.

Hospitals

- **I** **Barrow Hospital,** Barrow Gurney *tel Long Ashton 3162*
- **B** **Brentry Hospital,** Charlton Road, Westbury-on-Trym *tel 623443*
- **C** **Burden Neurological Hospital,** *tel 567444*
- **F** **Bristol Homeopathic Hospital,** 6 Cotham Hill *tel 312231*
- **H** **Cossham Memorial Hospital,** Kingswood *tel 671661*
- **I** **Farleigh Hospital,** Flax Bourton *tel Flax Bourton 3275*
- **D** **Frenchay Hospital** *tel 565656*
- **G** **Glenside Hospital,** Blackberry Hill, Stapleton *tel 653285*
- **E** **Ham Green Hospital,** Pill *tel Pill 2661*
- **L** **Hanham Hospital** *tel 677871*
- **E** **Leigh Court Hospital,** Pill *tel Pill 2109*
- **G** **Manor Park Hospital,** Manor Road, Fishponds *tel 656061*
- **G** **Meadowsweet Hospital,** Blackberry Hill *tel 653294*
- **G** **Purdown Hospital,** Bell Hill *tel 653554*
- **B** **Southmead General Hospital,** Westbury-on-Trym *tel 622821*

Sport and Recreation

- **I** **Ashton Hill Golf Course,** Clarken Coombe Road off B3128
- **I** **Bristol and Clifton Golf Course,** off Beggars Bush Lane B3129
- **G** **Bristol Lido Leisure Centre,** Alcove Road, Fishponds
- **F** **Bristol North Swimming Baths,** Gloucester Road
- **G** **Bristol Rovers Football Club and Greyhound Stadium,** Eastville

- **C** **Bristol Rugby Club,** Memorial Ground, Horfield
- **B** **Coombe Hill Golf Course,** off Henbury Road B4055
- **B** **Filton Golf Course,** off Charlton Road
- **K** **Filwood Swimming Baths,** Filwood Broadway
- **G** **Gloucester County Cricket Club,** Ashley Down
- **B** **Henbury Pool,** Crow Lane, Henbury
- **K** **Jubilee Swimming Baths,** Jubilee Road
- **F** **Redland Green,** Redland — tennis
- **A** **Shirehampton Swimming Baths,** Park Road, Shirehampton
- **G** **Speedwell Swimming Baths,** Whitefield Road
- **K** **Whitchurch Sports Centre,** Bamfield — badminton, squash, football, volleyball, tennis, basketball, netball and athletic track

Markets

- **G** **Bristol Stadium,** Stapleton Road, Eastville (Friday and Sunday)

Advertisers

- **C** **Crest** Bristol Esso Hotel

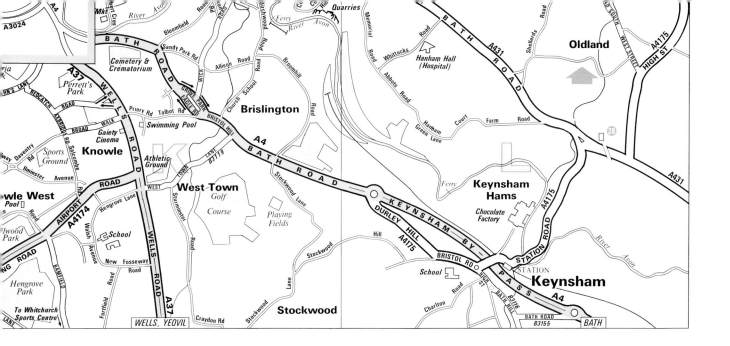

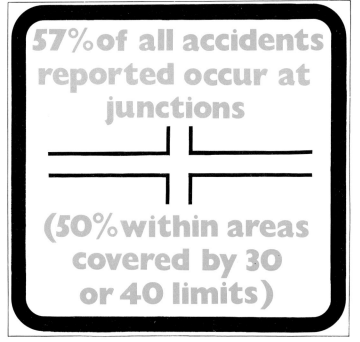

CAMBRIDGE

CENTRAL PLAN

K   **AA Service Centre** — Janus House, 46-48 St Andrew's Street *tel 63101*

K [i]   **Tourist Information Centre** — 4 Bene't Street *tel 58977*

K [i]   Information Kiosk, Market Square (summer only)

Public buildings and places of interest

COLLEGES

K(1) **Christ's College (1505)** The main gate bears the statue and insignia of the foundress, Lady Margaret Beaufort.

A(2) **Churchill College (1960)**

J(3) **Clare College (1326)** The present buildings date from 1638.

I(4) **Clare Hall**

K(5) **Corpus Christi College (1352)** The old court (14th-C) is the earliest complete court in Cambridge. The new court in Gothic style dates from 1827-32. The library contains a fine collection of Anglo-Saxon and medieval manuscripts.

N(6) **Darwin College (1964)**

O(7) **Downing College (1749)**

K(8) **Emmanuel College (1584)** The chapel of 1666 was designed by Sir Christopher Wren.

A(9) **Fitzwilliam College (1869)**

J(10) **Gonville (1348) & Caius College (1557)** Notable features are the 'Honour' and 'Virtue' gates.

P(11) **Hughes Hall (Teachers' Training) (1885)**

G(12) **Jesus College (1496)** Founded in buildings of former nunnery of St Radegund. The chapel, the former church of the nunnery, contains ceiling and windows by William Morris and Burne Jones.

J(13) **Kings College and Chapel (1441)** The magnificent chapel is the only completed medieval part of this college built 1441-1515 in Perpendicular style. It retains all its original stained glass and contains Rubens' *Adoration of the Magi.* Other buildings are mainly 19thC with the exception of the Fellows Building by Gibbs, a fine classical addition of 1723-9.

A(14) **Lucy Cavendish Collegiate Society**

F(15) **Magdalene College (1542)** The library of Samuel Pepys is housed here.

A(16) **New Hall (1954)** The third women's college.

M(17) **Newnham College (1871)** The second women's college.

K(18) **Pembroke College (1347)** The chapel built 1663-6 is the first completed building designed by Wren.

O(19) **Peterhouse College (1284)** The 13th-C Hall, which was greatly restored in the 19thC, now features a tiled fireplace by William Morris and windows by Ford Madox-Brown and Burne Jones.

J(20) **Queen's College (1448 & 1465)** Founded by the Queen's of Henry VI and Edward IV.

N(21) **Ridley Hall Theological**

J(22) **St Catherine's College (1473)**

A(23) **St Edmund's House**

F(24) **St John's College (1511)** Consists of three red-brick courts with a fine gate tower and chapel of the 1860s designed by Sir George Gilbert Scott.

M(25) **Selwyn College (1882)**

G(26) **Sidney Sussex College (1596)** Has associations with Cromwell.

F(27) **Trinity College (1546)** The Great Court is the largest of its kind in the world completed in 1676-90 by the addition of a library designed by Sir Christopher Wren. Statues of many famous men of the college, including Newton and Tennyson are to be found in the ante-chapel.

J(28) **Trinity Hall (1350)**

G(29) **Wesley House Theological**

G(30) **Westcott House Theological**

F(31) **Westminster College Theological and Cheshunt College** A fine red-brick building of 1889 in Tudor-style.

M(32) **Wolfson College (1964-65)**

CHURCHES

K(33) **Great St Mary's** The University church (1478-1514) in Perpendicular Gothic style with a fine tower and some Georgian screenwork.

G(34) **Holy Sepulchre, Round Church** Dates from 1104 and is the oldest surviving round church in England. Mainly Norman,

it has been extensively restored.

O(35) **Little St Mary's** Mostly 14thC, in decorated style.

K(36) **St Bene't's** Retains a notable early 11th-C Saxon tower, the oldest building in Cambridge.

MUSEUMS

F(37) **Cambridge and County Folk Museum** Exhibits include domestic items, agricultural tools and trade equipment illustrating the life of Cambridgeshire people since medieval times.

O(38) **Fitzwilliam Museum** Contains Egyptian Greek and Roman antiquities, paintings manuscripts, ceramics, textiles, Medieval and Renaissance objets d'art, an armoury and a library.

N(39) **Museum of Classical Archaeology** Houses casts of Greek and Roman statues.

P(40) **Scott Polar Research Institute** Includes sections on former polar expeditions, current research and the geography and geology of the Antarctic.

K(41) **Sedgwick Museum of Geology** Display of fossils of all ages and subordinate display of building and ornamental stones.

K(42) **University Museum of Archaeology and Ethnology** Comprises archaeogical collections from the Old Stone Age in Africa and the Near East; from prehistoric to medieval times in Britain and prehistoric America; and ethnological collections from Africa, the Americas, 'Asia and the Pacific.

K(43) **University Museum of Zoology** Includes sections on marine life, birds, insects and mammals, and also fossil specimens of extinct animals.

K(44) **Whipple Science Museum** A collection of scientific instruments and books mainly from the 16th to 18thC.

OTHER PLACES OF INTEREST

K(45) **Arts Theatre**

K(46) **Civic Centre**

K(47) **Guildhall and Central Library**

I(48) **History Faculty**

O(49) **Hobson's Conduit** Dates from 1614 and was transferred here from Market Hill in 1855.

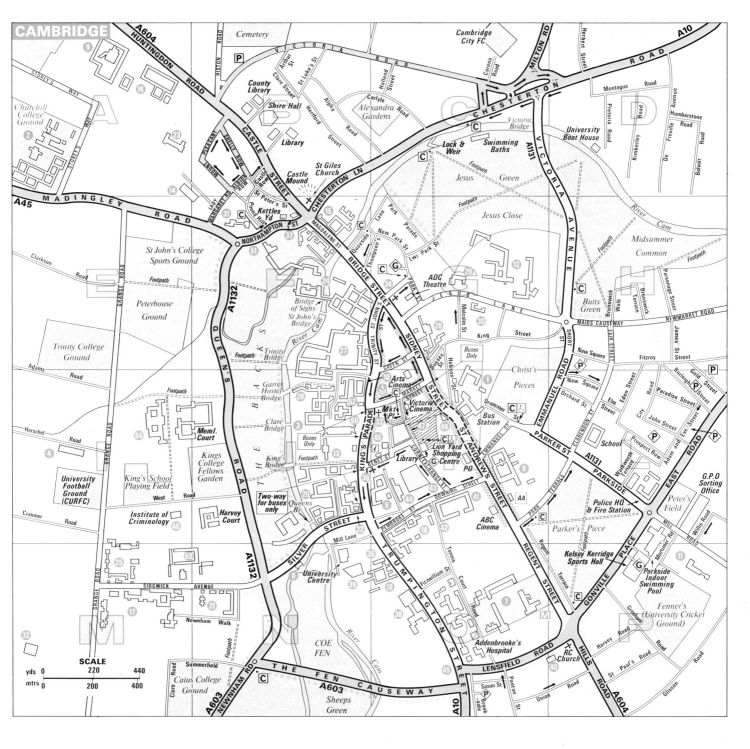

J(50) **Old Schools** These date from the 14thC and house the University's central administration.

F(51) **School of Pythagoras** An old house dating back in part to the 12thC.

K(52) **Senate House** A fine building of 1722-30 by James Gibb, noted for its wood and plasterwork.

M(53) **University Arts Faculty**

I(54) **University Library** An impressive design of 1931-34 by Sir George Gilbert Scott with a tower of 160ft.

B **Castle Mound** All that remains of Cambridge's Norman Castle.

Hospitals

O **Addenbrookes Hospital,** Trumpington Street *tel 55671*

Sport and Recreation

C **Cambridge City Football Club,** Milton Road

I **Cambridge University Rugby Football Club,** The Ground, Grange Road

P **Fenner's** (University Cricket Ground) Gresham Road

C **Jesus Green open-air swimming pool**

P **Kelsey Kerridge Sports Hall,** Gonville Place

P **Parkside Indoor Swimming Pool**

Theatres and Cinemas

K **ABC 1 & 2,** 37 St Andrews Street *tel 54572*

G **ADC Theatre,** Park Street *tel 59547*

K **Arts Cinema,** Market Pass *tel 52001*

K(45) **Arts Theatre,** Peas Hill *tel 52000* (see also public buildings and places of interest)

K **Victoria Cinemas 1 & 2,** 6 Market Hill *tel 52677*

Department Stores

Co-operative, Burleigh Street
Joshua Taylor Ltd, Sidney Street and Bridge Street
Laurie McConnal, Fitzroy Street
Marks and Spencer Ltd, Sidney Street
Mitchams, 34 Chesterton Road
Robert Sayle, 12/17 St Andrews Street
W Eaden and Lilly, Market Street
Early closing day Thursday, but some shops close all day Monday

Markets

K **Market Place** (daily but main market day Saturday)

Advertisers

P **Mercantile Credit**

K **THF** Blue Boar Hotel

DISTRICT PLAN

Public buildings and places of interest

A(55) **Girton College (1869)** The first college for women.

O(56) **Homerton College** Teachers' training.

K(57) **University Botanic Gardens** Lawns, flower beds, a notable rockery, scented garden and greenhouses containing many rare and exotic plants.

Hospitals

O **Addenbrookes Hospital,** Hill's Road *tel 45151*

L **Brookfields Geriatric Hospital,** 351 Mill Road *tel 45926*

C **Chesterton Hospital,** 29 Union Lane *tel 63415*

Sport and Recreation

H **Cambridge United Football Club,** Newmarket Road

Girton Golf Course, Dodford Lane, Girton 3½m NW via Girton Road (A)

Gog Magog Golf Course, Babraham Road 4m SE via Hills Road A604 (P)

Markets

K **Cattle Market** (Monday)

Advertisers

L **Godfrey Davis**

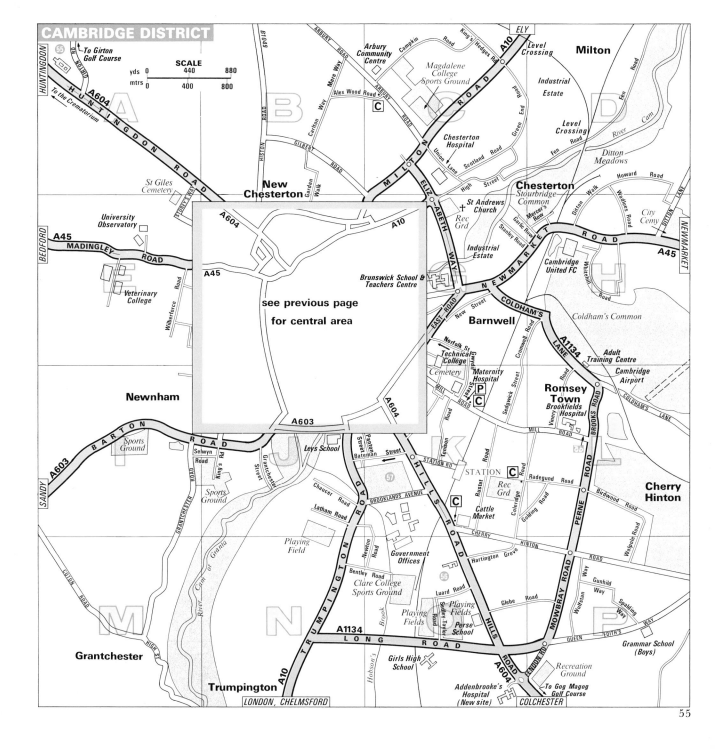

SCALE

yds 0   440   880
mtrs 0   400   800

To Girton Golf Course

To the Crematorium

Milton

New Chesterton

Chesterton

St Giles Cemetery

University Observatory

Veterinary College

Arbury Community Centre

Magdalene College Sports Ground

Industrial Estate

Level Crossing

Level Crossing

Ditton Meadows

Chesterton Hospital

St Andrews Church

Rec Grd

Stourbridge Common

Mercer's Row

Industrial Estate

City Cemy

Cambridge United FC

Barnwell

Brunswick School & Teachers Centre

see previous page

for central area

Newnham

Norfolk St Technical College

Cemetery

Maternity Hospital

Romsey Town

Brookfields Hospital

Coldham's Common

Adult Training Centre

Cambridge Airport

STATION

Cattle Market

Rec Grd

Cherry Hinton

Leys School

Sports Ground

Sports Ground

Chaucer Road

Latham Road

Playing Field

Clare College Sports Ground

Government Offices

Playing Fields

Perse School

Girls High School

Playing Fields

Grantchester

Trumpington

Recreation Ground

Addenbrooke's Hospital (New site)

To Gog Magog Golf Course

Grammar School (Boys)

LONDON, CHELMSFORD

COLCHESTER

ELY

HUNTINGDON

BEDFORD

MADINGLEY ROAD

A45

A604

A45

A604

A603

A1134 LONG ROAD

A10

SANDY

BARTON ROAD

TRUMPINGTON ROAD

HILLS ROAD

PERNE ROAD

MOWBRAY ROAD

FENDON RD

BROOKS ROAD

NEWMARKET ROAD

COLDHAM'S LANE

A1134

ELIZABETH WAY

MILTON ROAD

EAST ROAD

NEWMARKET

A45

River Cam

Ditton Walk

Howard Road

Wadloes Road

High Street

Scotland Road

Fen Road

Green End

Industrial Estate

Campkin Road

King's Hedges Road

ARBURY ROAD

Mere Way

Alex Wood Road

Carlton Way

HISTON

GILBERT ROAD

Garden Walk

Union Lane

Stanley Road

Garlic Row

Whitehill Road

Mill Road

Vinery Road

Cromwell Road

Sedgwick Street

Coleridge Road

Radegund Road

Golding Road

Birdwood Road

Walpole Road

Way

Gunhild Way

Wulfstan Way

Spalding Way

QUEEN EDITH'S WAY

Glebe Road

Hartington Grove

CHERRY HINTON ROAD

Rustat Road

Luard Road

Sedley Taylor Road

Newton Road

Bentley Road

Brooklands Avenue

Grantchester Street

Grantchester Road

King's Rd

Selwyn Road

Panton Street

Bateman Street

STATION RD

TENISON ROAD

HILLS ROAD

Hobson's Brook

River Cam or Granta

COTON ROAD

High St

B1049

55

CANTERBURY

G [i] Tourist Information Centres — The Longmarket *tel 66567* (summer only)

F [i] Sidney Cooper Centre, St Peters Street *tel 66567* (winter only)

Public buildings and places of interest

F(1) **Beaney Institute, Royal Museum, Art Gallery and Public Library** The museum displays the archaeology, including a hoard of Roman silver spoons and other finds, natural history and geology of the East Kent region.

F(2) **Black Friars Refectory** The refectory dates from c1300.

J(3) **Castle** The castle keep, one of the largest in the country, dates back to c1175.

G(4) **Cathedral** Founded in 602 by St Augustine. The present Cathedral, however is a beautiful 15th-C edifice, where Thomas à Becket was murdered in 1170. Of particular interest are the Trinity Chapel; the 12th-C choir; the "Corona" or Becket's Crown; the old glass; the Norman crypt; and the 15th-C Angel Steeple.

G(5) **Chequers of Hope** A few roof-beams of the famous old hostelry which stood here are still to be seen at the tobacconists. There are associations with Chaucer.

G(6) **Christ Church Gateway** A Tudor structure of 1507-17 with 17th-C gates.

H(7) **Christ Church Teachers' Training College** A modern building.

J(8) **Dane John Fortifications, Gardens and City Walls** The Dane John, an 80ft-high tumulus, has pleasant gardens partly enclosed by a dry moat. There are remains of the old city walls nearby.

F(9) **Grey Friars Monastery** Oldest Franciscan settlement in England of which one building, restored in 1920, remains. It has associations with the Royalist poet, Richard Lovelace.

F(10) **Holy Cross Church** Contains a notable font cover of the 15thC.

K(11) **"Invicta" Locomotive** One of the earliest steam locomotives, which ran on the Canterbury to Whitstable line which was opened in 1830.

G(12) **King's School** Founded originally in the 7thC and placed here as a grammar school by Henry VIII. The unique exterior Norman staircase is notable.

F(13) **Marlowe Theatre**

J(14) **Municipal Buildings**

F(15) **Poor Priests' Hospital and Buffs' Museum** The much altered buildings of the Hospital are of 14th-C date, and house a clinic and the Regimental Museum of the Buffs containing weapons, medals, uniforms, trophies, and pictures illustrating the history of the regiment.

F(16) **Queen Elizabeth's Guest Chamber** An old house dating back to 1573.

G(17) **Roman Pavement** Here are the remains of two mosaic floors, a hypocaust and other Roman relics.

A(18) **Roper Gateway** An elaborate 16th-C brick structure which once led to the home of Sir Thomas More's daughter.

F(19) **St Alphege's Church** A church of very old foundation, preserving some interesting brasses.

G(20) **St Augustine's Abbey and St Pancras Church** The restored abbey gateway of 1300 is impressive, and the nearby remains of St Pancras Church incorporate Roman brickwork.

G(21) **St Augustine's College** A college of the Anglican church founded in 1848 which incorporates some remains of the former abbey.

E(22) **St Dunstan's Church** Saxon work is preserved here, and in the vault is the head of Sir Thomas More, executed in 1535.

G(23) **St George's Church** Only the tower survives from this church where Marlowe was baptised.

C(24) **St John's Hospital** A foundation of 1074, with an old gatehouse and chapel.

H(25) **St Martin's Church** Probably England's oldest church still in use, preserving early Saxon work, notably the font.

J(26) **St Mildred's Church** In this 13th-C church Izaak Walton was married.

F(27) **St Peter's Church** Possibly of Saxon origin and preserving a massive Norman font.

F(28) **St Thomas (or Eastbridge) Hospital** This was re-established in 1342 and preserves a Norman hall and crypt with two chapels.

F(29) **Weavers** Picturesque gabled 15th-C houses with bay windows overlooking the River Stour.

F(30) **West Gate** Of 14th-C date and considered to be the finest city gate in England. It houses an armoury relating to its former use as city gaol.

University of Kent at Canterbury A modern university which opened in 1965. 2m NW via Whitstable Road A290 (A)

Hospitals

P **Kent at Canterbury Hospital,** Ethelbert Road *tel 66877*

O **Nunnery Fields Hospital,** *tel 66877*

Sport and Recreation

C **Canterbury City Football Club,** Kingsmead Stadium

P **Kent County Cricket Club,** St Lawrence Ground, Old Dover Road

C **Kingsmead Indoor Swimming Pool**

C **Speedway,** Kingsmead Stadium

Canterbury Golf Club, Littlebourne Road 1½m E via St Martins Hill A257 (H)

Theatres and Cinemas

K **ABC Cinema,** 43 St George's Place *tel 62022*

A **Gulbenkian Theatre,** at the University of Kent at Canterbury, Giles Lane *tel 69075*

F(13) **Marlowe Theatre,** St Margarets Street *tel 64747* (see also public buildings and places of interest)

F **Odeon Cinema,** The Friars *tel 62480*

Department Stores

Debenhams, Guildhall Street
Marks and Spencer Ltd, 4 St George's Street
Ricemans (Canterbury) Ltd, St George's Lane

Markets

B **General Market** (Wednesday)

B **Cattle Market** (Monday)

Advertisers

K **Mercantile Credit**

G **THF** Chaucer Hotel

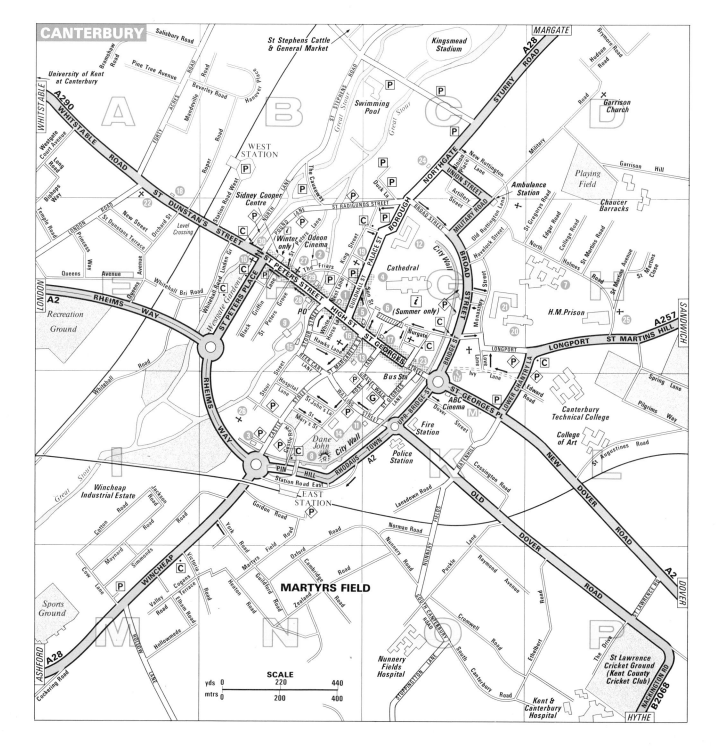

CARDIFF

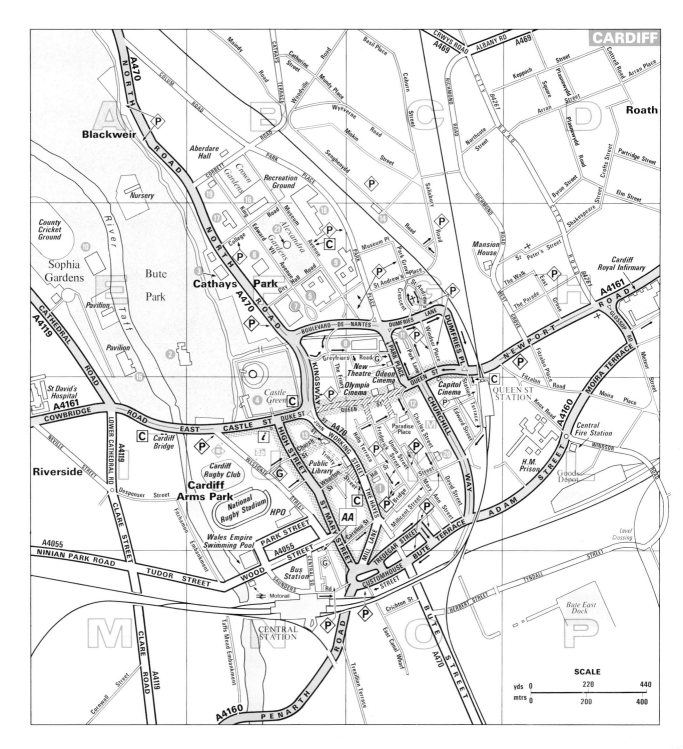

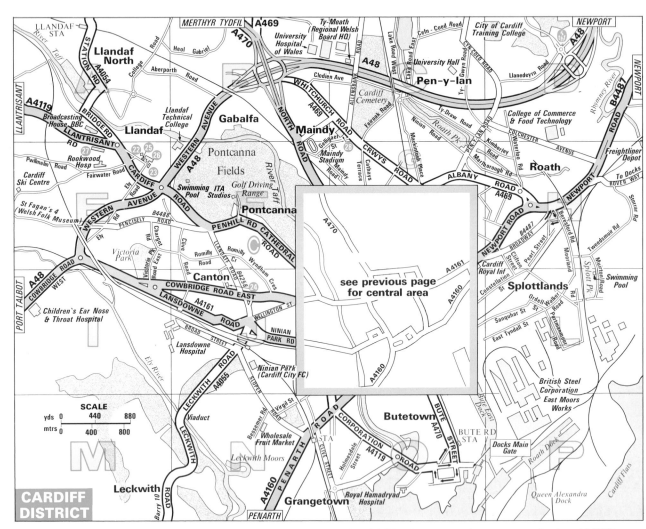

DISTRICT PLAN

Public buildings and places of interest

E(22) **Bell Tower** Remains of Llandaf Cathedral's 13th-C bell tower which once contained the 5½-ton bell 'Great Peter'.

E(23) **Bishops' Castle Gatehouse** The 14th-C gatehouse of the former Bishops' Castle which was sacked in 1402 by Owain Glyndwr.

J(24) **Chapter Arts Centre**

E(25) **City Cross**

E(26) **Llandaf Cathedral** The Cathedral which

dates from the 13thC has been restored after severe war damage.

E(27) **South Wales Gwent Training College of the Domestic Arts**

C(28) **Welsh Regiment Museum, Maindy Barracks**

Hospitals

I **Children's Ear, Nose and Throat Hospital,** Cowbridge Road West *tel 561371*

J **Lansdowne Hospital,** Sanatorium Road *tel 33651*

E **Rookwood Hospital,** Fairwater Road, Llandaf *tel 566281*

O **Royal Hamadryad Hospital,** Cardiff

Docks *tel 24895*

B **University Hospital of Wales,** Heath Park *tel 755944*

Sport and Recreation

J **Cardiff City Association Football Club,**

F **Llandaff Fields Open-Air Swimming Pool**

F **Pontcanna Fields Driving Range**

L **Splott Park Open-Air Swimming Baths**

Cardiff Golf Course, Sherbourne Avenue 3¾m N via Allesbank Road (C)

Advertisers

F **Crest** Beverley Hotel

D **THF** Post House

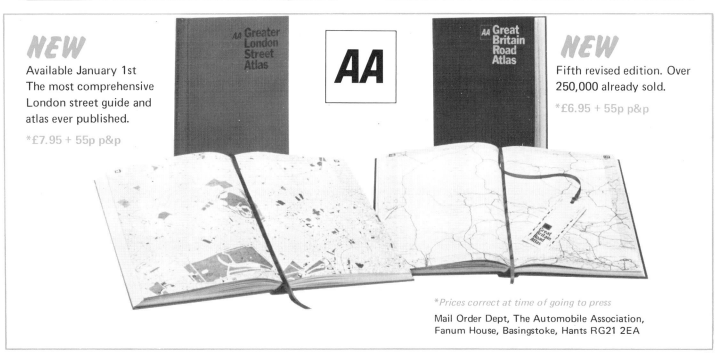

G(6) **Tourist Information Centre** — Municipal Offices, The Promenade *tel 22878* (see also public buildings and places of interest)

Public buildings and places of interest

O(1) **Cheltenham College** A well-known boys' public school, with a fine chapel, founded in 1841.

G(2) **Holst Museum** A Regency house where the composer Gustav Holst was born, with period rooms, paintings and Holst memorabilia.

J(3) **Ladies College** A well-known girls' school, founded in 1835.

G(4) **Library, Art Gallery and Museum** The library houses the historic archives of the borough. The art gallery is rich in 17th-C Dutch and Flemish paintings and 19th- and 20th-C British art. The museum displays English ceramics, Chinese porcelain, Cotswold bygones and furniture, and local geology.

J(5) **Montpellier Gardens** Nearby stands the Rotunda, a fine building of the Regency period, partly by Papworth. In Montpellier Walk, which adjoins, the shops are spaced between replicas of the Erectheon Caryatids.

G(6) **Municipal Buildings** Housed in a typical Regency terrace.

F(7) **St Gregory's Church (RC)**

G(8) **St Mary's Church** This 14th- to 15th-C church, which bears traces of an earlier building of the 12thC, is the town's oldest building. A rare and beautiful example of a rose window is to be seen in the north transept.

N(9) **St Mary's College**

B(10) **St Paul's College**

K(11) **Town Hall and Spa**

Pittville Pump Rooms, Pittville Park. A masterpiece of the Greek revival, built between 1825 and 1830 by Forbes and Papworth and restored after the war. Notable colonnaded façades, portico and pillared balcony and hall. It is situated in the Pittville Gardens off the Evesham road north of the town centre (C).

Hospitals

K **Cheltenham General Eye, Ear and Throat Hospital**, Sandford Road *tel 21344*

B **St Paul's Hospital (Maternity)**, Swindon Road *tel 56291*

Sport and Recreation

C **Approach Golf Course**, Pittville Park

H **Cheltenham Cricket Club**, Victoria Ground

H **Cheltenham Rugby Football Club**, Athletic Ground

D **Cheltenham Town Football Club**, Robbins, Whaddon Road

B **Pittville Swimming Pool**, Tommy Taylors Lane

K **Sandford Park Open-Air Swimming Pool**

Cheltenham Racecourse, Prestbury Park 1½m N via Evesham Road A435 (C)

Cotswold Hills Golf Club, at Cleeve Hill 4¾m NE via Prestbury Road A46 (D)

Lilleybrook Golf Club, Charlton Kings 2m SE via A40 and Cirencester Road A435 (C)

Theatres and Cinemas

G **ABC Cinema**, The Promenade *tel 52603*

K **Cheltenham Playhouse Theatre**, Bath Road *tel 22852*

G **Everyman Theatre**, Regent Street *tel 25544*

G **Odeon 3 Screen Cinema**, Winchcombe Street *tel 24081*

Department Stores

Cavendish House, Cambray Galleries
Daniel Neal and Sons Ltd, 19 Clarence Street
Habitat Designs Ltd, 108 The Promenade
Marks and Spencer Ltd, 179 High Street
Shirers and Lances Ltd, The Promenade
Early closing day Wednesday but most shops are open six days a week

Markets

F **Cattle Market** (Thursday)

Advertisers

F **THF** George Hotel
J **THF** Queen's Hotel

Cheltenham College

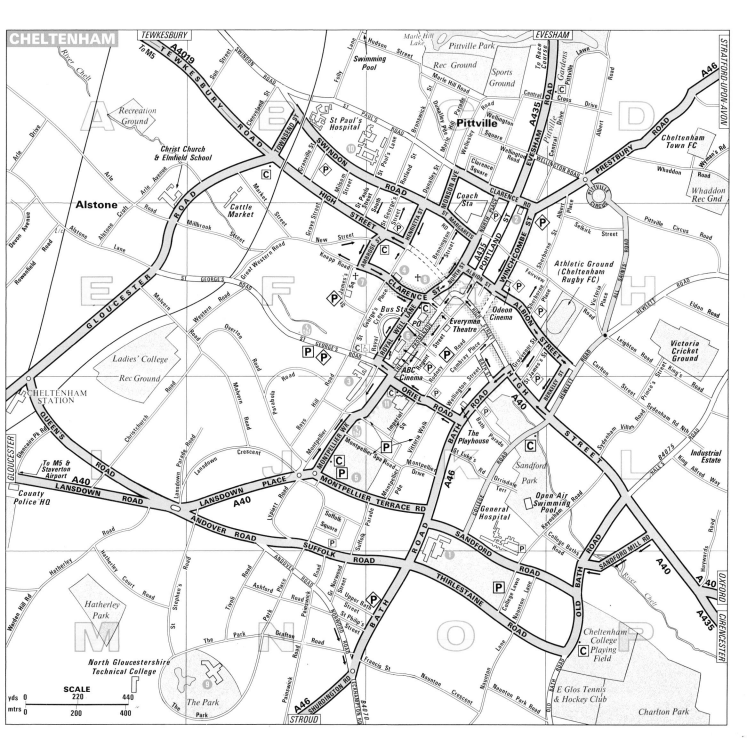

G   AA Service Centre — Mercia Square, Frodsham Street *tel 20438* (07.00-23.00hrs)

F(26)   Tourist Information Centre — Town Hall *i* *tel 40144* (see also public buildings and places of interest)

Public buildings and places of interest

F(1)   **Bishop Lloyd's House** One of the city's finest half-timbered houses dating from 1615, with a richly-carved panelled front showing scenes from sacred history and series of animals. (Closed until further notice for repairs).

F(2)   **Boneswaldesthorne Tower** Situated at the north-west corner of the city walls and linked to the Water Tower by an embattled spur wall.

K(3)   **Bridge Gate** Built 1782, this gate replaced an earlier medieval structure.

G(4)   **British Heritage Centre** Exhibition of Roman, Medieval and present day Chester.

J(5)   **Castle** Mainly 19thC, but the square Agricola Tower dates back to the 13thC and contains an old chapel and the Regimental Museum of the Cheshire Regiment, with relics, photographs, plans and maps covering over 250 years of service.

G(6)   **Cathedral** A mainly 14th-C red sandstone structure, which prior to its dissolution in 1540 was an abbey of ancient foundation. Of particular interest are the monastic remains, including cloisters, chapter house and refectory; the shrine of St Werburgh in the Lady Chapel; the choir stalls with carved misericords of 1380 and the only example of an old consistory court (1636) to be found in England.

G(7)   **Chester Heritage Centre** St Michael's Church Exhibition of Chester's architectural heritage including 20-minute audio-visual shows.

K(8)   **County Hall** Modern administrative offices, opened in 1957.

G(9)   **East Gate** A gateway of 1769, replacing earlier Roman and medieval structures, which is surmounted by a clock tower erected in 1897 to commemorate Queen Victoria's Jubilee.

F(10)   **God's Providence House** A timbered house of 1652 in the Rows. Altered in 1862.

J(11)   **Grosvenor Museum** Well-known for its collection of Roman antiquities but also contains natural history and art galleries and in an adjacent house, period rooms and displays of furniture, costume and folk-life.

F(12)   **Guildhall Museum** Documents, regalia, records and silver of 23 city companies dating from the 14thC.

F(13)   **High Cross** The original High Cross, destroyed in 1646, has now been restored and re-erected in its original position near the south door of St Peter's Church.

C(14)   **King Charles or Phoenix Tower** Although much restored in 1613 and 1658, it retains its medieval appearance. It contains a Civil War Exhibition.

G(15)   **New Gate** Opened in 1938 to provide a wider entranceway to the city than was previously afforded by the Wolfe Gate of 1768, which stands immediately to the north.

G(16)   **Nine Houses** An unusual terraced group of timber-framed buildings of the 17thC, restored in 1969.

B(17)   **North Gate** An early 19th-C structure, once used as a prison.

F(18)   **Pemberton's Parlour** Known also as the Goblin Tower, this was rebuilt in 1894.

G(19)   **Roman Amphitheatre** This is the site of the largest Roman building to have been excavated in Britain (1939). Later excavations have revealed large granaries.

G(20)   **Roman Garden** Contains a collection of Roman columns which have been re-erected here along with other architectural fragments.

G(21)   **St John's Church** A partly-ruined church which preserves a fine Norman nave.

K(22)   **St Mary-on-the-Hill** Mainly of the 15th and 16thCs and preserving a splendid medieval timber roof in the nave.

K(23)   **St Mary-without-the-Walls** A church of 1887 in Perpendicular style.

F(24)   **St Peter's Church** The principal city church which occupies the site of the headquarters of the Roman fortress.

F(25)   **Stanley Palace** A gabled and timbered former 16th-C home of the Earls of Derby, which has been much restored and is now the local headquarters of the English-speaking Union.

F(26)   **Town Hall** A Gothic-style building opened in 1869.

E(27)   **Water Tower** This outwork dates from 1322 and was once washed by the River Dee. It contains an exhibition on medieval Chester.

J   **Grosvenor Bridge.** A single stone span of 200ft built in 1832.

K   **Old Dee Bridge** Dating from the 13thC, it was until 1832, the only bridge crossing the Dee at Chester.

F   **The City Walls** These encircle the town for a distance of two miles and provide a splendid example of a fortified medieval town. Fine views can be obtained from a walk around the walls on their raised rampart walk.

G   **The Rows** Unique in England, these are continuous arcades or galleries running along the first floor of houses in Eastgate Street, Watergate Street and Bridge Street, and may be compared with somewhat similar examples in the Swiss town of Thun.

Zoological Gardens Interesting collection of animals displayed in natural surroundings, amid fine gardens. Tropical house, aquarium and walk-through aviary. 3m N via Liverpool Road A5116 (B)

Hospitals

F   **Chester Royal Infirmary,** St Martins Fields *tel 28261*

Sport and Recreation

E   **Chester Golf Course,** Curzon Park
J   **Chester Racecourse,** Roodee
H   **Swimming Baths,** Union Street
Chester Football Club, Sealand Road 1m NW via Sealand Road A548B (A)
Greyhound Racing Track, Sealand Road 1¼m NW via Sealand Road A548B (A)

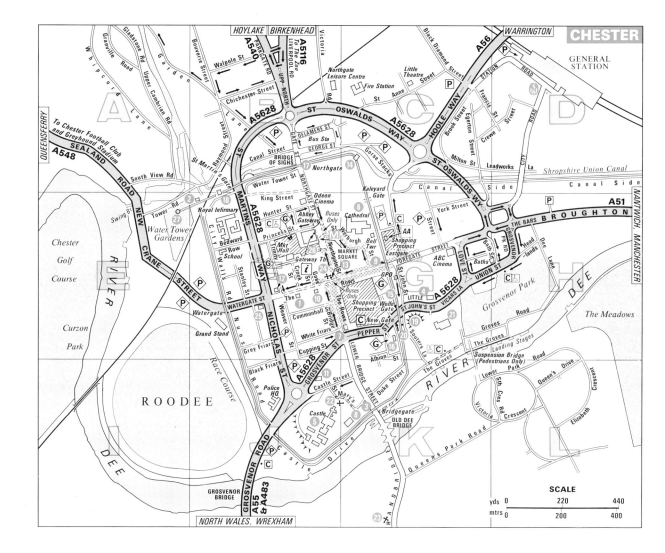

Theatres and Cinemas

G	**ABC Cinema,** Foregate Street *tel 22931*
C	**Chester Theatre Club,** Little Theatre, Gloucester Street *tel 22674*
F	**Gateway Theatre,** Hamilton Place *tel 40393*
F	**Odeon Theatre,** Northgate Street *tel 24930*

Department Stores

Army and Navy Stores (Coates), Mercia Square
Browns of Chester Ltd, Eastgate Street
Burrells Ltd, 28 & 30 Foregate Street
Famous Army Stores, 102 Northgate Street
King L and Co (Chester) Ltd, 20 Handbridge
Marks and Spencer Ltd, 22 Foregate Street
Owen Owen Ltd, Eastgate Street
Early closing day Wednesday

Markets

F	**Public Market,** Market Hall (at rear of Town Hall) (daily)

Cattle Market, Bumpers Lane (Tuesday and Thursday) 1m NW via Sealand Road A5488 (A)

Advertisers

G	**Mercantile Credit**
D	**THF** Queen Hotel

AA Road Service Centre (7) — 1m E via Westhampnett Road at junction of A285 and A27 (H) *tel 83111*

J(4) i **Tourist Information Centres** — Council House, North Street *tel 82226* (summer) (see also public buildings and places of interest)

J i Greyfriars, North Street *tel 842555* (winter)

Public buildings and places of interest

J(1) **Canon Gate** A 16th-C gateway leading from South Street into the Cathedral precincts along Canon Lane. To the south of Canon Lane is the Chantry with its 13th-C Hall and Chapel.

J(2) **Cathedral** Norman and later, with the only example in England of a detached bell-tower. Two 12th-C sculptures and the retrochoir are of particular note. Close to the Cathedral are the Bishop's Palace, Chapel and 14th-C Palace Gatehouse.

M(3) **College of Further Education**

J(4) **Council House,** An interesting 17th- and 18th-C town hall containing the City Council Chamber. Preserved at the front of the building is the Roman Neptune and Minerva Stone discovered in 1723.

N(5) **County Court**

F(6) **Festival Theatre** Opened in 1962, its summer season has acquired an international reputation.

J(7) **Library**

J(8) **Market Cross** Restored and renovated 16th-C cross which is arguably the finest example of its type in the country.

J(9) **Museum** Local relics and a display of material from the Royal Sussex Regiment are housed in this 18th-C building.

J(10) **Priory Park** In the park stands the Early English Choir of Greyfriars Church, later used as a Guildhall and now housing pottery and other archaeological material from the City museum.

K(11) **Roman Amphitheatre Site** This was the ampitheatre of the Roman town of Regnum.

J(12) **St Andrew's Church** A 15th-C structure built above a Roman pavement. Although now in an unsafe condition, its situation shows how valuable building space was wisely used in medieval times.

K(13) **St John's Church** Completed in 1813, the church contains a three-decker pulpit.

J(14) **St Mary's Hospital and St Martin's Square** The almshouses, refounded c1240, preserve a fine hall, with a wagon roof and an interesting Chapel screen. In St Martin's Square are some attractive Georgian houses.

J(15) **St Olave's Church** A partly-Norman Church, converted into a bookshop. It rests on Roman foundations and has an elaborate piscina in the North wall.

N(16) **St Richard's Church (RC)** A recent building which contains some notable modern French stained glass.

Fishbourne Roman Palace One of the major archaeological finds of this century in Britain. Mosaic-floored rooms, a museum and formal gardens are on display. 2m W via Westgate A259 and A27(I)

Hospitals

C **Graylingwell (Mental) Hospital,** College Lane *tel 85171*

G **St Richard's Hospital (Royal West Sussex),** Spitalfield Lane *tel 88122*

Sport and Recreation

F **Chichester City Football Club,** Oaklands Park *tel 82517*

F **Chichester Rugby Football Club,** Oaklands Park *tel 85545*

K **Swimming Pool,** Eastgate Square *tel 86587*

Theatres and Cinemas

F(6) **Festival Theatre** *tel 86333*

J **Granada Cinema,** East Street *tel 82407*

Department Stores

Geerings, 79 North Street
Marks and Spencer Ltd, 16 East Street
Morants (Army & Navy Stores), West Street
Portsea Island Mutual Co-operative, North Street
Early closing day Thursday

Markets

K **Cattle Market,** Market Road (alternate Wednesdays).

Advertisers

J THF Dolphin and Anchor Hotel

Chichester Cathedral bell-tower

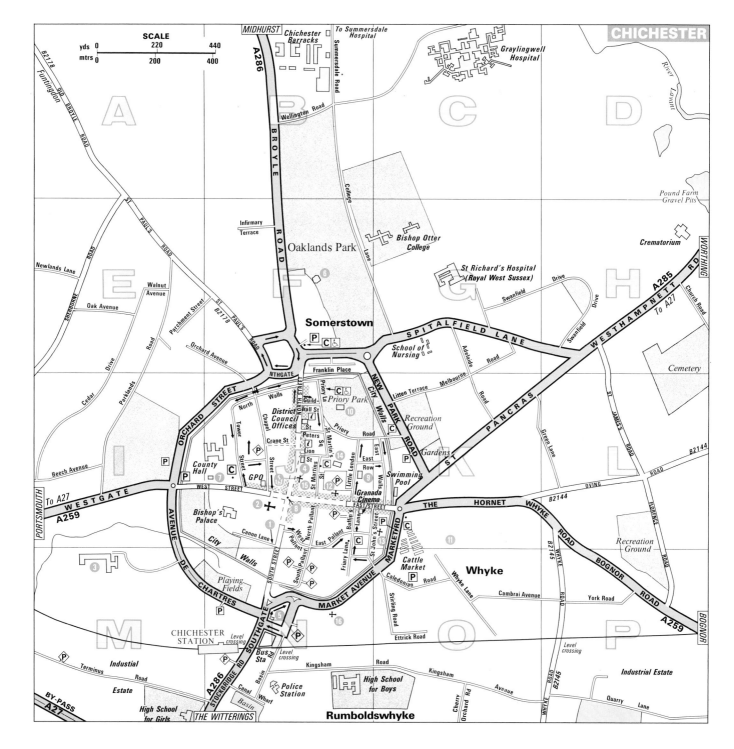

SCALE

yds 0   220   440
mtrs 0   200   400

CHICHESTER

MIDHURST
A286

To Summersdale Hospital

Chichester Barracks

Summersdale Road

Graylingwell Hospital

River Lavant

B2178
Funtington
OLD BROYLE ROAD

Wellington Road

BROYLE ROAD

Pound Farm Gravel Pits

Newlands Lane

ST PAUL'S ROAD

SHERBOURNE ROAD

Walnut Avenue

Oak Avenue

Parchment Street

Orchard Avenue

B2178
ST PAUL'S ROAD

Infirmary Terrace

Oaklands Park

College Lane

Bishop Otter College

St Richard's Hospital (Royal West Sussex)

Crematorium

WORTHING RD

A285
WESTHAMPNETT RD
To A27

Church Road

Cemetery

Cedar Drive

Parklands

Beech Avenue

ORCHARD STREET

AVENUE DE CHARTRES

Somerstown

P C &

Franklin Place

NTHGATE

North Walls

HIGH STREET

Tower Street

Crane St

Chapel Street

Little London

GPO

County Hall

P

C

WEST STREET

Bishop's Palace

City Walls

Playing Fields

P

CHICHESTER STATION

Terminus Road

Industrial Estate

P

A286
STOCKBRIDGE RD
SOUTHGATE

High School for Girls

THE WITTERINGS

Canal Basin

Wharf

Police Station

Bus Sta

Level crossing

Level crossing

Kingsham Road

High School for Boys

Rumboldswhyke

Kingsham Road

Cherry Orchard Rd

Caledonian Road

Stirling Road

Ettrick Road

Whyke Lane

Cattle Market

Whyke

MARKET AVENUE

MARKET RD

THE HORNET

Recreation Ground

Swimming Pool

Granada Cinema

EAST STREET

Priory Park

District Council Offices

School of Nursing

NEW PARK ROAD

CITY WALLS

SPITALFIELD LANE

ST PANCRAS

Gardens

Recreation Ground

Adelaide Road

Melbourne Road

Litten Terrace

Swanfield Drive

Swanfield

James's Road

Green Lane

OVING ROAD

B2144

B2144

FLORENCE ROAD

Recreation Ground

Cambrai Avenue

York Road

WHYKE ROAD
BOGNOR ROAD
B2145

A259
BOGNOR

Quarry Lane

Industrial Estate

Level crossing

B2145
WHYKE ROAD

PORTSMOUTH
To A27
WESTGATE
A259

BY-PASS
A27

Canon Lane

West Pallant

South Pallant

North Pallant

East Pallant

Baffin's Lane

Friary Lane

St John's Street

Priory Lane

Priory Road

East Row

East Walls

East Street

St Martin's

St Martin's Sq

Lion Street

Peters St

Guildhall St

Priory Park

COVENTRY

F   **AA Service Centre** — 19 Cross Cheaping
tel 021-550 4858

F 🛈   **Tourist Information Centre** — Broadgate
tel 25555/20084/51717/51718

Public buildings and places of interest

F(1) **Belgrade Theatre** Opened in 1958 and incorporating softwood from Yugoslavia in its construction.

F(2) **Bond's Hospital and Bablake Old School** An enchanting Tudor almshouse, with half-timbered and stone facade and nearby the picturesque old school building.

F(3) **Broadgate** Here are the Lady Godiva statue and New Clock Tower, with figures of Lady Godiva and Peeping Tom.

L(4) **Charter House** There are slight remains of these buildings, founded in 1381.

J(5) **Cheylesmore Manor House (Registry Office)** Dates back originally to 1230 and is built over a lane.

J(6) **Christ Church** Noted for its tall, restored 14th-C spire, which survived the bombing of 1940.

G(7) **City Walls and Gate** Slight remains of the 14th-C walls, together with two gates, are still to be seen.

J(8) **Council House**

G(9) **Coventry Theatre**

J(10) **Ford's Hospital** A half-timbered almshouse with interior courtyard considered to be an exceptional example of 16th-C domestic architecture.

G(11) **"Golden Cross Inn"** A gabled and restored half-timbered inn, probably dating from the 17thC.

K(12) **Herbert Museum and Art Gallery** The museum contains a collection of old motor vehicles, particularly of Coventry manufacture; a Warwickshire natural history section; a full-scale working loom; Stevengraphs (silk pictures); and silk woven bookmarks. The art gallery's permanent collection relates to British life and landscape, in particular of Warwickshire.

G(13) **Holy Trinity Church** A 15th-C church with a 231ft-high spire. The 15th-C brass eagle lecturn and west window of 1955 are notable.

G(14) **Lanchester College of Technology**

K(15) **Martyrs' Memorial** This memorial of 1910 is in memory of the Coventry martyrs of the 16thC.

F(16) **St John's Church** A restored 14th-to 15th-C church.

F(17) **St John's Hospital** Mainly 14th-C and formerly a school, with a fine hall. It has now been restored.

K(18) **St Mary's Guildhall** A building of 1340 and later, with restored Great Hall adorned with much fine, stained glass, in particular the North Wall window; portraits and a 15th-C Arras tapestry; minstrel's gallery, and 13th-C Caesar's watch-tower, rebuilt after bomb damage.

G(19) **St Michael's Cathedral** Only the walls, the 303ft-high, 15th-C tower and spire of the medieval cathedral survived the bombing of 1940. The new cathedral by Sir Basil Spence was completed in 1962 and is in a striking, modern style, incorporating richly-coloured glass; Epstein sculptures; an engraved glass screen by John Hutton and a vast Aubusson altar tapestry of *Christ in Glory* by Graham Sutherland.

F(20) **Spon Street** An attempt is being made to create a medieval street by rebuilding here ancient buildings from other parts of the town.

K(21) **Whitefriars Monastery and Museum** A beautifully-restored, old sandstone building housing an archaeological collection of the Coventry area with exhibits dating from the stone age.

Bond's Hospital

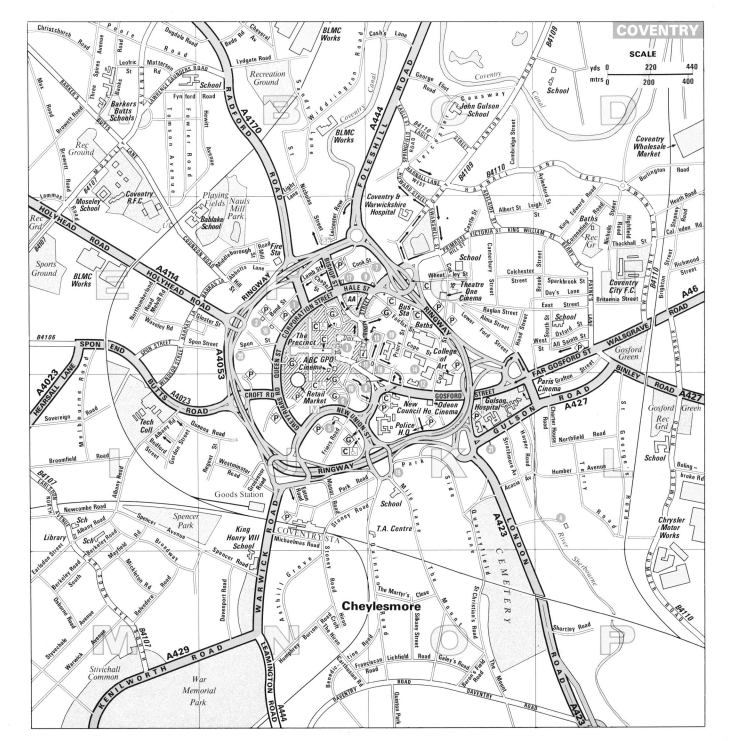

Hospitals

G	**Coventry and Warwickshire Hospital** *tel 24055*	
K	**Gulson Hospital** *tel 28331*	

Sport and Recreation

G	**Coventry Baths,** Fairfax Street
H	**Coventry City Football Club,** Highfield Road
E	**Coventry Rugby Football Club,** Coundon Road
H	**Primrose Hill Baths,** Coronation Road

Theatres and Cinemas

F	**ABC Cinema,** Hertford Street *tel 23600*
F(1)	**Belgrade Theatre,** Corporation Street *tel 20205* (see also public buildings and places of interest)
G(9)	**Coventry Theatre,** Hales Street *tel 23141* (see also public buildings and places of interest)
K	**Odeon Cinema,** Jordan Well *tel 22042*
K	**Paris Cinema,** Far Gosford Street *tel 26526*
G	**Theatre One Cinema,** Ford Street *tel 24301*

Department Stores

Co-operative, Lower Precinct
Marks and Spencer Ltd, The Precinct
Owen Owen Ltd, Broadgate
Early closing day Thursday, but most shops remain open six days

Markets

J	**Coventry Market** (Wednesday, Friday and Saturday)
D	**Coventry Wholesale Market,** Barras Heath

Advertisers

J	**Mercantile Credit**
F	**Godfrey Davis**

DISTRICT PLAN

Public buildings and places of interest

O(22)	**Lunt Roman Fort** Reconstruction of Roman Fort, which stood on this site AD71-75, with interpretive centre housed in reconstructed granary.	
M(23)	**University of Warwick**	
O(24)	**Zoo** Covers a wide representation of the animal kingdom.	

Hospitals

E	**Paybody Hospital** *tel 20455*
H	**Walsgrave Hospital** *tel 613232*
K	**Whitley Hospital** *tel 20455*

Sport and Recreation

N	**Coventry Golf Club,** Finham Park
K	**Grange Golf Course**
J	**Hearsall Golf Club,** Beechwood Avenue
K	**Humber Bowling Centre,** Forum Bowl, Longfellow Road
F	**Livingstone Road Baths**
L	**Speedway,** Brandon

Markets

K	**Coventry Wholesale Market,** Barras Heath

Advertisers

O	**Crest** Coventry Crest Motel
H	**Crest** Coventry Esso Motel
E	**THF** The Post House

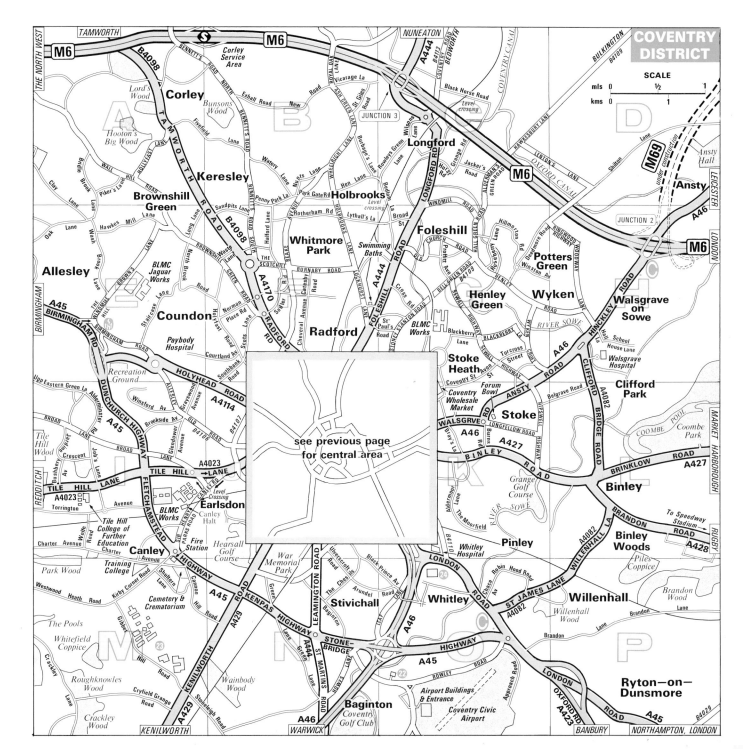

DERBY

CENTRAL PLAN

F(1) Tourist Information Centre — The
ⓘ Reference Library, Central Library,
The Wardwick *tel 31111 ext 2185/6*
(see also public buildings and places of
interest)

Public buildings and places of interest

F(1) **Art Gallery, Museum and Central Library**
Contains antiquities, local and social
history and natural history collections,
Derby porcelain, costumes, militaria,
Bonnie Prince Charlie room (1745
rebellion), a scaled working layout of
the former Midland Railway and paintings
by Joseph Wright of Derby (1734-97).

B(2) **Art School** St Helen's House, 18th-C.

B(3) **Brigg Chapel** A restored 14th-C chapel
situated on the 18th-C bridge spanning
the River Derwent.

F(4) **Cathedral** Formerly the Parish Church
until 1927. It was rebuilt by James
Gibbs in 1725 and is noted for its
16th-C Western tower, an 18th-C wrought
iron screen by Robert Bakewell and
modern windows by Ceri Richards
executed by Patrick Reynteins.

F(5) **Civic Halls**

F(6) **County Hall** The notable façade dates
from 1660.

F(7) **Guildhall and Market Hall**

K(8) **New Market Hall,** Eagle Centre

K(9) **New Playhouse Theatre,** Eagle Centre

O(10) **Royal Crown Derby Porcelain Company**
Factory tours on written application.

B(11) **St Mary's Church (RC)** A building by
the famous 19th-C architect Pugin.

F(12) **St Michael's Church** Rebuilt in the
19thC.

J(13) **St Peter's Church** This church has
preserved a fine Flemish chest.

F(14) **St Werburgh's Church** Dr Johnson was
married in this church.

F(15) **Silk Mill, Industrial Museum and Art
Gallery** Housed in an early 17th-C silk
mill which was substantially rebuilt in
1910, this museum contains a Rolls Royce
aero engine collection, exhibitions on
the history of aviation from the Wright
Brothers to the present day and 'An
Introduction to Derbyshire Industries'.

Hospitals

J **Derby Chest Clinic,** Green Lane *tel 40366*
B **Derbyshire Children's Hospital,** North
Street *tel 47141*
E **Derbyshire Hospital for Women,** Friar Gate
tel 47141
O **Derbyshire Royal Infirmary,** London
Road *tel 47141*
O **Nightingale Maternity Home,** London Road
tel 47141

Theatres and Cinemas

K **ABC Cinema,** East Street *tel 43964*
K(9) **New Playhouse Theatre,** Eagle Centre
tel 363275 (see also public buildings
and places of interest)
K **Odeon Cinema,** London Road *tel 40139*
F **Odeon Pennine Cinema,** Colyear Street
tel 45026

Department Stores

Debenhams Departmental Store, 17 Victoria
Street
Marks and Spencer Ltd, 11 St Peter's Street
Early closing day Wednesday, but most shops are
open six days a week

Markets

F(7) **Market Hall** (General retail, meat,
poultry, fish — daily) (see also public
buildings and places of interest)
K(8) **New Market Hall,** Eagle Centre (daily)
(see also public buildings and places
of interest)
G **Morledge Open Market** (Fruit, veg & misc)
(Tuesday, Thursday, Friday, Saturday)

Advertisers

F **Mercantile Credit**

DISTRICT PLAN

F **AA Road Service Centre (25)** — On A52 at
junction with A5111 *tel 41496*

Public buildings and places of interest

B(16) **Darley Abbey** (ruins)
A(17) **Kedleston Hall** Outstanding Robert Adam
mansion, with unique marble hall, state
room and collection of fine pictures,
which stands in a lake-watered 500-acre
park.

Hospitals

I **Derby City Hospital,** Uttoxeter Road
tel 40131
G **Derwent Hospital,** Mansfield Road
tel 47141
I **Kingsway Hospital,** Kingsway *tel 362221*
I **Manor Hospital,** Uttoxeter Road *tel
49694*
I **Pastures Hospital,** Mickleover *tel
53921*
M **Rykneld Hospital** *tel 53656*
F **Queen Mary Maternity Home,** Duffield
Road *tel 47141*

Sport and Recreation

B **Allestree Park Golf Course**
K **Derby County Football Association**
N **Derby Golf Course,** Sinfin
B **Derby Rugby Football Club,** Pavilion,
Kedleston Road
F **Greyhound Stadium,** Vernon Street
A **Kedleston Park Golf Course**
I **Mickleover Golf Course,** Uttoxeter Road
O **Municipal Sports and Athletic Stadium,**
Moor Lane, Osmaston Park Road
K **Reginald Street Baths**
O **Regional Swimming Pool,** Municipal Sports
Ground, Moor Lane, Allerton

Cinemas

H **Lucky Seven Film Centre,** Nottingham
Road, Chaddesden *tel 674161*

Markets

O **Allenton Open Market** (Friday and
Saturday)
G **Cattle and Wholesale Markets,** Chequers
Road (daily, except cattle — Tuesday
and Saturday)

Advertisers

I **Crest** Derby Crest Motel

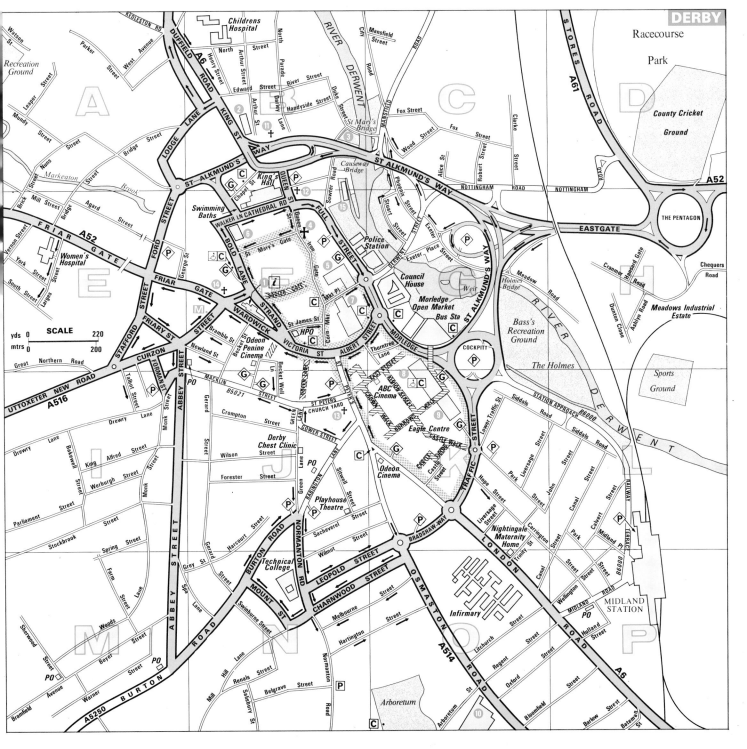

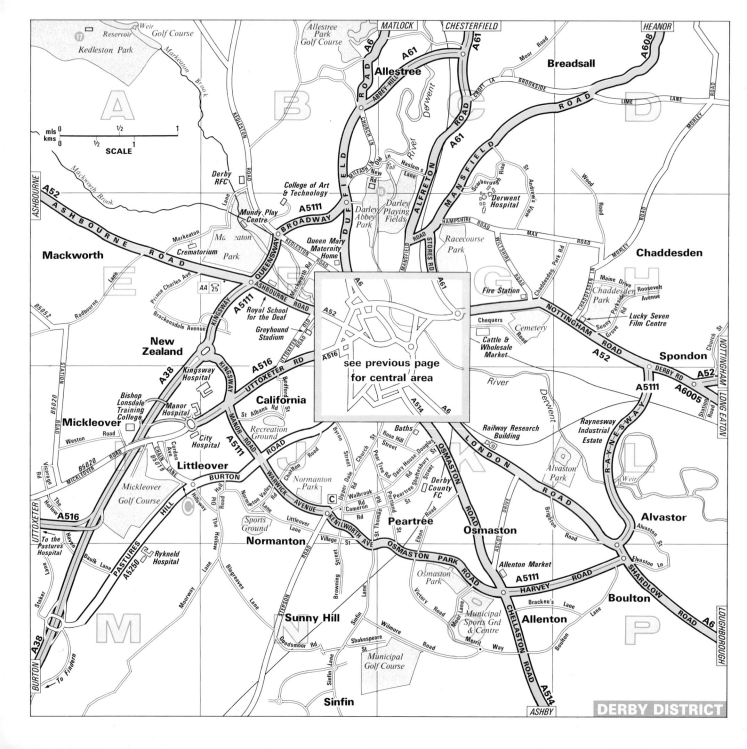

DERBY DISTRICT

DRIVE
DRIVE AA

**If you're a motorist
you daren't go without it.**

DRIVE

**Now six times a year.
From any newsagent.**

DOVER

H   **AA Service Centre** – Fanum House, Russell Street *tel 203580*

H *i*   **Tourist Information Centre** – Townwall Street *tel 205108*

Public buildings and places of interest

D(1)   **Bleriot Memorial** A granite aeroplane commemorates Louis Bleriot's epic flight across the English Channel in 1909.

D(2)   **Castle, St Mary de Castra Church and Roman Lighthouse** The impressive Norman Castle, the 'Key to England' overlooks the Channel. The Keep dates from 1181. The Church of St Mary de Castra is a pre-Conquest structure of the 10th or 11thC and has been used as the garrison church since the restoration by Scott in 1860-62. Nearby stands the Roman 'pharos' or lighthouse.

G(3)   **Dover College** The College preserves portions of the monastery of St Martin of the New Wark, often called Dover Priory.

G(4)   **Library** This is housed in the attractive 17th-C building, Maison Dieu House, a former pilgrim's hostel.

G(5)   **St Edmund's Chapel** This was consecrated by St Richard of Chichester in 1253 and fell into disuse as a chapel in 1544. It has now been restored and was reconsecrated in 1968.

H(6)   **St Mary's Church** Retains a Norman Tower, much of the structure having been rebuilt in 1843.

G(7)   **Town Hall, Museum and Information Bureau** The building includes the 13th-C Hall of Maison Dieu. The museum contains exhibits on local history, diorama, early furniture, textiles, pictures, ceramics, ships etc.

Hospitals

F   **Buckland Hospital,** Coombe Valley Road *tel 201624*

F   **Eye Hospital,** Noah's Ark Road *tel 201624*

G   **Royal Victoria Hospital,** High Street *tel 204508*

Sport and Recreation

G   **Maison Dieu Gardens** – bowls.

H   **Sports Centre,** Townwall Street.

Theatres and Cinemas

H   **ABC Cinema,** Castle Street *tel 206750*

Department Stores

The Co-operative, Biggin Street

Marks and Spencer Ltd, 28 Biggin Street

Early closing day Wednesday

Advertisers

M   **Godfrey Davis**

The Roman 'pharos'

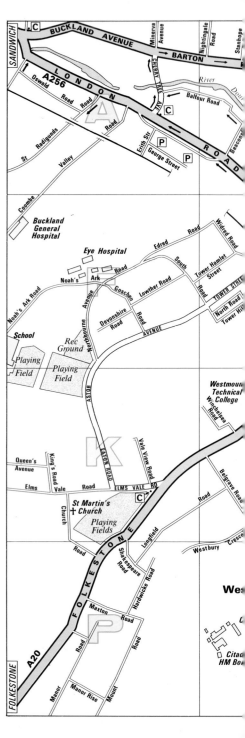

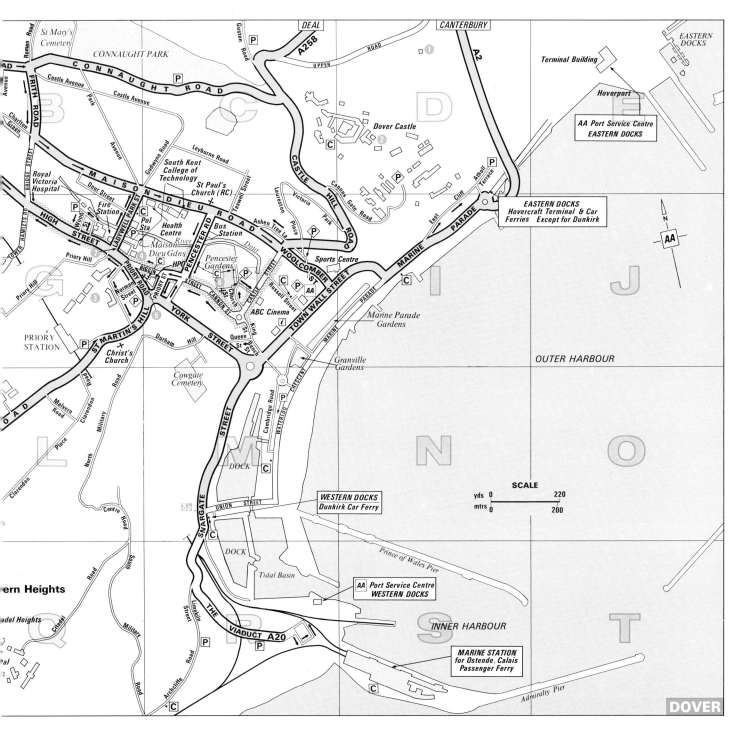

DUNDEE

CENTRAL PLAN

F   **AA Service Centre** – 124 Overgate *tel 25585*

G 🛈   **Tourist Information Centre** – 98 Nethergate *tel 23141* (May-Sep)

Public buildings and places of interest

G(1)   **Albert Institute** Contains the city museum, library and art gallery, housing collections on local archaeology; history; natural history; geology and botany; a display on the life and works of Mary Slessor, the missionary; and works of art by principal British and European masters.

F(2)   **Barrack Street Museum** Contains shipping and industrial exhibits relating to the city.

G(3)   **Caird Hall** Built 1914-23, comprises the city hall and council chambers.

C(4)   **Cowgate Port** The only surviving gate of the old town walls. George Wishart is said to have preached from the gate during the plague of 1544.

A(5)   **Dudhope Castle** A restored 13th-C castle, now used as a meeting place for clubs and societies.

G(6)   **HMS Unicorn** The oldest floating warship, it was completed in the early 19thC.

F(7)   **Mercat Cross** A replica of 1874 of the original cross that stood in Seagate.

F(8)   **St Mary's Tower** A 15th-C steeple or bell-tower, 160ft-high, which is part of the three city churches. A small museum displaying the history of the churches is housed here.

G(9)   **St Paul's Cathedral** Designed by Sir Gilbert Scott and completed in 1853, it stands on the site of the old Dundee Castle.

E(10)   **University**

F   **The Howff** Old burial ground, founded by charter of Mary, Queen of Scots in 1564, and used until 1878. Also formerly used as a meeting place for local craftsmen until 1778.

Hospitals

F   **Dundee Eye Institution,** 138 Nethergate *tel 23639*

B   **Dundee Royal Infirmary,** Barrack Road *tel 23125*

Sport and Recreation

K   **Swimming and Leisure Centre**

Theatres and Cinemas

G   **ABC Cinema,** Seagate, *tel 26865*

A   **Dundee Repertory Theatre,** 113 Lochee Road *tel 23530*

C   **Little Theatre,** 58 Victoria Road *tel 25835*

G   **Odeon Cinema,** Cowgate *tel 26767*

C   **Tivoli Cinema,** Bonnybank Road *tel 24258*

A   **Tryp Repertory Theatre,** 113 Lochee Road *tel 24532*

C   **Victoria Cinema,** Victoria Road *tel 26186*

E   **Whitehall Theatre,** Bellfield Street *tel 22200*

Department Stores

Arnotts, 80 High Street
Draffens, Nethergate
Lawsons Ltd, Whitehall Crescent
McGill Brothers Ltd, 5 Victoria Road
Marks and Spencer Ltd, 41 Murraygate
Robertsons, Barrack Street
Smith Alex (Stores) Ltd, 100 Commercial Street
Telfer and Co Ltd, 26 Exchange Street
Early closing day Wednesday

Markets

G   **City Arcade,** Caird Hall Buildings, Shore Terrace (daily)

Advertisers

C   **Mercantile Credit**
F   **Godfrey Davis**
J   **THF** Queen's Hotel
F   **Centre** Tay Centre Hotel
F   **Centre** Royal Centre Hotel

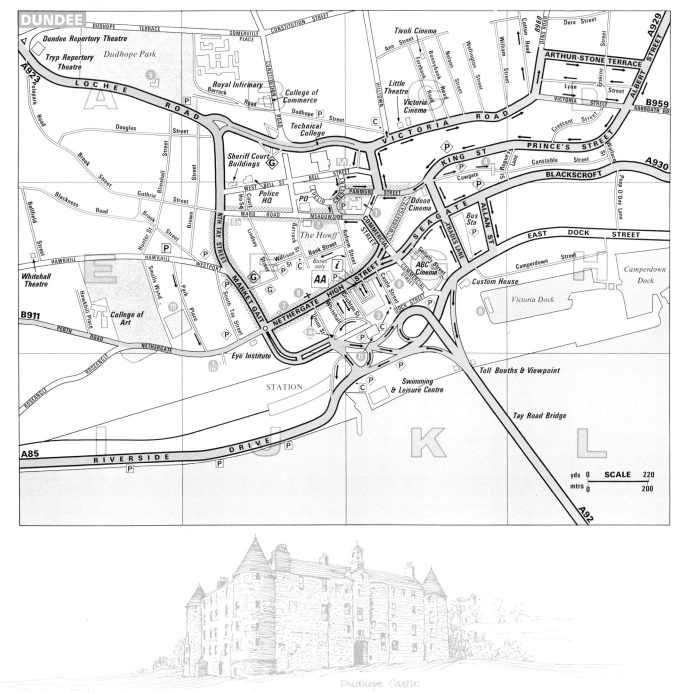

DUNDEE

Dudhope Park

Dundee Repertory Theatre

Tryp Repertory Theatre

DUDHOPE TERRACE

SOMERVILLE PLACE

CONSTITUTION STREET

A923 Polepark Road

LOCHEE ROAD

CONSTITUTION ROAD

Royal Infirmary

Barrack Road

College of Commerce

Dudhope Street

Technical College

Douglas Street

Blinshall Street

Guthrie Street

Brook Street

Brown Street

Hunter St.

Sheriff Court Buildings

West Court HoSq

Police HQ

BELL ST

EUCLID

PO

BELL STREET

WARD ROAD

MEADOWSIDE

The Howff

Barrack Street

Lindsay Street

Willison St.

Bank Street

Blackness Road

Bellfield Street

Whitehall Theatre

HAWKHILL

WESTPORT

Smalls Wynd

College of Art

Hawkhill Place

B911

PERTH ROAD

ROSEANGLE

NETHERGATE

Eye Institute

STATION

A85 RIVERSIDE DRIVE

Tivoli Cinema

Ann Street

Forebank Road

Bonnybank Road

Nelson Street

Wellington Street

William Street

HILLTOWN

Little Theatre

Victoria Cinema

VICTORIA ROAD

Cotton Road

B960 DENS ROAD

Dura Street

Street

A929 ALBERT STREET

ARTHUR-STONE TERRACE

Lyon Street

Erskine Street

VICTORIA STREET

B959

ARBROATH RD

KING ST

Crescent Street

PRINCE'S STREET

Wallace St.

A930

Cowgate

St Roque's Lane

Constable Street

BLACKSCROFT

Peep O'Day Lane

Odeon Cinema

PANMURE STREET

MURRAYGATE

COMMERCIAL STREET

REFORM STREET

HIGH STREET

SEAGATE

TRADES LANE

ALLAN ST

Bus Sta

EAST DOCK STREET

Camperdown Street

Camperdown Dock

Gellatly Street

ABC Cinema

Castle Street

DOCK STREET

Custom House

Victoria Dock

NETHERGATE

Crichton St.

Whitehall Union St.

Swimming & Leisure Centre

Toll Booths & Viewpoint

Tay Road Bridge

A92

| yds | 0 | SCALE | 220 |
| mtrs | 0 | | 200 |

Dudhope Castle

DISTRICT PLAN
Public buildings and places of interest

C(11) **Dundee Law** A 571ft-high viewpoint.

C(12) **Mains of Fintry Castle** Ruins of a late 16th-C castle standing in Caird Park.

F(13) **Mills Observatory** Stands in Balgay Park and can be visited.

A(14) **Spalding Golf Museum,** Camperdown Park. This museum portrays the history of golf through three centuries and includes an iron club of c1680. It is housed in Camperdown House, a classical mansion of 1824-28. The park also contains a children's zoo and aviary.

H(15) **The Tay Bridge** This bridge carries dual two-lane carriageways each 22ft wide, and there is a 10ft-wide central reservation for pedestrians. The toll booths are on the Dundee side. Situated 2m downstream from the Tay railway bridge, it is 7,365ft (1.4m) long.
Begun in May 1963, the Tay road bridge was opened by HM The Queen Mother on 18 August 1966. It consists of 42 spans with twin concrete columns of an unusual developing parabolic shape, and the deck rises from 32ft to 125ft above mean water level. There are two public viewing platforms; one above the tollbooths, and one above the navigation span, half a mile from the Fife shore.

K(16) **The Tay Railway Bridge** A double track structure 11,653ft long, and opened in 1887. It was built to replace the single line bridge opened in 1878, part of which collapsed during a great storm in December 1879 with the loss of a train and 75 passengers. The remains of the old piers can be seen alongside the present bridge.

Hospitals

E **Ninewells Hospital** *tel 60111*
C **Kings Cross Hospital,** West Clepington Road *tel 85241*
C **Maryfields Hospital,** Mains Loan *tel 40011*
F **Royal Victoria Hospital,** Jedburgh Road *tel 66246*

Sport and Recreation

C **Caird Park Golf Course**
A **Camperdown Golf Course,** Camperdown Park
B **Dundee-Angus Ice Rink,** Kingsway West
C **Dundee Football Club,** Dens Park, Sandeman Street
C **Dundee United Football Club,** Tannadice Street
B **Downfield Golf Club**
B **Swimming Baths,** High Street, Lochee

Markets

D **Cattle Market,** Broughty Ferry Road (Tuesday; general agricultural sales Friday and Saturday)
C **Dens Road Market,** 39 Dens Road (Tuesday mornings)
B **Lorne Street Market,** Lochee

Mains of Fintry Castle

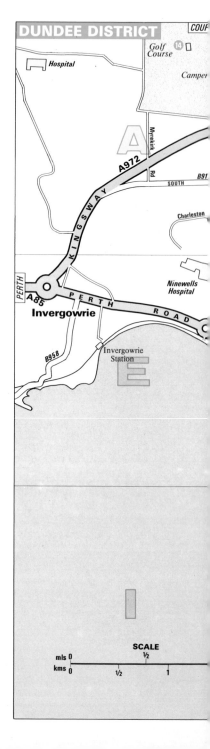

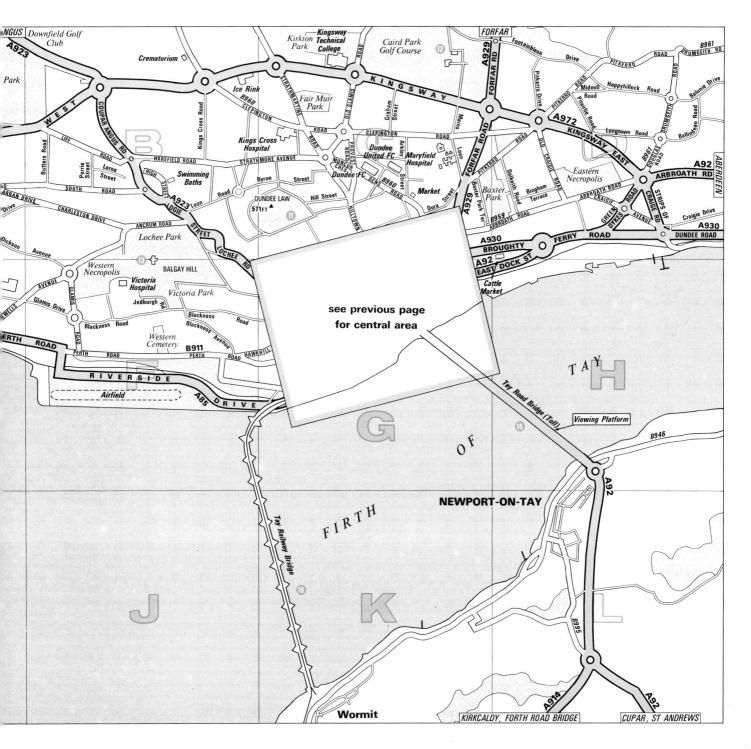

DURHAM

AA Road Service Centre (18) — *tel 62894*
2½m E at Carville via A690 (H)

G **i**   **Tourist Information Centre** — 13 Claypath
tel 3720

Public buildings and places of interest

L(1)   **Assize Courts**

K(2)   **Castle** A fine, mainly 12th- to 14th-C
building with a notable hall and 11th-C
chapel. It is now used by Durham
University.

K(3)   **Cathedral and Monastic Buildings**
A splendidly-situated cathedral dating
from the Norman period and later. It is
famous for the great Norman piers of
the nave; the Galilee Porch containing
Bede's tomb; the 13th-C chapel of the
Nine Altars; the Sanctuary Knocker;
and the Neville Screen of 1380. There
are considerable remains of the
Monastic buildings.

O(4)   **College** A peaceful close containing
dwellings of the Cathedral dignitaries.

B(5)   **County Hall**

K(6)   **Dunelm House, Student Union**

C(7)   **Durham Light Infantry Museum and Arts
Centre** Collection of military relics,
exhibitions, recitals and lectures.

K(8)   **Elvet Bridge** A 12th-C bridge, widened
in 1805.

K(9)   **Framwelgate Bridge** The bridge dating
from c1128 was rebuilt 1388-1405.

R(10)   **Gulbenkian Museum of Oriental Art**
The only museum in the country devoted
entirely to Oriental art and
archaeology.

M(11)   **Neville's Cross** The ruined cross
commemorates a battle of 1346 when the
Scots were defeated.

O(12)   **Prebends Bridge** (no cars). A bridge
of the late 18thC.

K(13)   **Public Library**

H(14)   **St Giles' Church** Partly Norman,
containing a wooden effigy of 1591.

O(15)   **St Oswald's Church** A 12th- to 15th-C
building.

G(16)   **Town Hall**

K(17)   **University Library**

Hospitals

F   **County Hospital** *tel 64911*
J   **St Margaret's Hospital** *tel 64911*

Sport and Recreation

D   **Durham City Association Football Club,**
Ferens Park

L   **Durham City Rugby Football Club,** Green
Lane

G   **Durham Ice Rink,** Freemans Place

L   **Durham Swimming Pool,** Elvet Waterside

Theatres and Cinemas

F   **Classic Cinema,** North Road *tel 3184*

Department Stores

Marks and Spencer Ltd, Silver Street
Early closing day Wednesday

Markets

G   **Market Place** (Saturday — covered and
open)

Note

North Road, Framwelgate Bridge, Silver Street
Saddler Street, and Elvet Bridge are closed to
traffic from 10.00hrs. They are open at night
and early morning for access.

Cathedral

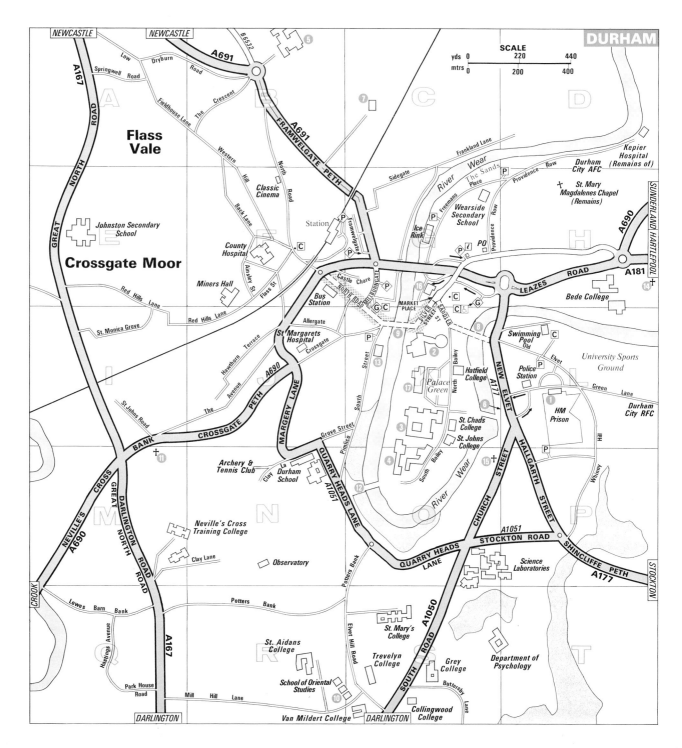

DURHAM

Flass Vale

Crossgate Moor

NEWCASTLE NEWCASTLE

A167 A691 B6532

GREAT NORTH ROAD

Springwell Low Dryburn Road
Fieldhouse Lane The Crescent
Western Hill North Road
Back Lane
Classic Cinema

FRAMWELGATE PETH

Johnston Secondary School

County Hospital
Ainsley St. Flass St.
Miners Hall

Red Hills Lane
St. Monica Grove Red Hills Lane

Hawthorn Terrace
The Avenue
A690 CROSSGATE PETH
St Johns Road
BANK

GREAT DARLINGTON NORTH ROAD
NEVILLE'S CROSS

A690
A167

CROOK

Lowes Barn Bank
Hastings Avenue
Clay Lane

Neville's Cross Training College

Observatory

MARGERY LANE

St Margarets Hospital
Crossgate
Allergate
Street Street
South Street

Archery & Tennis Club
Clay La Durham School
A1051

QUARRY HEADS LANE

Pimlico
Grove Street

Potters Bank

QUARRY HEADS LANE

Potters Bank

Elvet Hill Road

St. Aidans College

School of Oriental Studies

Mill Hill Lane
Park House Road

A167

DARLINGTON

Station
Framwelgate
Castle Chare
Bus Station
NORTH ROAD MILLBURNGATE

MARKET PLACE SILVER STREET SADDLER ST.

Palace Green
Hatfield College
North Bailey
South Bailey
St. Chads College
St. Johns College

River Wear

St. Mary's College
Trevelyan College
Grey College
Collingwood College

A1050 SOUTH ROAD

Van Mildert College DARLINGTON

River Wear The Sands
Sidegate Place
Freemans
Wearside Secondary School
Providence Row
Frankland Lane

Ice Rink
PO
P i

LEAZES ROAD
A181
A690

SUNDERLAND HARTLEPOOL

Kepier Hospital (Remains of)
St. Mary Magdalenes Chapel (Remains)

Bede College

Swimming Pool Old Elvet
Police Station
Green Lane
University Sports Ground
Durham City RFC

NEW ELVET
Bailey

HM Prison

A177

HALLGARTH STREET
CHURCH STREET

A1051 STOCKTON ROAD
SHINCLIFFE PETH
A177 STOCKTON

Science Laboratories

Department of Psychology

Butterby Lane

Durham City AFC

SCALE
yds 0   220   440
mtrs 0 200 400

EDINBURGH

G   **AA Service Centre** — Fanum House, 18-22 Melville Street *tel 031-225 8464*

CENTRAL PLAN

H   **Tourist Information Office** — 1 Cockburn Street *tel 031-226 6591*

Public buildings and places of interest

I(1)   **Acheson House** The headquarters of the Scottish Craft Centre is housed in this 17th-C mansion.

H(2)   **Assembly Rooms and Music Hall**

M(3) **Castle and Scottish National War Memorial** The historical castle on its commanding site has many Royal associations. The Norman St Margaret's Chapel is Scotland's oldest ecclesiastical building still in use. The Scottish National War Memorial was opened in 1927.

I(4)   **City Chambers** Originally erected in 1753 as the Royal Exchange.

I(5)   **Canongate Tolbooth** Once a prison and courthouse dating back to 1591. It has a curious projecting clock.

H(6)   **Edinburgh Festival Office**

H(7)   **Floral Clock** This is the oldest floral clock in the world. It dates from 1903.

G(8)   **Freemasons' Hall**

M(9) **George Heriot's School** Dates from 1628 and was founded by George Heriot.

H(10) **Gladstone's Land** Built in 1620 it preserves Edinburgh's last arcaded ground floor.

M(11) **Greyfriars Church and Greyfriars Bobby Fountain** The church dates from 1612 and is famous for the signing of the National Covenant in 1638. There is also a memorial to the Covenanters. The fountain recalls an Edinburgh dog who watched over his master's grave from 1858 to 1872.

J(12) **Holyroodhouse and Abbey** The Palace of Holyroodhouse dates from 1500 and is noted for its historical apartments, State Rooms and picture gallery. There are associations with Mary, Queen of Scots, and Prince Charles Edward. The Abbey (now in ruins) was founded in 1128.

I(13) **Huntly House** Dating from 1570, Huntly House now houses the City Museum of local history.

I(14) **John Knox's House** A 15th-C house, preserving wooden galleries. Built by the goldsmith to Mary, Queen of Scots, and probably lived in by John Knox.

H(15) **Lady Stair's House** A restored house, built in 1622. It is now a literary museum.

I(16) **Museum of Childhood** Contains an extremely large collection of items relating to childhood in the past.

H(17) **National Gallery of Scotland** Contains a comprehensive collection of paintings of a number of schools.

M(18) **National Library of Scotland** Contains a large collection of books and manuscripts.

I(19) **National Monument and Nelson Monument** Commenced in 1822, but left unfinished. It commemorates the Scottish dead in the Napoleonic Wars and forms a notable viewpoint. The nearby Nelson Monument is 108-ft high.

C(20) **National Portrait Gallery and Museum of Antiquities** The Portrait Gallery was founded in 1882 and contains a collection of portraits of famous Scots. The museum contains a representative collection of history and everyday life of Scotland from the Stone Age to modern times.

N(21) **New University**

N(22) **Old University** A Robert Adam design of 1789, with 19th-C additions. It was founded in 1582.

M(23) **Outlook Tower** This tower contains a fine camera obscura, which has been in use since 1892.

N(24) **Parliament House** Built 1633-40 but now masked by later buildings. The Hall has a fine hammer-beam roof.

I(25) **Register House** Built between 1774-89 from designs by Robert Adam. It houses the Archives of Scotland.

H(26) **Royal Scottish Academy** Founded in 1826 to promote Fine Arts in Scotland.

N(27) **Royal Scottish Museum** Opened in 1866, it contains the United Kingdom's largest display of the decorative arts, natural history, geology and technology under one roof.

I(28) **St Andrew's House** Government Offices

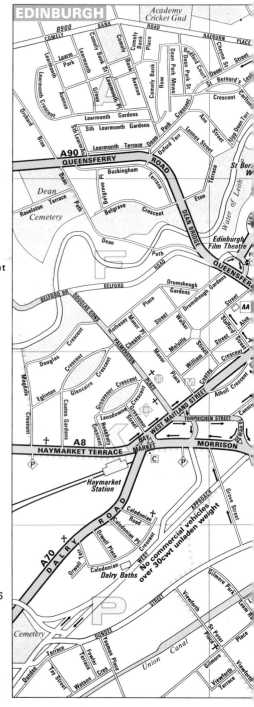

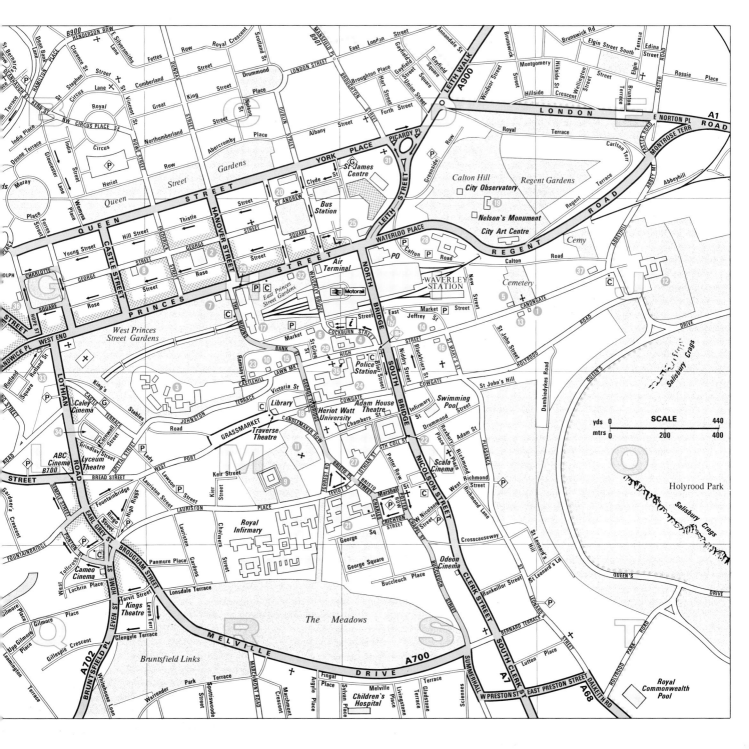

H(29) St Giles Cathedral and Mercat Cross
The Cathedral is an imposing and lofty
Gothic building. The tower is the
oldest part and is surmounted by the
famous 'Crown' steeple. The ornate
Thistle Chapel dates from 1911. The
Mercat Cross, which incorporates the
original shaft, was erected in 1885 by
Gladstone.

K(30) St Mary's Episcopal Cathedral Designed
by Sir Gilbert Scott and completed in
1917.

D(31) St Mary's Cathedral (RC)

H(32) Scott Monument A 19th-C memorial to Sir
Walter Scott, designed by George Kemp.

**G(33) Scottish Tourist Board Information
Centre**

L(34) Usher Hall

I(35) Wax Museum The museum contains an
interesting collection of over 100 wax
figures from the 11thC to the present
day.

G(36) West Register House The former St
George's Church is now an annexe of the
Record Office.

J(37) White Horse Close An original coaching
terminus.

Hospitals

S Royal Hospital for Sick Children,
Sciennes Road *tel 031-667 6811*

M Royal Infirmary of Edinburgh, Lauriston
Place *tel 031-229 2477*

Sport and Recreation

P Dalry Baths, Caledonian Crescent

N Swimming Pool, Infirmary Street

T Royal Commonwealth Pool, Dalkeith
Road

Theatres and Cinemas

L ABC Film Theatre, Lothian Road *tel 031-
229 3030*

N Adam House Theatre, Chambers Street *tel
031-225 3744*

L Caley Cinema, 31 Lothian Road *tel
031-229 7670*

Q Cameo Cinema, 138 Home Street,
Tollcross *tel 031-229 6822*

G Edinburgh Film Theatre, Randolph
Crescent *tel 031-225 1671*

Q King's Theatre, Leven Street, Tollcross
tel 031-229 1201

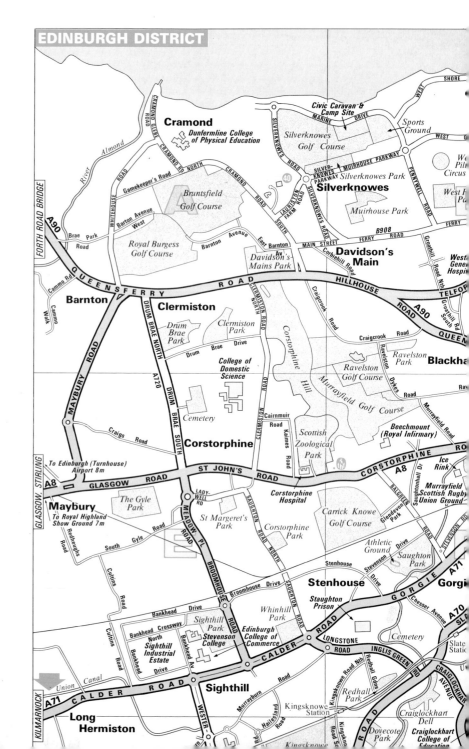

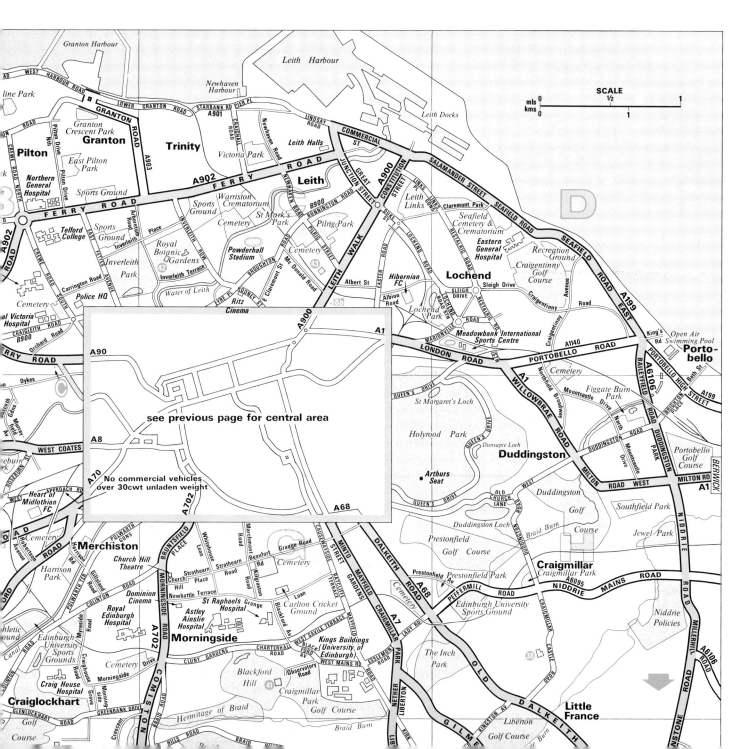

S **Odeon Cinema**, 7 Clerk Street *tel* 031-667 3805
L **Royal Lyceum Theatre**, Grindlay Street *tel 031-229 4353*
N **La Scala Cinema**, Nicolson Street *tel 031-667 1839*
M **Traverse Theatre Club**, 112 West Bow *tel 031-226 2633*

Department Stores

Binns Ltd, Princes Street
A Goldberg and Sons Ltd, Tollcross
Jenners, Princes Street, St David Street
J Lewis and Son, St James Centre
Marks and Spencer Ltd, 53 Princes Street
P Thomson, 15 North Bridge
Early closing day various parts of the town close Tuesday, Wednesday and Saturday

Advertisers

K **Mercantile Credit**
I **Centre** Royal Mile Centre
K **Centre** Grosvenor Centre Hotel
I **THF** Carlton Hotel

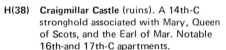

Canongate Tolbooth

DISTRICT PLAN

Public buildings and places of interest

H(38) Craigmillar Castle (ruins). A 14th-C stronghold associated with Mary, Queen of Scots, and the Earl of Mar. Notable 16th-and 17th-C apartments.

K(39) Hillend Ski Centre Situated south of the city on the Pentland Hills the 400-metre artificial ski slope is the largest in Britain.

A(40) Lauriston Castle A late 16th-C mansion with furniture and antiques displaying English and French styles. Associated with John Law, the early 18th-C broker.

G(41) Royal Observatory The Royal Observatory was moved from Calton Hill to Blackford Hill at the end of the 19thC, and is now a research establishment of the Science Research Council.

C(42) Scottish National Gallery of Modern Art A modern building set in the surrounds of the Royal Botanic Gardens. Contains a large collection of paintings of various important schools.

C(43) Transport Museum Contains several old trams and buses, a collection of old uniforms, and model exhibits which together illustrate the trend of transport in Edinburgh over the centuries.

E Zoo Set in 80 acres of grounds the zoo is one of the finest in Europe. Also magnificent views of Edinburgh and the surrounding countryside.

Hospitals

G **Astley Ainslie Hospital**, Grange Loan *tel 031-447 3399*
F **Beechmount Hospital**, 102 Corstorphine Road *tel 031-337 2888*
J **City Hospital**, Greenbank Drive *tel 031-447 1075*
E **Corstorphine Hospital**, 136 Corstorphine Road *tel 031-334 4952*
F **Craig House Hospital**, Craig House Road *tel 031-447 2011*

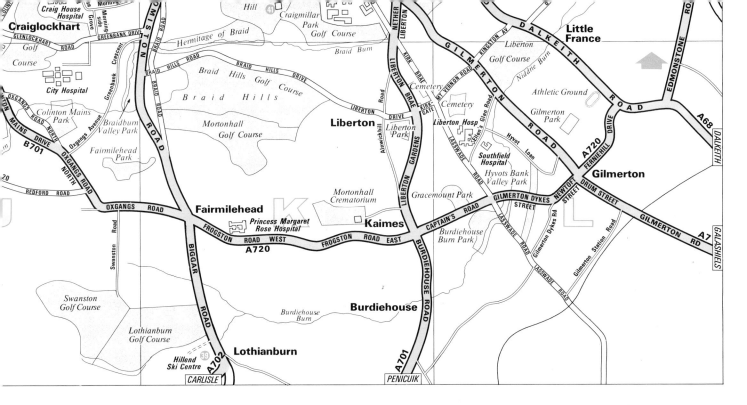

D	**Eastern General Hospital**, Seafield Street *tel 031-554 2266*	D	**Craigentinny Golf Course**	**Broughton Road**
L	**Liberton Hospital**, Lasswade Road *tel 031-664 4997*	J	**Craiglockhart Golf Course**	H	**Prestonfield Golf Course**

D   **Eastern General Hospital**, Seafield Street *tel 031-554 2266*

L   **Liberton Hospital**, Lasswade Road *tel 031-664 4997*

B   **Northern General Hospital**, Ferry Road *tel 031-332 2511*

K   **Princess Margaret Rose Hospital**, Fairmilehead *tel 031-445 2007*

F   **Royal Edinburgh Hospital**, Morningside *tel 031-447 2011*

B   **Royal Victoria Hospital**, Craigleith Road, Comeley Bank *tel 031-332 1221*

G   **St Raphael's Hospital**, 6 Blackford Avenue *tel 031-667 3604*

L   **Southfield Hospital**, Lasswade Road *tel 031-664 1788*

B   **Western General Hospital**, Crewe Road South *tel 031-332 2525*

Sport and Recreation

I   **Baberton Golf Course**

K   **Braid Hills Golf Courses**

A   **Bruntsfield Golf Course**

F   **Carrick Knowe Golf Course**

D   **Craigentinny Golf Course**

J   **Craiglockhart Golf Course**

G   **Craigmillar Park Golf Course**

H   **Duddingston Golf Course**

F   **Heart of Midlothian Football Club**, Tynecastle Park

C   **Hibernian Football Club**, Easter Road Park

K(39)   **Hillend Ski Centre** (see also public buildings and places of interest)

I   **Kingsknowe Golf Course**

L   **Liberton Golf Course**

K   **Lothianburn Golf Course**

D   **Meadowbank International Sports Centre**, London Road

D   **Meadowbank Thistle Football Club**, Meadowbank International Sports Centre

K   **Mortonhall Golf Course**

F   **Murrayfield Golf Course**

F   **Murrayfield Ice Rink**

D   **Open Air Swimming Pool**, Rosebank Lane

H   **Portobello Golf Course**

C   **Powderhall Greyhound Stadium**, off Broughton Road

H   **Prestonfield Golf Course**

B   **Ravelston Golf Course**

A   **Royal Burgess Golf Course**

F   **Scottish Rugby Union Football Ground**, Murrayfield

A   **Silverknowes Golf Course**

J   **Swanston Golf Course**

I   **Torphin Hill Golf Course**

Department Stores

Presto Discount Centre, Wester Hailes Centre

Advertisers

B   **Crest** Edinburgh Esso Hotel

C   **Godfrey Davis**

F   **THF** The Post House

EXETER

J   **AA Service Centre** — Fanum House, Bedford Street *tel 32121*

G(4)   **Tourist Information Centre** — Civic
[i]   Centre, Paris Street *tel 77888 ext 2297/8* (see also public buildings and places of interest)

Public buildings and places of interest

F(1)   **Albert Memorial Museum and Art Gallery** Founded in 1865. It contains natural history, ethnographical, industrial, and technological displays; collections of English water colours, oil paintings and silverware.

J(2)   **Cathedral** A Norman to Decorated structure. Points of interest are the twin Norman transeptal towers; minstrel's gallery; carved-stone screen; clock — originally constructed in the 14thC; wood carvings and a wealth of carved roof bosses.

J(3)   **City Walls** Roman Wall with medieval buttresses, of which the best remains are seen in Southernhay, and from Northernhay and Bartholomew Street.

K(4)   **Civic Centre**

N(5)   **Custom House** A fine Georgian quayside house.

J(6)   **Guildhall** A picturesque building dated 1330, and altered in 1446 and 1593, regarded as the oldest municipal building in the United Kingdom.

N(7)   **Maritime Museum** Over 70 sail and steam vessels from all over the world, in a setting of quays and old warehouses.

J(8)   **Mol's Coffee House** A tall, late 16th-C house with an oak-panelled room. Now an art dealers.

F(9)   **Rougemont Castle Grounds, Museum, Public Library and Northernhay Park** The grounds contain the scanty remains of the Norman Castle (keep and gateway), a Saxon tower (Athelstan's) and portions of the city walls. Rougemont House Museum (late 18thC) contains exhibits on the archaeology of Devon and Exeter since the Ice Ages.

J(10)   **St Mary Arches Church** A mainly 12th-C structure, but with some Saxon work. The double Norman arcade, c1130 is the only example in Devon.

J(11)   **St Mary Steps Church** In this church are a Norman font, a good screen and a curious old clock.

J(12)   **St Nicholas' Priory** A restored Norman to Tudor building.

J(13)   **Tucker's Hall** An old hall, used as a guild house since 1471, with a wagon roof and panelling dated 1634.

F(14)   **Underground Passages** The entrance to these medieval aqueducts, of which the earliest channel dates from the 14thC, is in Eastgate. Open to the public at certain times (organised parties on application to the Town Clerk's Office).

B(15)   **University**

K(16)   **Wynard's Almshouses** Founded in 1436 and has a restored chapel.

Hospitals

P   **Exe Vale Hospital (Wonford),** Dryden Road *tel 77358*

P   **Princess Elizabeth Orthopaedic Hospital,** Barrack Road *tel 54217*

L   **Royal Devon and Exeter Hospital,** Heavitree *tel 77991*

P   **Royal Devon and Exeter Hospital,** Wonford *tel 77833*

K   **West of England Eye Infirmary,** Magdalen Street *tel 72261*

Sport and Recreation

H   **Clifton Hill Athletic Ground and Ski Slope**

K   **Corporation Baths,** Heavitree Road

C   **Exeter City Football and Athletic Club,** St James Park

B   **Exeter Cricket Club,** Prince of Wales Road

M   **Exeter Rugby Football Ground and Greyhound Stadium,** County Ground, Church Road, St Thomas

Theatres and Cinemas

F   **ABC Cinema,** New North Road *tel 75274*

K   **Barnfield Theatre,** Barnfield Road *tel 70891*

B   **Northcott Theatre,** Stocker Road *tel 54853*

G   **Odeon Cinema,** Sidwell Street *tel 54057*

Department Stores

Debenhams Ltd, 123 Sidwell Street
Marks and Spencer Ltd, 247 High Street

Markets

J   **Corn Exchange,** St George's Hall (Friday)
J   **Market,** Fore Street (Daily)

Advertisers

O   **Crest** Buckerell Lodge Hotel
G   **Godfrey Davis**
G   **Mercantile Credit**
A   **THF** Great Western Hotel

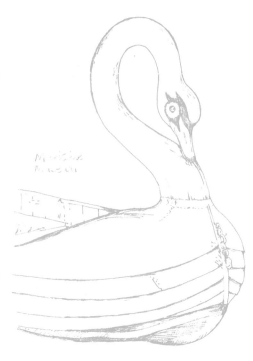

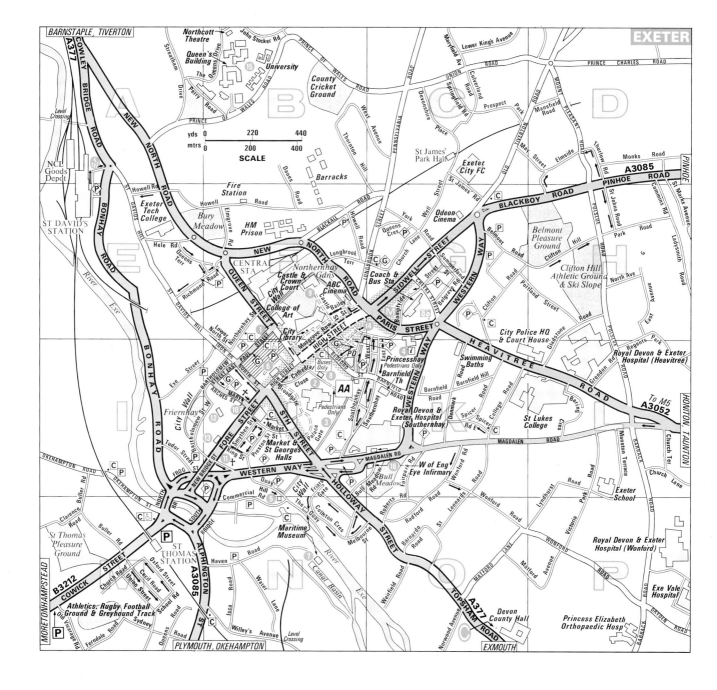

EXETER

91

GLASGOW

H   **AA Service Centre** — 269 Argyle Street *tel 041-812 0101*

H [i]   **Tourist Information Centre** — Municipal Information Bureau, George Square *tel 041-221 9600*

Public buildings and places of interest

A(1)   **Art Gallery and Museum** The art gallery's collection of Italian, Flemish, Dutch, French and British paintings constitutes Britain's finest civic art collection. The museum contains sections on armour, archaeology and history, technology, ethnography and natural history.

J(2)   **Cathedral** This 12th- to 15th-C structure is considered to be a perfect example of pre-reformation Gothic architecture. The fan vaulting over the tomb of St Mungo in the crypt is notable.

I(3)   **City Chambers** This fine building of 1883-8 by William Young in Italian Renaissance style has a rich and lavish interior including a marble staircase and notable banqueting hall.

I(4)   **City Hall** A concert hall built in 1841, now refurbished to house the Scottish National Orchestra.

I(5)   **George Square** Contains statues of many famous people, including Sir Walter Scott, Queen Victoria, Prince Albert, Robert Burns, James Watt, William E Gladstone and Sir Robert Peel.

N(6)   **Mercat Cross** Erected in 1929, it is a replica of the medieval cross.

N(7)   **Merchants Hall Steeple** The only remaining part of the old Merchants House which was built in 1651-9 and is now surrounded by the fish market. The tower is noted for its effect of diminishing storeys.

B(8)   **Mitchell Library** Founded in 1874 and contains numerous rare books including a valuable Burns collection.

B(9)   **Museum of the Royal Highland Fusiliers** Housed in the regiment's headquarters is a chronological display showing the histories of the Royal Scots Fusiliers and The Highland Light Infantry from their foundation to amalgamation in 1959.

N(10)   **Peoples Palace** Incorporates the Old Glasgow Museum which displays a visual record of the history of the city.

I(11)   **Provands Lordship** Built in 1471 it is the oldest house in the city. It now houses a museum, mainly of domestic articles and 17th- and 18th-C furniture.

M(12)   **St Andrew's Cathedral (RC)**

G(13)   **St Vincent Street Church** A striking design of 1857-59 by 'Greek' Thomson.

I(14)   **Sheriff Court Buildings** Built in 1842 and enlarged in 1874. They were once the Municipal Buildings.

H(15)   **Stirling Library** Contains special collections of books on music and pictorial arts and is housed in the Royal Exchange Building, originally a suburban residence built in 1780.

I(16)   **Stow College**

I(17)   **Strathclyde University** One of the leading institutions in the field of applied science.

N(18)   **Tolbooth Steeple** The surviving portion of the tolbooth of 1626. It is surmounted by a 'Crown' somewhat similar to examples in Edinburgh and Aberdeen.

N(19)   **Tron Steeple** This forms an arch over the footpath and is all that remains of St Mary's Church dating from 1637 which was burnt down in 1793 by the Hellfire Club.

A(20)   **University** The university, founded in 1450, occupies buildings dating from 1868-70 which were designed by Sir Gilbert Scott. The Bute Hall is an addition of 1882, and the old Lodge is built of stones from the former structure. The Hunterian Museum and Library are outstanding.

Hospitals

J   **Duke Street Hospital,** Duke Street *tel 041-554 1221*

B   **Glasgow Dental Hospital,** 378 Sauchiehall Street *tel 041-332 7020*

G   **Glasgow Ear, Nose and Throat Hospital,** 306 St Vincent Street *tel 041-221 7921*

A   **Glasgow Eye Infirmary,** 174 Berkeley Street *tel 041-221 7464;* Orthoptic Department, 3 Sandyford Place *tel 041-248 5363*

B   **Royal Beatson Memorial Hospital,** 132 Hill Street *tel 041-332 0286*

J   **Royal Infirmary,** Castle Street *tel 041-552 3535*

I   **Royal Maternity Hospital,** Rottenrow *tel 041-552 4513*

Sport and Recreation

F   **Cranstonhill Baths,** 68 Elliot Street

M   **Gorbals Baths,** 144 Gorbals Street

L   **Kingston Baths,** Paterson Street

C   **North Woodside Baths,** 10 Moncrieff Street

I   **Townhead Baths,** 49 Collins Street

Theatres and Cinemas

C   **ABC 1 & 2 Cinemas,** Sauchiehall Street *tel 041-332 1592 & 9513*

C   **Apollo Centre,** Renfield Street *tel 041-332 1199*

M   **Citizens Theatre,** 119 Gorbals Street *tel 041-429 0022*

H   **Classic Cinemas Ltd,** 15 Renfield Street *tel 041-221 3400*

H   **Classic Grand Cinema,** 18 Jamaica Street *tel 041-248 4620*

M   **Coliseum Cinema,** Eglinton Street *tel 041-429 1500*

C   **Glasgow Film Theatre,** 12 Rose Street *tel 041-332 6535*

B   **King's Theatre,** Bath Street *tel 041-248 5153*

C   **La Scala Cinema,** 155 Sauchiehall Street *tel 041-332 1228*

H   **Odeon Film Centre,** 56 Renfield Street *tel 041-322 8701*

C   **Pavilion Theatre,** Renfield Street *tel 041-332 0478*

H   **Regent Cinema,** 72 Renfield Street *tel 041-332 3303*

C   **Theatre Royal,** Hope Street *tel 041-332 6431*

Department Stores

Arnotts, 193 Argyle Street
Arnotts, 83 Sauchiehall Street
Bremner and Co Ltd, 44 Glassford Street
Campbells and Stewart and McDonald Ltd, 137 Ingram Street
David Elder Ltd, 335 Argyle Street
Frasers, Buchanan Street

Goldberg A and Sons Ltd, 270 Crownpoint Road
Goldberg A and Sons, Candleriggs
Holbourne (Granite House) Ltd, Trongate
Lewis's Ltd, Argyle Street
Marks and Spencer Ltd, 12 Argyle Street
Marks and Spencer Ltd, 172 Sauchiehall Street
Paisley's, Jamaica Street
Telfer and Co Ltd, 74 Miller Street
Treron Ltd, 254 Sauchiehall Street
Wilson John and Son (Belfast) Ltd, 219
Sauchiehall Street
Early closing day Tuesday or Saturday

Markets

O	**Cattle and Meat Market**, Gallowgate
N	**Fishmarket**
N/O	**The Barrows — General** (Saturday and Sunday)

Advertisers

H	**Godfrey Davis**
H	**Centre** Glasgow Centre Hotel
B	**Mercantile Credit**

DISTRICT PLAN

Public buildings and places of interest

B(21) **Botanic Gardens** 42 acres of grounds with glasshouses including notable collections of orchids and begonias and Kibble Palace with its unique collection of tree ferns and plants from temperate areas.

J(22) **Camphill Museum** Contains pictures and art objects from the Burrell Collection, as well as some natural history exhibits.

I(23) **Crookston Castle** Probably 13th-C with an earlier defensive ditch. Visited by Mary, Queen of Scots and Darnley in 1565.

J(24) **Haggs Castle** A new museum of history for children.

F(25) **Kelvin Hall and Arena** Rebuilt in 1926, it is the largest hall in Scotland and is used for exhibitions and concerts.

J(26) **Langside Monument** This memorial in Queen's Park, recalls the battle of 1568, which was fatal to the cause of Mary, Queen of Scots.

Continued on page 96

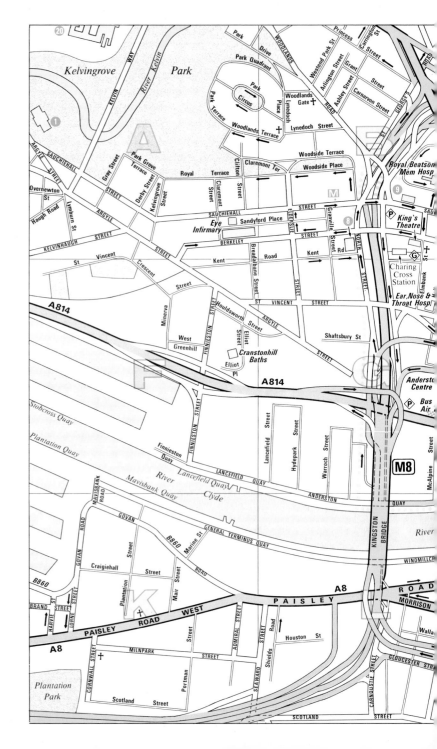

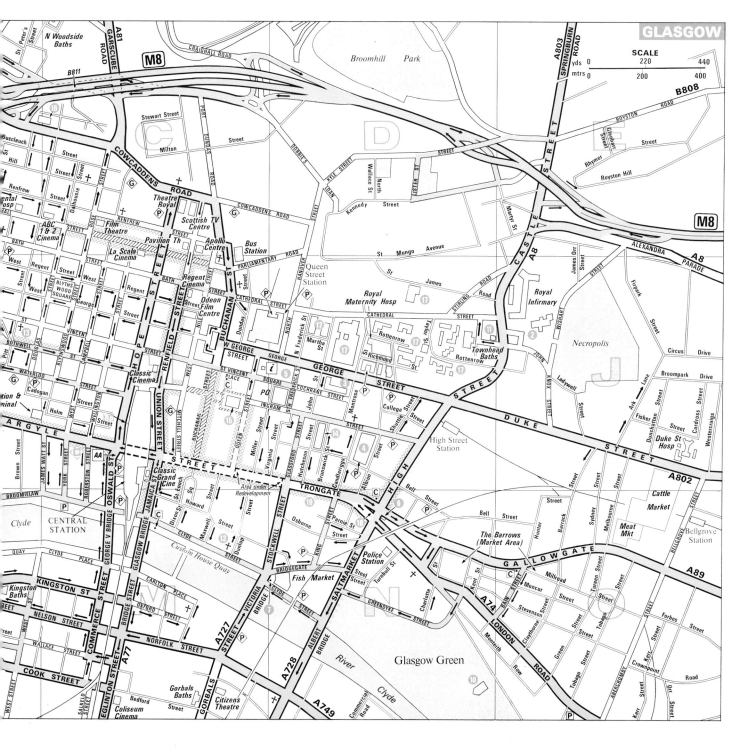

J(27)   **Pollok House** This building of 1752 was designed by William Adam and stands in extensive wooded grounds. It houses the famous Stirling-Maxwell Collection of Spanish and other paintings, as well as some fine furniture, silver and porcelain.

H(28)   **Tollcross Museum** A children's museum containing a collection of dolls, attractive pictures and an exhibit *The Story of Cock Robin*.

J(29)   **Transport Museum** A museum displaying the development of the bicycle, horse-drawn vehicles, tram cars, Scottish motor cars from vintage to the present day, and a collection of railway locomotives.

A(30)   **Victoria Park** The park contains the best-known fossilized tree stumps of the prehistoric Coal Age period; they were discovered in 1887 and are housed in the Fossil Grove Building.

Calderpark Zoo, Uddingston. A variety of birds, mammals, fish and reptiles housed in spacious new enclosures and buildings. 6m ESE off A74 (L) **Provan Hall** 15th-C house, formerly the mansion of the lairds of Provan. Well-restored and considered the most perfect example of a simple pre-Reformation house remaining in Scotland. 5m E via A8 (H), then Bartiebeith Road and Auchinlea Road.

Hospitals

H   **Belvidere Hospital,** London Road *tel* 041-554 1855

A   **Blawarthill Hospital,** Holehouse Drive *tel* 041-959 1864

I   **Cowglen Hospital,** Boydstone Road *tel* 041-632 9106

C   **Foresthall Hospital,** Petershill Road *tel* 041-558 5684

B   **Gartnavel General Hospital,** 1055 Great Western Road *tel* 041-334 8122

B   **Gartnavel Royal Hospital,** 1055 Great Western Road *tel* 041-334 6241

B   **Glasgow Homeopathic Hospital,** 1000 Great Western Road *tel* 041-339 0382

A   **Knightswood Hospital** *tel* 041-954 9641

I   **Leverndale Hospital,** 510 Crookston Road *tel* 041-882 6255

H   **Lightburn Hospital,** Carntyne Road *tel* 041-774 5102

F   **Queen Mother's Maternity Hospital and Royal Hospital for Sick Children,** Yorkhill *tel* 041-339 8888

K   **Royal Samaritan Hospital for Women,** Coplaw Street *tel* 041-423 3033

C   **Ruchill Hospital,** Bilsland Drive *tel* 041-946 7120

F   **St Francis Maternity Home,** Merryland Street *tel* 041-445 1118

E   **Southern General Hospital,** 1345 Govan Road *tel* 041-445 2466

C   **Stobhill Hospital,** Springburn *tel* 041-558 0111

J   **Victoria Infirmary,** Langside *tel* 041-649 4545

B   **Western Infirmary,** Dumbarton Road *tel* 041-339 8822

Sport and Recreation

C   **Ashfield Stadium,** 404 Hawthorn Street — greyhound racing

E   **Bellahouston Sports Centre,** Bellahouston Drive

L   **Cambuslang Golf Club,** Western Green

G   **Celtic Football and Athletic Club,** Celtic Park, 95 Kerrydale Street

J   **Clydesdale Cricket Club,**

K   **Clyde Football Club,** Shawfield Park

I   **Cowglen Golf Club,** Pollokshaws

J   **Crossmyloof Ice Rink,** Titwood Road

J   **Haggs Castle Golf Club,** Dumbreck Road

A   **Knightswood Park Golf Course**

C   **Littlehill Golf Course**

D   **Lethamhill Golf Course**

G   **Osborne Street Baths**

B   **Partick Thistle Football Club,** Firhill Road

J   **Poloc Cricket Club,**

J   **Pollok Golf Club,** 90 Barrhead Road

K   **Queen's Park Football Club,** Hampden Park

E   **Ralston Golf Club**

F   **Rangers Football Club,** Ibrox Stadium

H   **Sandyhills Golf Club**

K   **Shawfield Stadium** — greyhound racing

B   **West of Scotland Cricket Club,** Peel Street

Advertisers

J   **Godfrey Davis**

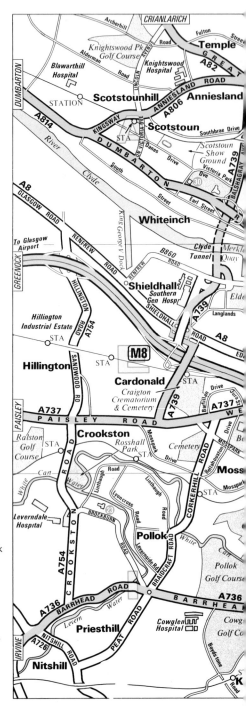

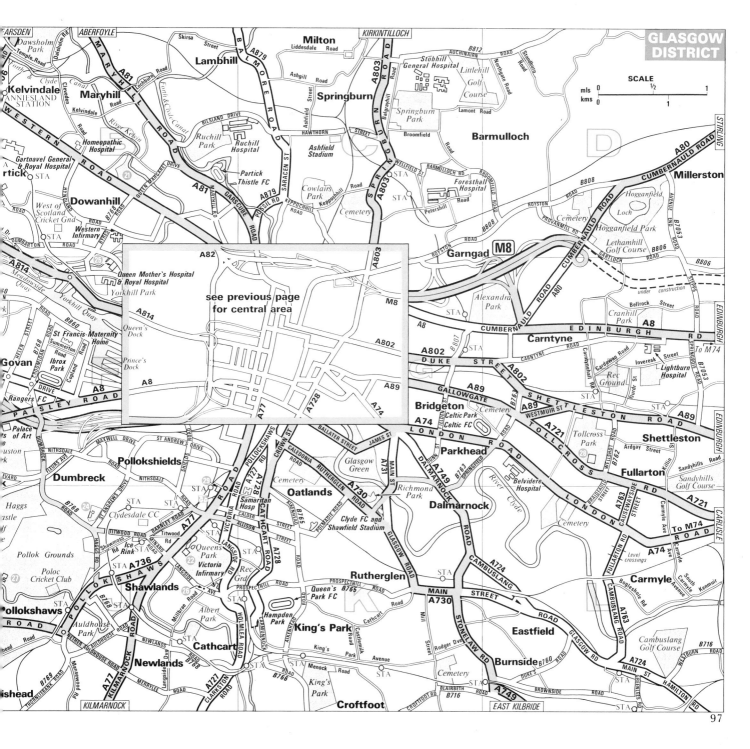

see previous page
for central area

GLOUCESTER

AA Road Service Centre (21) – *tel 23278* 2¼m NE on Cheltenham Road A40 at its junction with the B4063 (D)

J(6) [*i*] **Tourist Information Centre** – The Gloucester Leisure Centre, Station Road *tel 36788* (see also public buildings and places of interest)

Public buildings and places of interest

I(1) **Blackfriars Priory** The Priory remains include some early library buildings and an Early English church vestry.

F(2) **Cathedral** A magnificent Norman to Perpendicular building especially notable for the imposing central tower; the 14th-C east window; the choir stalls; and the beautiful cloisters.

J(3) **City Museum, Central Library and Art Gallery** Collections include local archaeology, geology, and natural history; period furnishings; silver; glass; clocks and watches. Temporary art exhibitions are held.

E(4) **Folk Life and Regimental Museum** Housed in three timber-framed buildings of the 15th to 17thCs, one of which is supposed to be the place where the Protestant Bishop Hooper spent the night before he was martyred in 1555. Collections include the history and agriculture of Gloucester and the surrounding countryside; Civil War relics and the Gloucestershire Regiment.

J(5) **Guildhall** A handsome building of 1890 with large assembly hall which is the headquarters of the City's administration.

J(6) **Leisure Centre and Tourist Information Centre**

I(7) **Llanthony Priory** There are slight remains of this 12th-C priory near the river.

F(8) **"New Inn"** An exceptionally picturesque open-galleried pilgrim's inn dating back to the 15thC.

F(9) **Parliament House** A well-restored, timbered, 15th-C building on the site where a parliament was held in 1378.

J(10) **Raikes' House** A 16th-C timber-framed house associated with Robert Raikes, often held to have been the founder of Sunday schools.

J(11) **St Mary-de-la-Crypt Church** Dating from the 12thC, but with tower, nave and chancel of the 15thC, this church contains the tomb of Robert Raikes.

E(12) **St Mary-de-la-Lode Church** This church which rests on Roman foundations features a late Norman tower and Early English vaulted chancel.

E(13) **St Nicholas Church** A Norman to Perpendicular style church with 15th-C spire, which was shortened and topped with a pinnacled cap in 1783.

F(14) **St Oswald's Priory** The Norman and Early English north nave arcade incorporates an arch which may derive from the priory church begun in 909.

F(15) **St Peter's Church (RC)**

E(16) **Shire Hall** Built in 1814 to the designs of Sir Robert Smirke RA; with extensive additions and reconstructions in recent years.

G(17) **United Hospitals Almshouses** These include the partly-Norman Chapel of St Mary Magdalene and also the remains of St Margaret's Chapel.

I **The Docks** The canal basin which opened in 1827, retains several of its old warehouses.

Hospitals

G **Gloucestershire Royal Hospital,** Great Western Road *tel 28555*

I **Gloucestershire Royal Infirmary,** Southgate Street *tel 21021*

G **Horton Road Hospital,** Horton Road *tel 20324*

Sport and Recreation

L **Gloucester City Association Football Club,** Sports Stadium, Horton Road

N **Gloucester City Cricket Club,** Spa Pleasure Ground

J(6) **Gloucester Leisure Centre,** Station Road – swimming pools etc (see also public buildings and places of interest)

B **Gloucester Rugby Football Club,** Kingsholm Road

Gloucester Engineering Sports Ground (for Gloucester County cricket matches), Tuffley Avenue. 1¼m S via Bristol Road A430 (M)

Greyhound Racing Track, Cheltenham Road 2m NE via Cheltenham Road A40 (D)

Theatres and Cinemas

F **ABC Cinema,** St Aldate Street *tel 22399*

J **Gloucester Operatic and Dramatic Society,** Olympus, Kingsbarton Street *tel 25917*

J **Odeon Cinema,** Barton Street *tel 23757*

Department Stores

Browns of Chester Ltd, Northgate Street
Debenhams Ltd, King's Square
Marks and Spencer Ltd, 13 Northgate Street

Early closing day Thursday

Markets

B **Cattle Market,** St Oswald's Road (Monday and Thursday; open market Saturday)

J **New Eastgate Retail Market,** Bell Walk (Daily)

Eastbrook Road Market (off Eastern Avenue) 2m E via London Road, Barnwood Road A417 and Eastern Avenue A38 (H)

Advertisers

J **Godfrey Davis**
F **Mercantile Credit**

New Inn

GLOUCESTER

SCALE
yds 0   220   440
mtrs 0   200   400

TEWKESBURY

ESTCOURT   ROAD   A40

A38

KINGSHOLM   ROAD

Cattle Market

Deans Way
Deans Way
Deans Walk
St Mark Street

Gloucester RFC Ground

Lansdown   Road

Denmark   Road

Lansdown   Road

Gloucestershire College of Education

To Greyhound Stadium

CHELTENHAM ROAD (Northbound)

A40   CHELTENHAM ROAD

Uxstalls Lane

CHELTENHAM

Pitch & Putt Course & Boating Lake

ROSS

A40

LOWER WESTGATE ST

RIVER SEVERN

THE QUAY

WESTGATE STREET

QUAY ST

St Catherine Street
St Mary's Street
Archdeacon St
Pitt Street
Park Street
Hare Lane
Worcester Street

St Oswald's Road

Skinner St
Alvin Street

Denmark Road
Oxford Road
Oxford Street
Heathville Road

Hillfield Garden

St Catherine's Church

Kenilworth Avenue
Merevale Road

LONDON   ROAD

ESTCOURT RD   A417   BARNWOOD RD

CIRENCESTER
A417

To M5
A40

14

12

St John's Church
St John's Lane

St Mary's Street

13

9

2

15

17

Gloucestershire Royal Hospital

County Library

Pol Sta

HM Prison

NORTHGATE STREET

ABC Cinema

EASTGATE

Market Pde
Bruton Way

Great Western Road

Horton Road Hospital

Goods Depot

16

8

GREYFRIARS Priory (ruins)

Eastgate Retail Market

PD

Clarence Street
Russell Street
Nettleton Rd

Bus Sta

GLOUCESTER STATION

STATION ROAD

Horton Road

Football Ground (Gloucester City AFC)

COMMERCIAL ROAD

THE DOCKS

Llanthony Rd
Llanthony Road
Severn Road

Gloucester & Sharpness Canal

7

1

10

11

Tech College

Eastgate St
Southgate Street
Ladybellegate St
Longsmith St

3

Odeon Cinema

Gloucestershire College of Art

BARTON

6

Olympus Theatre
Arthur Street
Wellington Street

Brunswick Square
Brunswick Road

GLOUCESTER STATION

Level Crossing

SOUTHGATE STREET

Gloucestershire Royal Hospital

St Michael's Square
Park Square
Cromwell Street

Montpellier

Albion Street

Spa Road

War Memorial

Goodyere St
Dinah St
St Victoria St
Midland Road

All Saints Road

Millbrook Street

Jersey Road

Derby Road

St James Street

Barton Street

PARKEND ROAD
PARK ROAD

The Park

Spa Pleasure Ground

New Street

Seymour Road

A430 BRISTOL ROAD (Southbound)
To M5

BRISTOL

STROUD ROAD

B4072

STROUD

Falkner Street
Ryecroft Street
Conduit Street
High Street
Hopewell St
Upton Street
B4073

EASTERN AVENUE A38

Cemetery

Coney Hill

99

GUILDFORD

CENTRAL PLAN

G(8) **Tourist Information Centre** — Central
Library, North Street *tel 68496* (see
also public buildings and places of
interest)

Public buildings and places of interest

G(1) **Archbishop Abbot's (Trinity) Hospital**
A picturesque brick-built building
founded by George Abbot — a native of
Guildford and Archbishop of Canterbury
from 1611 to 1633 — in 1619 as an
almshouse for 12 men and 8 women.

J(2) **Castle Keep and Gardens** A rectangular
Norman keep of three storeys, situated
in attractive gardens. Fine view from
the summit.

F(3) **Citizens' Advice Bureau**

C(4) **Civic Hall** A modern building opened
in 1962 and home of the Guildford
Philharmonic Orchestra.

G(5) **Guildford House** A fine town house of
1660, noted for its beautifully-
carved staircase and finely-decorated
plaster ceilings. Frequently changing
art exhibitions are held here.

F(6) **Guildhall** The picturesque 17th-C
façade of this building which overlooks
the High Street, is noted for its
projecting clock.

G(7) **Holy Trinity Church** A late 18th-C
red-brick church standing at the top
of the High Street, which contains
the tomb of Archbishop Abbot.

G(8) **Library and Tourist Information Centre**

G(9) **Municipal Buildings**

J(10) **Museum, Castle Arch** Contains
collections on local history, geology
and archaeology, including those of the
Surrey Archaeological Society.

G(11) **Royal Grammar School** A 16th-C building
famous for its collection of chained
books in the library.

G(12) **St Joseph's Church (RC)**

J(13) **St Mary's Church** Guildford's oldest
and most interesting church which
preserves specimens of Saxon, Norman,
Early English and Transitional
architecture.

J(14) **St Nicholas' Church** Rebuilt in the
late 19thC, but preserving the
Perpendicular Loseley Chapel, with
interesting monuments of the Mores
of Loseley family.

B(15) **St Saviour's Church** A late 19th-C
structure with a prominent tower.

E(16) **Sports Centre**

F(17) **Treadwheel Crane** Restored 18th-C
treadwheel crane of the old town wharf.

G(18) **Tunsgate** With its tall Tuscan columns
this is what remains of the old corn
exchange and law courts.

J(19) **Yvonne Arnaud Theatre** Opened in 1965.

F/G/J **High Street and Quarry Street** These
two streets, the former of which is
paved with granite setts, have been
designated a Conservation Area. The
elegant Georgian fronts of many of

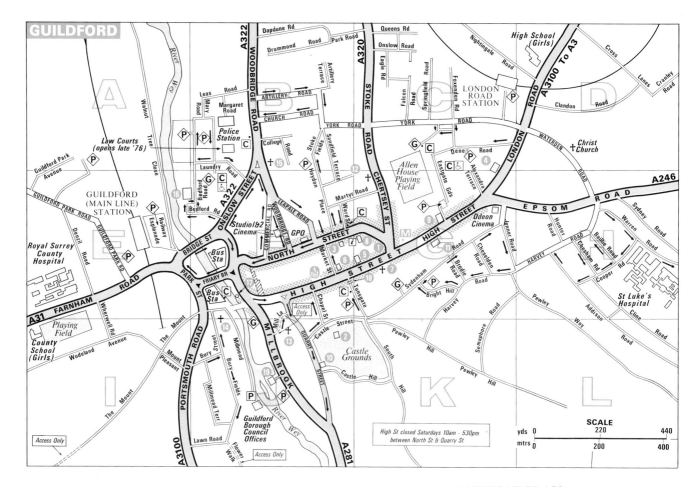

the buildings often hide far older backs.

Hospitals

E **Royal Surrey County Hospital,** Farnham Road *tel 71122*

H **St Luke's Hospital,** Warren Road *tel 71122*

Sport and Recreation

E(16) **Sports Centre,** Bedford Road — swimming pools etc (see also public buildings and places of interest)

Theatres and Cinemas

G **Odeon Cinema,** Epsom Road *tel 4990*

F **Studio 1 & 2 Cinemas,** Woodbridge Road *tel 4234*

J(19) **Yvonne Arnaud Theatre,** Millbrook *tel 64571* (see also public buildings and places of interest)

Department Stores

Debenhams Ltd, Millbrook
Harveys Ltd, High Street
Marks and Spencer Ltd, High Street
Early closing day Wednesday

Markets

F **Fruit and Vegetable Market,** North Street (Friday and Saturday)

Advertisers

G **Mercantile Credit**
F **THF** Angel Hotel

DISTRICT PLAN

H **AA Service Centre** — Fanum House, London Road *tel 72841*

Public buildings and places of interest

J(20) **Cathedral** On a magnificent site on the summit of Stag Hill, overlooking the town and surrounding countryside. Designed by Sir Edward Maufe, and consecrated in 1961, it is a fine example of modern materials and methods of construction.

G(21) **St John the Evangelist Church** The oldest parts, dating from the early 14thC, are the nave and south chapel. The tower was added in the 15thC.

J(22) **University of Surrey** A modern university

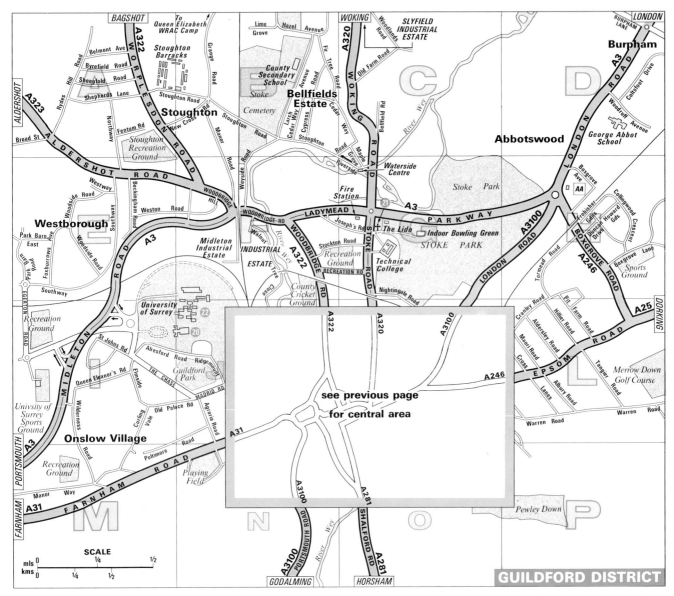

GUILDFORD DISTRICT

SCALE
mls 0 · ¼ · ½
kms 0 · ¼ · ½

which was granted its charter in 1966. The main site is on Stag Hill, below the Cathedral.

Loseley House An Elizabethan house of 1562 with fine panelling, furniture, ceilings, fireplaces and tapestries. 3m S of Guildford via Portsmouth Road A1300 then B3000 (N)

St Catherine's Chapel A ruined chantry chapel built c1308 on top of a steep sandy hill, which affords a splendid view of Guildford and the Wey valley. ¾m S of Guildford via Portsmouth Road A3100 (N)

Sutton Place Gardens A beautiful 16th-C house in red brick and terracotta, situated in an extensive and picturesque garden layout. (Gardens only open to the public). 4m NE via London Road A3 (D)

Madley, Hereford HR2 9NA England
Telephone: Madley (09815) 244
Telegrams: Antiques Hereford

Great Brampton House Antiques

We have one of the largest and finest collections of period furniture in the country.

Free delivery, in our own vehicles, to most parts of the United Kingdom.

Goods packed and shipped to any part of the world.

We are situated 7 miles SW of Hereford on Madley to Kingstone Road.

Open Monday to Saturday 9am to 5pm and on Sundays and in the evenings by appointment.

HEREFORD

H [i] **Tourist Information Centre** – Town Hall
tel 68430

Public buildings and places of interest

H(1) **All Saints' Church** An Early English
to Perpendicular church, noted for its
library of 300 chained books, 14th-C
carved stalls, and twisted spire.

H(2) **Booth Hall** A hall of c1400, with an
unusual restored timber roof, having
tie-beams and hammer-beams.

D(3) **Bulmers Railway Centre**

H(4) **Castle Green** Once the site of the
massive Norman castle keep.

H(5) **Cathedral** A Norman foundation with
many later additions and alterations.
Features of note are the 14th-C tower
with ball-flower decoration; The Early
English Lady Chapel of 1220 and the
chained library of over 1,600 books.
Nearby are some 15th-C houses, the
College of Vicars Choral, Foundations
of Chapter House gardens and the
bishops cloisters.

F(6) **Churchill Gardens Museum** Located in
a Regency House with fine grounds and
containing costumes, furniture, watercolours and paintings by local artists
in particular those of Brian Hatton.

H(7) **City Walls** The most extensive remains
of the medieval walls, once over 1,900yd
long, are the western section. Recently
restored and incorporating two of the
once fifteen bastions.

E(8) **Coningsby Hospital and Black Friars
Monastery Ruins.** The Hospital was founded
as an almshouse in 1614 and incorporated
earlier buildings, including a dining
hall of c1170, of the Knights of St
John of Jerusalem. The monastic ruins
are of 14th-C date.

H(9) **Library, Museum and Art Gallery** Contains
local natural history, archaeological,
geological and folk life collections;
English water colours; glass; silver;
and ceramics.

H(10) **Old House, Butchers' Guild** A restored
half-timbered building of 1621, preserved
as a period house and furnished in the
Jacobean style.

H(11) **St Peter's Church** A 12th- to 14th-C
church with 15th- to 16th-C timber
roofing and 15th-C canopied choir
stalls.

H(12) **Shire Hall** A building of 1817-19 by
Robert Smirke in the Grecian style.

H(13) **Town Hall**

H(14) **Wye Bridge** Dates back to 1490 and
was widened in 1826. Four of the six
arches are original. A new bridge has
recently been built alongside.

Belmont Abbey The Abbey church in Victorian
Gothic style was opened in 1859. Later additions
include the 112ft tower of the 1880s.
2m SW via Belmont Road A465(J)

Herefordshire Waterworks Museum Broomy Hill.
Housed in a Victorian pumping station of 1856
and containing two steam pumping engines of 1895
and 1906. ¾m W via Broomy Hill Road(G)

Hospitals

F **County Hospital** *tel 68161*
L **General Hospital** *tel 2561*
G **Victoria Eye Hospital** *tel 65961*

Sport and Recreation

A **Hereford Racecourse**

F **Hereford Rugby Club**
E **Hereford United Football Club,** Edgar
Street
K **Swimming Baths**
Wormsley Golf Course 8m NW via White Cross
Road A438 then A480 (D)

Cinemas

F **ABC Cinema,** Commercial Road *tel 3164*
H **Focus Cinema,** High Town *tel 2554*

Department Stores

Black M and Sons (Hereford) Ltd, 29 Widemarsh
Street
Chadds of Hereford Ltd, 40/43 Commercial Street
Marks and Spencer Ltd, High Town
Early closing day Thursday

Markets

Main Market Day Wednesday
E **Fruit and Cattle Market** (Monday to
Friday)
H **Market** (indoor) (Monday to Saturday).

Advertisers

H **THF** Green Dragon Hotel

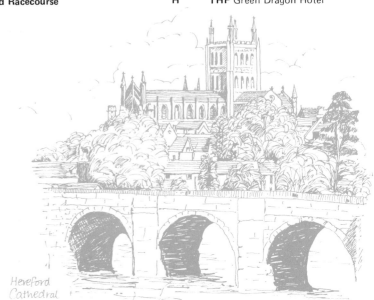

Hereford Cathedral

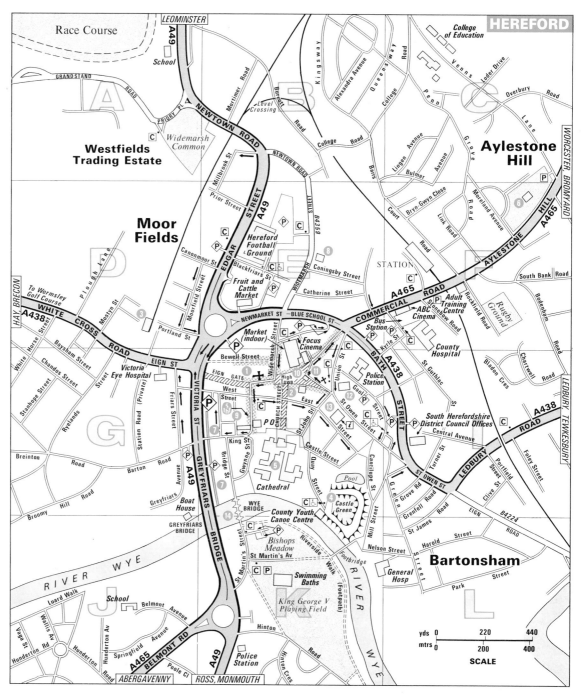

Race Course

LEOMINSTER
A49

School

GRANDSTAND
ROAD

College
of Education

Venns
Loder Drive

Overbury
Road

Lane

WORCESTER
BROMYARD

Kingsway

PRIORY PL

NEWTOWN ROAD

Mortimer Road

Level
Crossing

Burcott
Road

College
Road

Queensway
Road

Alexandra Avenue

College

Penn
Grove

**Aylestone
Hill**

Widemarsh
Common

**Westfields
Trading Estate**

Milbrook St

Prior Street

EDGAR STREET
A49

NEWTOWN ROAD

B4359

Barrs

Lingen Avenue

Bulmer

Court

Bryn Gwyn Close

Moreland Avenue

Link Road

AYLESTONE HILL
A465

**Moor
Fields**

Canonmoor St

Mostyn St

Moorfield Street

Hereford
Football
Ground

Blackfriars St

WIDEMARSH

Coningsby Street

STATION

Road

South Bank Road

A465

COMMERCIAL ROAD

Rockfield Road

Bodenham

Rugby
Ground

HAY BRECON
A438

WHITE CROSS ROAD

To Wormsley
Golf Course

Plough Lane

White Horse Street

Baysham Street

Chandos Street

Portland St

3

Fruit and
Cattle
Market

Catherine Street

NEWMARKET ST — BLUE SCHOOL ST

Market
(indoor)

Focus
Cinema

8

Bus
Station

Kyrle St

ABC
Cinema

Adult
Training
Centre

Stonebow Road

County
Hospital

St Guthlac

Bladen Cres

Chartwell

Road

South Herefordshire
District Council Offices

A438

LEDBURY ROAD

LEDBURY TEWKESBURY

Stanhope Street

Ryelands

Station Road (Private)

Friars Street

Victoria
Eye Hospital

EIGN ST

VICTORIA ST

EIGN
GATE

West
Street

P

Bewell Street

1

High Town

10

2

CHURCH STREET

P.O.

Union St

11

East
Street

St John St

12

Gaol

13

St Owen
Street

Police
Station

BATH STREET

A438

ST OWEN ST

Central Avenue

Turner St

Breinton

Road

Barton Road

Avenue

GREYFRIARS
A49

King St

Bridge St

Gwynne St

POOL

9

7

7

5

Castle Street

Quay Street

Cantilupe St

Pool

4

Castle
Green

Green Grove Rd

Grenfell Road

St James

EIGN

B4224

Broomy

Hill Road

Greyfriars

Boat
House

Cathedral

WYE
BRIDGE

County Youth
Canoe Centre

Castle Green

Riverside

RIVER WYE

14

GREYFRIARS
BRIDGE

BRIDGE

St Martin's St

Bishops
Meadow

St Martin's Av

Walk

Footbridge
(Footpath)

RIVER
WYE

Mill Street

Nelson Street

General
Hosp

Bartonsham

Park

Street

School

Luard Walk

Belmont Avenue

Vaga St

Wallis Av

Hunderton Av

Springfield Avenue

Hunderton
Road

Poole Ci

A465
BELMONT RD

A49

Hinton

Hinton Cres

Swimming
Baths

P

King George V
Playing Field

Hinton Road

ABERGAVENNY

ROSS, MONMOUTH

Police
Station

yds 0   220   440
mtrs 0   200   400

SCALE

HULL

CENTRAL PLAN

F   **AA Service Centre** — 27 Carr Lane *tel 28580*

B(1) [i]   **Tourist Information Centre** — City Information Service, Central Library, Albion Street *tel 223344* (see also public buildings and places of interest)

Public buildings and places of interest

B(1)   **Central Library, City Information Service and Film Theatre**

F(2)   **City Hall**

C(3)   **College of Technology**

F(4)   **Customs and Excise Buildings**

F(5)   **Dock Offices and Maritime Museum** The museum which was transferred to these premises during 1975, has a display on 'Whales and Whaling'. Other sections devoted to the history of shipping and fishing will be opened 1976-77.

F(6)   **Ferens Art Gallery** Contains a permanent collection of modern British paintings, 20th-C sculpture, 19th-C marine paintings and Old Masters, particularly of the English and Dutch schools. Also frequent temporary exhibitions.

G(7)   **Guildhall and Law Courts**

G(8)   **Holy Trinity Church** A 14th- and 15th-C structure and one of the largest parish churches in England. It is noted for its early brickwork, a fine font and a massive stone tower.

G(9)   **Maister's House (NT)** A Georgian merchant's house of 1743 with an impressive staircase, and entrance hall with finely-carved doors.

F(10)   **Municipal Offices**

E(11)   **Regional College of Art**

G(12)   **St Mary's Church** Early 14th-C, with a brick tower of 1697, later encased in stone.

F(13)   **Telephone House** The only municipal telephone service in the United Kingdom operates from here.

G(14)   **Transport and Archaeology Museum** Contains exhibits of transport through the ages; the Mortimer Archaeological Collection; and three 4th-C Roman pavements from a site at Rudston.

G(15)   **Trinity House** Formerly the offices of a Guild of Humber pilotmen. It is now concerned with seamen's welfare. The building dates from 1753 and contains paintings associated with its history.

G(16)   **Wilberforce House** An early 17th-C Elizabethan mansion where William Wilberforce, the slave emancipator was born in 1759. Now the Wilberforce Historical Museum exhibiting relics of the slave trade; many rooms in period styles from Stuart to Victorian; and personal items relating to William Wilberforce.

C(17)   **Wilberforce Monument**

Hospitals

E   **John Symon's Home**, Park Row, Park Street *tel 29515*

Theatres and Cinemas

E   **ABC Cinema**, Ferensway *tel 23530*

A   **Arts Centre** (Humberside Theatre), Spring Street *tel 23638*

F   **Cecil Cinema**, Anlaby Road *tel 224981*

F(2)   **City Hall**, Queen Victoria Square *tel 20123* (see also public buildings and places of interest)

B   **Dorchester Cinema**, George Street *tel 29450*

B(1)   **Film Theatre**, Central Library *tel 25017* (see also public buildings and places of interest)

E   **Regent Cinema**, Anlaby Road *tel 212433*

E   **Tower Cinema**, Anlaby Road *tel 212356*

Department Stores

Binns Ltd, Paragon Square

Boyes W and Co Ltd, 226-232 Hessle Road

Boyes W and Co Ltd, 310a Holderness Road

Debenhams Ltd, Prospect Street

Dunn Clifford Ltd, Prospect Street

Hull and East Riding Co-operative Society, Jameson Street

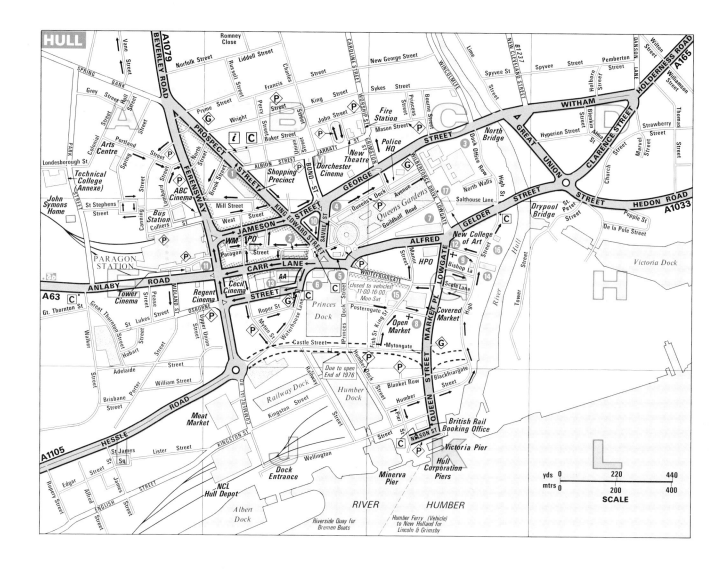

Markers

Marks and Spencer Ltd, 42-3 Whitefriargate
Willis Ludlow Ltd, Carr Lane
Early closing day Thursday. A few shops close all day Monday

107

DISTRICT PLAN
Public buildings and places of interest

C(18) Endsleigh Training College (RC)
Associated with Hull University.

B(19) University of Hull A modern university
in a pleasant setting north-west of the
city centre. Most of the Halls of
Residence are located in Cottingham.

Hospitals

B   Hull Hospital for Women, Cottingham
Road *tel 442191*

N   Hull Maternity Hospital, Hedon Road
tel 76215

L   Hull Royal Infirmary, Anlaby Road
tel 28541

E   Hull Royal Infirmary, (Sutton Annexe)
tel 701151

H   Kingston General Hospital, Beverley
Road *tel 28631*

B   Townend Maternity Home, Cottingham
Road *tel 42199*

Sport and Recreation

H   Beverley Road Swimming Baths

I   East Park Lido, (Open-air Swimming Pool)

I   East Hull Baths, Holderness Road

K   Hull City Association Football Club,
Boothferry Park

L   Hull Cricket Club, Anlaby Road

**L   Hull and East Riding Rugby Union
Football Club,** West Park, The Circle,
Anlaby Road

I   Hull Kingston Greyhound Stadium, Craven
Park, Holderness Road

I   Hull Kingston Rovers Football Club,
Craven Park, Holderness Road

F   Hull Municipal Golf Course, Springhead
Park, Willerby Road

L   Hull Rugby League Football Club,
Boulevard Ground

L   Hull Vikings Speedway Club, Boulevard
Stadium

E   Sutton Park Golf Course, Salthouse Road

Theatres and Cinemas

G   Open-Air Theatre, West Park, Anlaby
Road

Hull Docks

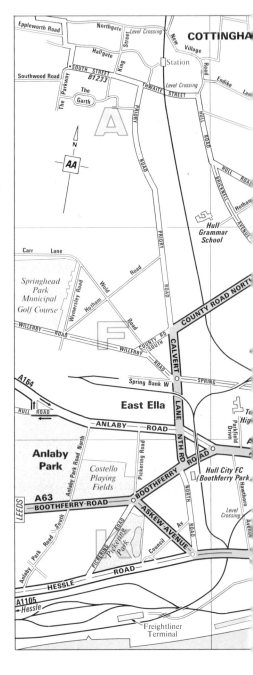

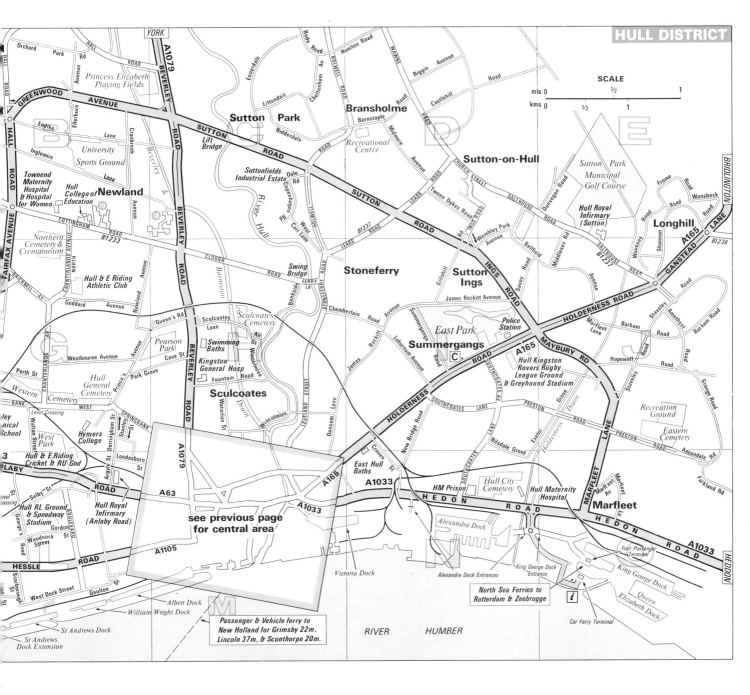

SCALE

mls 0 ½ 1

kms 0 ½ 1

YORK

Orchard Park

Princess Elizabeth Playing Fields

GREENWOOD AVENUE

HALL ROAD

FAIRFAX AVENUE

Endike Lane

Ellerburn

Inglemire Lane

University Sports Ground

Townend Maternity Hospital & Hospital for Women

Hull College of Education

Newland

COTTINGHAM ROAD

Northern Cemetery & Crematorium

Hull & E Riding Athletic Club

Goddard Avenue

Chanterlands Avenue

Perth St

Westbourne Avenue

Pearson Park

Hull General Cemetery

Western Cemetery

West Park

Hymers College

Hull & E. Riding Cricket & RU Gnd

Hull RL Ground & Speedway Stadium

HESSLE ROAD

West Dock Street

Goulton St

Albert Dock

William Wright Dock

St Andrews Dock

St Andrews Dock Extension

A1079 BEVERLEY ROAD

SUTTON ROAD

Lift Bridge

Sutton Park

Suttonfields Industrial Estate

Copenhagen Rd

Oslo Rd

West Carr Lane

River Hull

Swing Bridge

Stoneferry

CLOUGH ROAD

Barmston Drain

Bankside

FERRY LA

Queen's Rd

Sculcoates Cemetery

Sculcoates Lane

Air St

Swimming Baths

Kingston General Hosp

Fountain Rd

Sculcoates

SPRINGBANK

Argyle St

Derringham St

Stanley St

Londesboro St

Waterloo St

Wincolmlee

LEVELAND STREET

Dansom Lane

A1079

A63 ROAD

A1105

see previous page for central area

Passenger & Vehicle ferry to New Holland for Grimsby 22m, Lincoln 37m, & Scunthorpe 20m.

Bransholme

Recreational Centre

Barnstaple

Nidderdale

Littondale

SUTTON ROAD

LEADS ROAD

Sutton-on-Hull

CHURCH STREET

SALTHOUSE

Tween Dykes Road

B1237

Wembley Park Avenue

Bellfield

Stoneferry

Chamberlain Road

Sutton Ings

East Park

James Reckitt Avenue

Summergangs

Police Station

Summergangs

Lambourne Avenue

C

James Reckitt Avenue

HOLDERNESS ROAD

Southcoates Lane

New Bridge Road

Craven St

East Hull Baths

A1033

HM Prison

Hull City Cemetery

HEDON ROAD

Victoria Dock

Alexandra Dock

Alexandra Dock Entrances

North Sea Ferries to Rotterdam & Zeebrugge

Car Ferry Terminal

RIVER HUMBER

Sutton Park Municipal Golf Course

Hull Royal Infirmary (Sutton)

Longhill

BRIDLINGTON

GANSTEAD LANE

A165

B1238

Frome Road

Wansbeck

Shannon Road

Waveney

Middlesex Rd

SALTHOUSE ROAD

Dunvegan Road

Staveley Road

Amethyst Road

Barham Road

Barham Road

INGS ROAD

Savoy Road

MAYBURY RD

A165

HOLDERNESS ROAD

Hull Kingston Rovers Rugby League Ground & Greyhound Stadium

Preston Grove

Holderness Drain

MARFLEET LANE

PRESTON ROAD

Recreation Ground

Eastern Cemetery

Hopewell Road

Stoveley

Grange Road

Parkland Rd

Annandale Rd

Bilsdale Grove

Exeton Road

Marfleet Lane

Marfleet Av

Hull Maternity Hospital

Marfleet

King George Dock Entrance

Foot Passenger Terminal

King George Dock

Queen Elizabeth Dock

HEDON ROAD

A1033

HEDON

i

N   **AA Road Service Centre (80)** — Bishops Road Car Park *tel 33213*

K [i]   **Tourist Information Centre** — Inverness, Loch Ness Tourist Organisation, 23 Church Street *tel 34353*

Public buildings and places of interest

J(1)   **Abertarff House** Built c1592, it retains its old turnpike stair and now houses a highland craft and information centre.

K(2)   **Castle** The present castle built between 1834 and 1846, which replaced an earlier building destroyed by the Jacobite army in 1746, houses the Sheriff's Court House and Police Headquarters. In the courtyard is the old castle well, discovered and restored in 1909, and in the castle esplanade is the Flora MacDonald Monument erected in 1899.

N(3)   **County Buildings**

B(4)   **Cromwell's Clock Tower** This is all that remains of the Citadel built by Cromwell between 1652 and 1657, for a garrison of 1,000 men, which was demolished in 1661.

F(5)   **Dunbar's Hospital** An almshouse dating from 1688.

F(6)   **High Parish Church** Largely rebuilt 1770-2, but retaining its 14th-C vaulted tower. The execution stone in the courtyard bears bullet marks recalling the spot where prisoners from the Battle of Culloden were executed.

K(7)   **Library, Museum and Art Gallery** The museum contains many interesting Jacobite and Highland folklore relics. The art gallery has mainly temporary exhibitions.

J(8)   **St Andrew's Cathedral** The Episcopal Cathedral of the Diocese of Moray, Ross and Caithness, completed in 1869. Of particular interest are the illuminated windows, carved pillars and the baptismal font which is a copy of Thorwalden's font in Copenhagen Cathedral.

K(9)   **Tolbooth Steeple** A fine 130ft-high steeple of 1791, which was formerly used as a gaol.

M(10)   **Tomnahurich Cemetery** A fine view of Inverness and its surroundings, can be obtained from the 220ft summit of this cemetery, once claimed to be the most beautiful cemetery in the world.

K(11)   **Town House** A Gothic-style town hall, completed in 1882, and containing many fine paintings and stained glass. A framed document in the Council Chambers bears the signatures of the cabinet ministers who attended the first cabinet meeting held outside London, in 1921 under Lloyd George. In front is the Mercat Cross, surmounting the Clach-na-Cudaiann, or Stone of the Tubs, which recalls the spot where women rested when carrying home their tubs or pails of water.

Clava Cairns A group of burial cairns with three concentric rings of great stones, of late Neolithic or Early Bronze Age date. 5½m E via Millburn Road A9 and B9006 (H)

Craig Phadrig An Iron Age vitrified fort probably dating from the 1stC AD, situated on the summit of a hill (556ft). 2¼m W via Telford St A9 (E)

Culloden Battlefield The site of the battle, where the Jacobite army of 'Bonnie' Prince Charlie was defeated by British forces under the Duke of Cumberland, on April 16 1746. The old Leanach farmhouse around which the battle was fought is now a museum, and nearby are the Graves of the Clans, Wells of the Dead, and Cumberland Stone. 6m E via Millburn Road A9 and B9006 (H)

Ness Islands Situated in the River Ness, just south of the town (N) and the venue of open-air concerts and other entertainments.

Hospitals

P   **Hilton Hospital** (Geriatric) *tel 34151*

N   **Royal Northern Infirmary**, Ness Walk *tel 34411*

Sport and Recreation

E   **Caledonian Football Club Ground**, Telford Street

A   **Clachnacuddin Football Club Ground**, Grant Street

F   **Inverness Baths**, Riverside Street

P   **Inverness Golf Club**, Culcabock Road

L   **Inverness Thistle Football Club Ground**, Kingsmills Park

Inverness Ice Rink, Bught Park — skating and curling (September to April) 1m SW via Glenurquart Road A82 and Bught Drive (M)

Torvean Municipal Golf Course, Glenurquart Road. 1¼m SW via Glenurquart Road A82 (M)

Theatres and Cinemas

N   **Eden Court Theatre**, Bishop's Road *tel 221719*

G   **La Scala Cinema**, Academy Street *tel 33302*

G   **Little Theatre**, Farraline Park

Department Stores

Arnotts, 7 Union Street

F A Cameron, High Street

Early closing day Wednesday

Advertisers

K   **THF** Royal Hotel

Flora Macdonald's monument

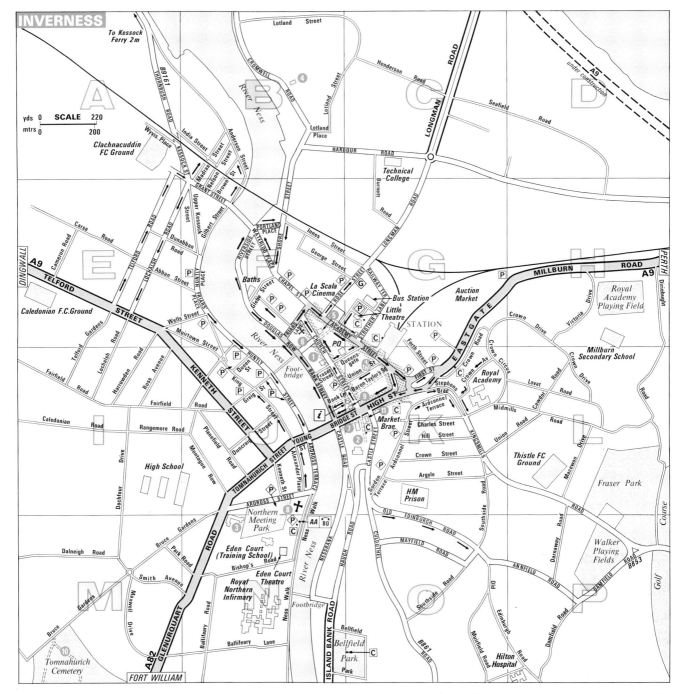

INVERNESS

To Kessock
Ferry 2m

Lotland Street

CROMWELL ROAD

River Ness

Henderson Road

LONGMAN ROAD

A9
under construction

SCALE
yds 0 — 220
mtrs 0 — 200

Clachnacuddin
FC Ground

Wyvis Place

B9161 THORNBUSH ROAD

KESSOCK ST

India Street

Madras Street

Nelson Street

Brown St

Anderson Street

Lotland Street

Lotland Place

HARBOUR ROAD

Seafield Road

Technical College

DINGWALL

A9

TELFORD STREET

Caledonian F.C.Ground

Cameron Road

Corse Road

GRANT STREET

Upper Kessock Street

Gilbert Street

Dunabban Road

Abban Street

HUNTLY PLACE

NORTH FRIARS PLACE

LOCHALSH ROAD

TELFORD ROAD

Wells Street

Muirtown Street

Baths

PORTLAND PLACE

WATERLOO PLACE

RIVERSIDE STREET

SHORE STREET

Chapel St

Glebe Street

Friars St

Innes Street

George Street

La Scala Cinema

RAILWAY TER

RISE STREET

ACADEMY STREET

Little Theatre

Bus Station

Auction Market

STATION

EASTGATE

MILLBURN ROAD

PERTH Diriebught

A9

Royal Academy Playing Field

Crown Drive

Victoria Drive

Millburn Secondary School

Caledonian Road

Telford Gardens

Lochalsh Road

Harrowden Road

Ross Avenue

Fairfield Road

Fairfield Road

Rangemore Road

KENNETH STREET

Planefield Road

Montague Row

Duncraig Street

Greig Street

King Street

Queen St

Huntly St

Douglas Row

Friars Lane

River Ness

Footbridge

Church St

PO

Queensgate

Fraser Street

Bank Street

Union Street

Baron Taylor's St

HIGH ST

Stephens Brae

Forth Street

Ardconnel Terrace

Crown Av

Crown Circus

Crown Street

Royal Academy

Lovat Road

Midmills Road

Union Street

Crown Road

Thistle FC Ground

Fraser Park

High School

Dochfour Drive

TOMNAHURICH STREET

YOUNG STREET

Alexander Place

ARDROSS TERRACE

Kenneth St

Ardross St

BRIDGE ST

CASTLE ROAD

Market Brae

Charles Street

Hill

Crown Street

Argyle Street

HM Prison

Gordon Terrace

Ardconnel Street

KINGSMILLS ROAD

Macewen Drive

Darnaway Road

Walker Playing Fields

River Ness

ROAD B853

River Ness

ARDROSS STREET

Ness Walk

Northern Meeting Park

AA 80

Eden Court (Training School)

Bishop's Road

Royal Northern Infirmary

Eden Court Theatre

Ness Walk

Footbridge

OLD EDINBURGH ROAD

MAYFIELD ROAD

Southside Road

Southside Road

OLD Edinburgh Road

Muirfield Road

Mayfield Road

ANNFIELD ROAD

DARNFIELD ROAD

Dalneigh Road

Bruce Gardens

Park Road

Smith Avenue

Mewar Drive

Bruce Gardens

Ballifeary Road

Ballifeary Road

Ballifeary Lane

ISLAND BANK ROAD

Bellfield Park

Bellfield Park

B861 ROAD

Hilton Hospital

Tomnahurich Cemetery

A82 GLENURQUART ROAD

FORT WILLIAM

111

Breakdown and Information Service *tel*
Chelmsford 61711 or Norwich 29401

J(11)   **Tourist Information Centre** — Town Hall,
ⓘ   Cornhill *tel 55851* (see also public
          buildings and places of interest)

Public buildings and places of interest

G(1)   **Central Library**
G(2)   **Christchurch Mansion** A fine brick house
        of 1548 now incorporating a museum of
        domestic antiquities. The kitchen has
        a 16th-C fireplace and domestic utensils.
        The Wolsey Art Gallery is at the rear
        of the house. Pictures displaying the
        life of the town are on display in the
        corridors.
L(3)   **Civic College**
J(4)   **Corn Exchange Entertainment and Arts
        Centre**
B(5)   **Ipswich School** Founded in 1400, the
        school has occupied its present site
        since 1852.
F(6)   **Museum** Houses collections devoted to
        archaeology and natural history. Other
        collections illustrate the geology,
        pre-history and history of Suffolk from
        earliest times to the medieval period.
J(7)   **St Lawrence's Church** The church has a
        flint tower originally built in the
        15thC then rebuilt in 1882, and a 15th-C
        stone screen.
G(8)   **St Margaret's Church** The church is noted
        for the double hammer-beam roof in the
        nave and has an exceptional example of
        the Royal Arms of Charles II.
G(9)   **St Mary-le-Tower Church** The civic
        church of the town, with a tower 176ft
        high and a pulpit carved by Grinling
        Gibbons.
J(10) **Sparrowe's (or Ancient) House** A
        picturesque, old pargetted house dating
        back to 1567, and now a book shop.
J(11) **Town Hall and Tourist Information Centre**
J(12) **Unitarian Meeting House** A plaster and
        timber building dating from c1700.
N(13) **Wolsey's Gateway and St Peter's Church**
        The gateway, a fine example of medieval
        brickwork, is a relic of a college
        built by Cardinal Wolsey in 1536. St
        Peter's Church contains one of the rare
        examples of a 12th-C black marble
        Tournai font.

Hospitals

B   **Ipswich & East Suffolk Hospital**,
        Anglesea Road Wing *tel 212477 or
        51021*

Sport and Recreation

O   **Fore Street Baths**, Fore Street
I   **Ipswich Town FC**, Portman Road
E   **St Matthews Baths**, St Matthews Street

Theatres and Cinemas

K   **ABC Cinema**, Butter Market *tel 53353*
K   **Gaumont Theatre**, St Helen's Street *tel
        53641*
J   **Ipswich Theatre**, Tower Street *tel 53725*
F   **Odeon Theatre**, Lloyds Avenue *tel 52082*

Department Stores

W R Bowman, 36 Norwich Road
Debenhams Ltd, Waterloo House
Marks and Spencer Ltd, 16 Westgate Street
Early closing day - Monday and Wednesday, most
shops are open 6 days a week

Markets

I   **Livestock Market**, Portman Road (Tuesday)

Advertisers

J   **Mercantile Credit**
J   **THF** Crown and Anchor Hotel
K   **THF** Great White Horse Hotel

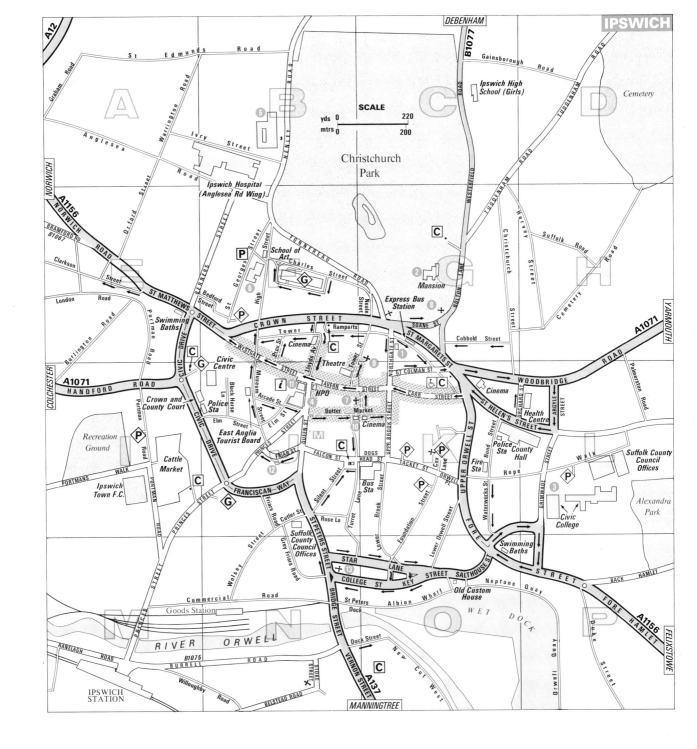

LEEDS

CENTRAL PLAN

P　　AA Service Centre – 95 The Headrow
　　　tel 38161
P(2)　Tourist Information Centre – Central
i　　Library *tel 31301/34485*

Public buildings and places of interest

V(1)　Black Prince Statue
P(2)　City Art Gallery, Library and Museum
　　　The art gallery contains a large
　　　collection of old masters; 19th- and
　　　20th-C British and French paintings;
　　　watercolours and contemporary British
　　　sculpture. The museum contains a
　　　world-wide archaeological collection
　　　but is chiefly concerned with Yorkshire.
P(3)　City Varieties Theatre The only place
　　　in the world where real music hall is
　　　played today and best known for the
　　　BBC series 'The Good Old Days'.
I(4)　Civic Hall A modern building, with an
　　　imposing porticoed front, flanked by
　　　twin towers 170ft high topped by gilded
　　　owls each 8ft high.
J(5)　Civic Theatre and College of Art
K(6)　College of Building
W(7)　Corn Exchange An unusual oval-shaped
　　　building with a domed interior dating
　　　from 1861.
B(8)　Grammar School Founded in 1552.
Q(9)　Grand Theatre A fine, late Victorian
　　　building dating from 1878.
V(10)　Holy Trinity Church The only surviving
　　　18th-C church in Leeds, built 1721-7
　　　and a perfect example of its period.
I(11)　Leeds Polytechnic
V(12)　Queen's Hall
P(13)　St Anne's Cathedral (RC) A Gothic-
　　　style church completed in 1904,
　　　possessing good timber tunnel vaulting
　　　and a reredos by Pugin in the south
　　　chancel chapel.
P(14)　St John's Church Built 1631-4, it
　　　retains highly interesting woodwork,
　　　notably the screen, pulpit and panelled
　　　wainscoting.
W(15)　St Peter's Parish Church The oldest
　　　foundation in Leeds. It was rebuilt in
　　　1839-41 and retains a notable Saxon

cross shaft discovered at that time.
O(16)　Town Hall Designed by Cuthbert
　　　Broderick in 1858, it has an impressive
　　　colonnaded front and a massive clock-
　　　tower rising to 225ft. The triennial
　　　Leeds Music Festival is held here.
C(17)　University The University, which
　　　received its charter in 1904, is
　　　expanding rapidly on a well laid-out
　　　site on the north-west side of the city
　　　centre.

Hospitals

I　　Leeds General Infirmary, Great George
　　　Street *tel 32799*
H　　Maternity Hospital at Leeds, Hyde
　　　Terrace *tel 459681*

Sport and Recreation

J　　Merrion Centre – Tenpin bowling
N　　International Swimming Pool, Westgate

Theatres and Cinemas

Q　　ABC Cinemas 1 & 2, Vicar Lane
　　　tel 451013
P(3)　City Varieties Music Hall, The Headrow
　　　tel 30808 (see also public buildings
　　　and places of interest)
J(5)　Civic Theatre *tel 455505* (see also
　　　public buildings and places of interest)
Q(9)　Grand Theatre *tel 40971/450891* (see
　　　also public buildings and places of interest)
I　　Leeds Playhouse, Calverley Street *tel
　　　42111*
J　　Odeon Cinema, Merrion Centre *tel 454322*
P　　Odeon Cinema, The Headrow *tel 452806*
P　　Plaza Cinema, New Briggate *tel 456882*
Q　　Tower Cinema, 54 New Briggate *tel
　　　458229*

Department Stores

Debenhams Ltd, 121 Briggate
Hemingways Department Store Ltd, 8 Harrison
Street
Lewis's Ltd, The Headrow
Marks and Spencer Ltd, 46 Briggate
Schofields (Yorkshire) Ltd, 79 The Headrow
Willis Ludlow Ltd, Vicar Lane
Early closing day Wednesday (A few shops close
Monday)

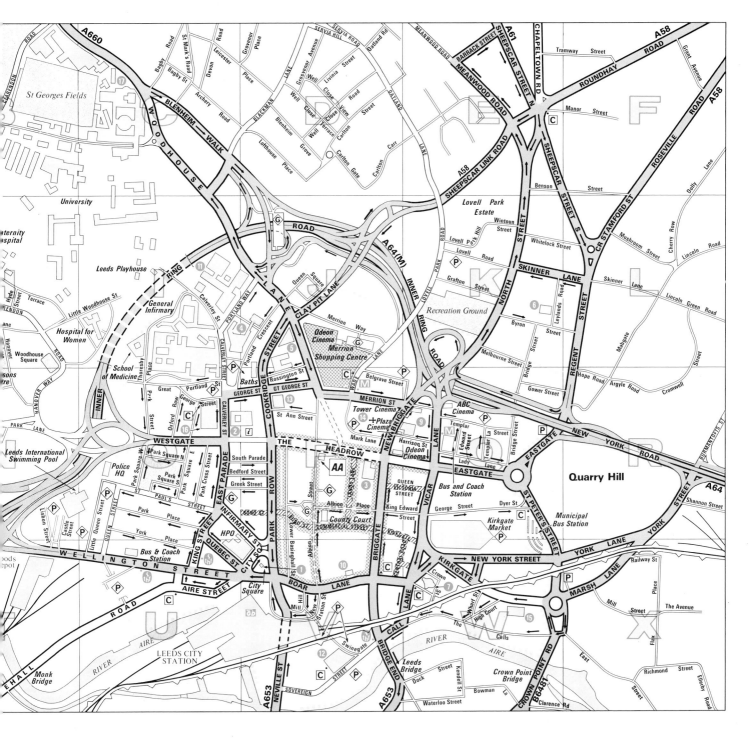

Markets

Q **Kirkgate Market** (General — Tuesday, Friday, Saturday; Corn and Hay — Tuesday; Fruit and Vegetables — each weekday)

Advertisers

V	**THF**	Golden Lion Hotel
U	**THF**	Hotel Metropole
U	**THF**	Wellesley Hotel
Q		Mercantile Credit (branch office)
P		Mercantile Credit (area office)
V		Godfrey Davis

DISTRICT PLAN
Public buildings and places of interest

G(18) Kirkstall Abbey and Abbey House Museum There are interesting remains of this 12th-C Cistercian Abbey set in a small park near the River Aire. The museum is housed in the abbey gatehouse and covers folk-life of Yorkshire of the last 300 years, including a full-scale model of streets and buildings connected with old trades in the Leeds area.

M(19) Middleton Colliery Railway The first railway authorized by Act of Parliament in 1758. Industrial locomotives and rolling stock are in use. Trains, normally steam-hauled, are run on weekend afternoons during the summer months.

O(20) Temple Newsam House A fine Tudor and Jacobean house set in a 935-acre park with woods, lakes and ornamental gardens. Lord Darnley (who married Mary, Queen of Scots) was born here in 1545. There are fine Georgian and Tudor rooms, and a collection of English furniture, paintings, silver and ceramics.

Hospitals

D Chapel Allerton Hospital *tel 623404*
B Cookridge Hospital *tel 673411*

B **Ida and Robert Arthington Hospital** *tel 677292*
J **Killingbeck Hospital,** York Road *tel 648164*
C **Meanwood Park Hospital** *tel 758721/783619*
N **St George's Hospital,** Rothwell *tel 822211*
G **St Mary's Hospital,** Green Hill Road *tel 638771*
I **St James's Hospital,** Beckett Street *tel 33144*
J **Seacroft Hospital,** York Road *tel 648164*

Sport and Recreation

G **Bramley Rugby League Football Club,** The Ground, Town Street
D **Cobble Hall Golf Course,** Elmete Lane
G **Gotts Park Golf Course**
M **Greyhound Racing,** Leeds Stadium, Elland Road
G **Headingley Rugby Union Club,** Bridge Road
M **Leeds United Association Football Club,** Elland Road
H **Leeds Rugby League Football Club,** St Michael's Lane, Headingley
M **Middleton Park Golf Course**
M **New Hunslett Rugby League Football Club,** off Dewsbury Road
D **Roundhay Golf Course,** Park Lane
D **Roundhay Park Open-air Swimming Pool,** Wetherby Road
M **South Leeds Golf Course,** Dewsbury Road Car Terminus
O **Temple Newsam Golf Course**
H **Yorkshire County Cricket Club,** Headingley Cricket Ground

Markets

J **Seacroft Town Centre** (Friday and Saturday)
I **Wholesale Fish, Fruit and Vegetable Market,** Pontefract Lane
I **Wholesale Meat Market and Abattoir,** Pontefract Lane

Advertisers

M **Godfrey Davis**

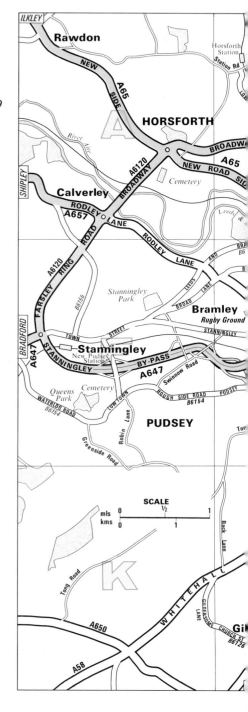

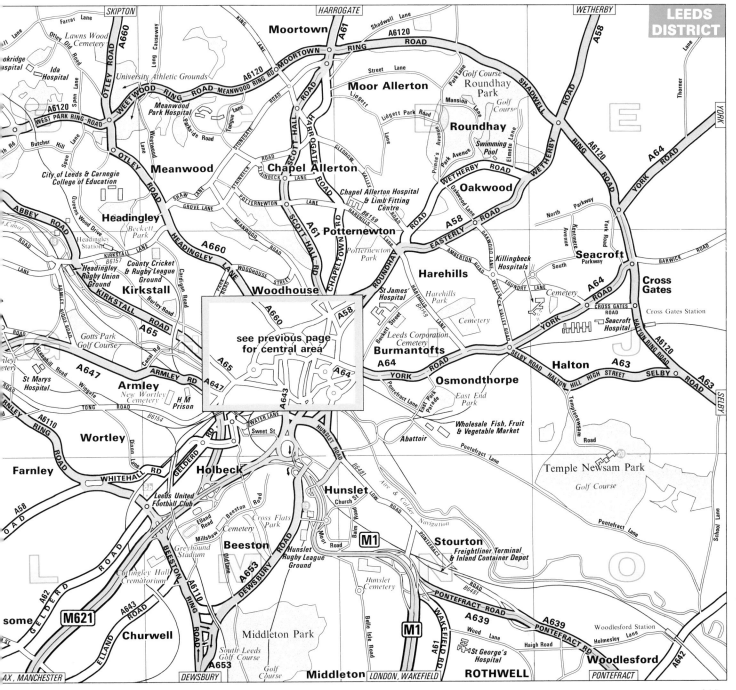

SKIPTON

HARROGATE

WETHERBY

Farrar Lane

Lawns Wood Cemetery

Otley Old Road

A660 OTLEY ROAD

A58

YORK ROAD

Moortown

A61

Shadwell Lane

A6120 ROAD

Golf Course

Roundhay Park

Moor Allerton

Roundhay

MOORTOWN RD RING ROAD

A6120 WEETWOOD RING ROAD MEANWOOD RING ROAD

University Athletic Grounds

Meanwood Park Hospital

Golf Course

Mansion

Swimming Pool

WETHERBY ROAD

SHADWELL ROAD

A6120 RING ROAD

York Road

A64 YORK ROAD

Thorner

brokridge Hospital

Ida Hospital

A6120

WEST PARK RING ROAD

Butcher Hill

OTLEY ROAD

Meanwood

Chapel Allerton

SCOTT HALL ROAD

HARROGATE ROAD

GLEDHOW VALLEY ROAD

Oakwood

WETHERBY ROAD

A58 EASTERLY ROAD

North Parkway

Kentmere Avenue

Parkway

WETHERBY RING ROAD

Seacroft

Cross Gates

City of Leeds & Carnegie College of Education

Headingley

HEADINGLEY LANE

A660

Chapel Allerton Hospital & Limb Fitting Centre

B6159

Potternewton

Potternewton Park

Killingbeck Hospitals

FOUNDRY LANE

Cemetery

South

BARWICK ROAD

A64

CROSS GATES ROAD

Cross Gates Station

ABBEY ROAD

Beckett Park

Headingley Station

County Cricket & Rugby League Ground

SCOTT HALL RD

A61

WOODHOUSE STREET

Harehills

Harehills Park

WYKEBECK VALLEY ROAD

AMBERTON ROAD

Seacroft Hospital

HALTON RING ROAD

A6120

Headingley Rugby Union Ground

Kirkstall

KIRKSTALL ROAD

A65

CHAPELTOWN RD

Woodhouse

St James' Hospital

Beckett Street

Cemetery

Leeds Corporation Cemetery

YORK ROAD

Halton

A63

SELBY ROAD

A63

Gotts Park Golf Course

see previous page for central area

Burmantofts

A64

SELBY ROAD

HALTON HILL HIGH STREET

St Marys Hospital

A647

ARMLEY RD

Armley

New Wortley Cemetery

H M Prison

Osmondthorpe

YORK ROAD

Pontefract Lane

East End Park

East Park Parade

Templenewsam Road

A643

A65 A647

Wortley

A6110 RING ROAD

A62

Wholesale Fish, Fruit & Vegetable Market

Abattoir

Temple Newsam Park

Farnley

WHITEHALL ROAD

GELDERD RD

Holbeck

Leeds United Football Club

Elland Road

Beeston Road

Cross Flats Park

HUNSLET ROAD

Hunslet

Church St

Aire & Calder Navigation

Golf Course

Pontefract Lane

School Lane

some

M621

A643 ROAD

Churwell

BEESTON ROAD

Greyhound Stadium

Millshaw

Cottingley Hall Crematorium

Beeston

A653 DEWSBURY ROAD

Hunslet Rugby League Ground

Moor Road

M1

Balm Road

Stourton

Freightliner Terminal & Inland Container Depot

PONTEFRACT ROAD

Woodlesford Station

GELDERD ROAD

ELLAND ROAD

A643

A653

Middleton Park

South Leeds Golf Course

Golf Course

Belle Isle Road

Hunslet Cemetery

M1

A61 WAKEFIELD RD

A639 PONTEFRACT RD

A639

Wood Lane

St George's Hospital

Haigh Road

Holmesley Lane

Woodlesford

A642

AX, MANCHESTER

DEWSBURY

Middleton

LONDON, WAKEFIELD

ROTHWELL

PONTEFRACT

117

LEICESTER

G   **AA Service Centre** — Fanum House, 132 Charles Street *tel 20491*

G [*i*]   **Tourist Information Centre** — 112 Bishop Street *tel 20644*

Public buildings and places of interest

F(1)   **Castle and Crown Court** Little remains of the Norman Castle with the exception of the motte and great hall. The latter, preserved behind an 18th-C façade, is now in use as a law court. Access to the Castle Yard is through two gateways, of 14th- and 15th-C date.

G(2)   **Clock Tower** Dates from 1866 and commemorates four of Leicester's benefactors.

G(3)   **Corn Exchange** An 18th-C building situated in the Market Place. It has an unusual outside staircase.

P(4)   **De Montfort Hall** A Grecian-style building, well-known as a venue for opera, ballet, dances, concerts, and music festivals.

O(5)   **Granby Hall** A large centre for exhibitions and shows.

F(6)   **GuildhalII (AM)** A magnificent timbered guildhall, dating in part from 1340, and containing the ancient town library.

C(7)   **Haymarket Theatre** Opened in 1973, it is part of the Haymarket development project.

J(8)   **Leicester Polytechnic**

G(9)   **Municipal Buildings**

K(10)   **Museum and Art Gallery** Dates from 1849 with displays of geology, natural history, painting and sculpture.

F(11)   **Museum of Costume, Roger Wygston's House** The house dates from the 15thC and displays English costume from 1760 to 1920.

F(12)   **Newarke Houses** Two buildings, Chantry House of 1511 and an adjacent house of c1600, together form a museum of the city's and county's social history from 1500 to the present day.

G(13)   **Reference Library and Tourist Information Centre**

F(14)   **Regimental Museum** The museum of the Leicestershire Regiment, housed in the massive 17th-C Magazine Gateway (AM) of the Newarke.

F(15)   **St Martin's Cathedral** A 13th- to 15th-C structure preserving a carved chancel roof and showing good modern woodwork.

F(16)   **St Mary de Castro Church** A Norman and later church with a lofty crocketted 14th-C spire, and notable Norman chancel sedilia.

F(17)   **St Nicholas Church, Jewry Wall Museum and Site** The Saxon to 13th-C church, the city's oldest, incorporates Roman materials and has a Norman south door. Museum of Leicestershire archaeology from the earliest times to the Middle Ages. Remains of 2nd-C Roman baths and Jewry Wall.

G(18)   **Town Hall and Magistrates Court** The Town Hall dates from 1875.

J(19)   **Trinity Hospital Almshouses** Part of the original Newarke (a 14th-C street), the almshouses date from 1331 and later. The Chapel is of interest.

P(20)   **University** A University college since 1921, it received full University status in 1957, and has expanded considerably in recent years.

P(21)   **War Memorial** Arch of Remembrance Designed by Sir Edwin Lutyens.

Hospitals

K   **Fielding Johnson Hospital,** Regent Road *tel 23281*

H   **Hillcrest Hospital,** Swain Street *tel 29761*

J   **Royal Infirmary,** Infirmary Square *tel 23281*

Sport and Recreation

O(5)   **Granby Halls** — roller skating (winter only) (see also public buildings and places of interest)

N   **Leicester City Football Club,** Filbert Street

O   **Rugby Football Club,** Welford Road

B   **St Margaret's Swimming Baths,** Vaughan Way

County Cricket Club, 1m S via Aylestone Road A426 (N)

Speedway and Greyhound Stadium, Parker Road ½m N via North Gate Street A5125 (A)

Theatres and Cinemas

C   **ABC Cinemas 1 & 2,** Belgrave Gate *tel 24346*

F   **Cameo Cinema,** High Street *tel 59791*

C   **Cinecenta Cinemas,** Abbey Street *tel 25892*

C(7)   **Haymarket Theatre,** Belgrave Gate *tel 52521*

G   **Little Theatre,** Dover Street *tel 21945*

G   **Odeon Cinema,** Rutland Street *tel 22892*

J   **Phoenix Theatre,** Newarke Street *tel 58832*

Department Stores

P B Hill, 388 Humberstone Road

Lewis's Ltd, Humberstone Gate

Mackay Bros Ltd, 63a King Street

Marks and Spencer Ltd, 18 Gallowtree Gate

Morgan Squire Ltd, Hotel Street

Early closing day — some small shops close half day Thursday, a few large stores close all day Monday

Markets

G   **Retail Market,** Market Place (general, meat, fish, poultry — Wednesday, Friday and Saturday)

Advertisers

G   **Mercantile Credit**

Guildhall

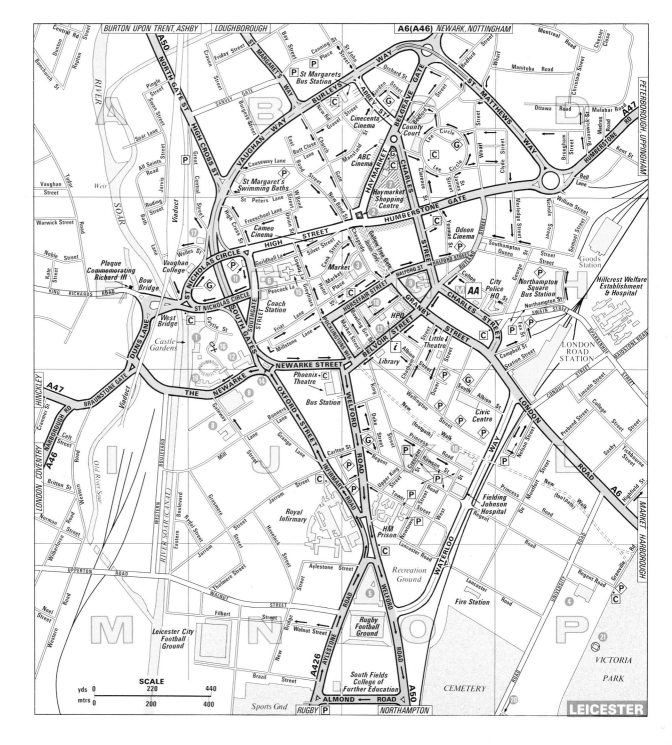

N   **AA Road Service Centre (93)** — Car Park in Tentercroft Street *tel 22873*

B(7) **Tourist Information Centres** — East
ⓘ   Midlands Tourist Board Offices, 90 Bailgate *tel 29828* (see also public buildings and places of interest)

F(5) **Information Bureau**, City Hall, Beaumont
ⓘ   Fee *tel 32151* (see also public buildings and places of interest)

Public buildings and places of interest

F(1) **Aaron the Jew's House** An important example of 12th-C domestic architecture.

F(2) **Cardinal's Hat** A magnificent late 15th-C timber-framed house, used as an inn in the 16thC, and one of the many fine timber buildings in the city centre.

B(3) **Castle (AM)** 11th-C and later structure retaining the Norman bailey and two motte mounds. The 18th- and 19th-C buildings within the walls are the former prison (now the County Archives Office) and the Assize Court.

C(4) **Cathedral** A splendid Norman and later building dominating the City and surrounding country. Of particular note are the west front, the triple towers, St Hugh's Choir and the beautiful Angel Choir, the 13th-C Chapter House, the black marble Tournai font and a copy of Magna Carta. Nearby are the fine buildings of Cathedral Close and Minster Yard, including the 13th-C Bishop's House and 19th-C Palace and the 14th-C Vicar's Court.

F(5) **City Hall and Information Bureau**

C(6) **East Gate** A massive Roman tower, dating from the 3rdC AD.

B(7) **East Midlands Tourist Board Offices**

B(8) **Exchequer Gate** The west gatehouse of the Close wall, dating from the 14thC.

J(9) **Greyfriars City and County Museum and City Library** A former friary dating from the 13thC with a fine barrel roof. Now a museum of antiquities. The library adjoins the museum.

J(10) **High Bridge** A Norman vaulted bridge spanning the Witham River, with a timber-framed 16th-C house on the west side.

F(11) **Jew's House** Another Norman house of c1170-80, and probably a better-known example than Aaron the Jew's House (1).

A(12) **Museum of Lincolnshire Life** Exhibits cover the period from Elizabethan times to the present day.

B(13) **Newport Arch (AM)** Dating from the 2nd-C AD it is the last Roman arch in England which still spans a road. To the east is a fragment of the Colonia wall and ditch — the latter was 30ft deep. To the south is Bailgate with remnants of a Roman colonnade.

G(14) **Potter Gate** Dates from the early 14thC.

C(15) **Priory Gate**

J(16) **St Benedict Church** Preserves an 11th-C tower.

J(17) **St Mary-le-Wigford Church** Mainly 13th-C with a Norman tower and a Roman memorial stone.

N(18) **St Mary's Guildhall (or John of Gaunt's stables) (AM)** A fine Norman guildhall dating from c1180.

N(19) **St Peter-at-Gowt's Church** The tower also dates from the 11th-C.

J(20) **St Swithin's Church** A modern church with a Roman altar stone.

J(21) **Stonebow and Guildhall** The Stonebow gateway is late 15th- and early 16th-C. Above it is the fine, partly timbered Guildhall which contains the Civic insignia and royal charters.

F(22) **Theatre Royal**

G(23) **Usher Gallery** Contains a fine collection of miniatures, glass, ceramics, watches and water-colours.

Hospitals

H   **County Hospital**, Sewell Road *tel 29921*
B   **Lawn Hospital**, Union Road *tel 26226*
St George's Hospital, Long Lays Road *tel 29921* 1¼m NW via Yarborough Road A1102(A)
St John's Hospital, London Road, Bracebridge Heath *tel 27401* 3m S via High Street and Cross O'Cliffe Road A15 (N)

Sport and Recreation

C   **Lincolnshire County Cricket Club**, Lindum Sports Club, Wragby Road
C   **Lincoln Rugby Union Football Club**, Lindum Sports Club, Wragby Road
City Sports Centre (including swimming pool), Skellingthorpe Road 2m S via High Street A15 (M) then Dixon Street A1180
Lincoln City Football Club, Sincil Bank 1m S via Canwick Road A158 (O) or High Street A15 (N)
Lincoln Racecourse (Point-to-point events) 1½m NW via Carholme Road A57 (E)
South Cliffe Golf Course 1m S via Canwick Road A158 (O)

Theatres and Cinemas

J   **ABC Cinema**, Saltergate *tel 23062*
N   **Odeon Cinema**, High Street *tel 20951*
F(22) **Theatre Royal**, Clasketgate *tel 25555*

Department Stores

Bainbridges (Lincoln) Ltd, 233 High Street
Marks and Spencer Ltd, 204 High Street
Mawer and Collingham, High Street and Mint St
Early closing day Wednesday

Markets

J   **Central Market**, Sincil Street (Fruit and Vegetables — Weekdays; General — Friday and Saturday)
J   **Corn Market**, Corn Exchange (Friday)

Advertisers

F   **Mercantile Credit**
C   **THF** Eastgate Hotel

The following streets shown on the plan are closed to traffic between 10.00 and 16.00hrs. At other times they are open for access only: High Street (north of St Mary Street), Cornhill, Sincil Street (south of Waterside South), Saltergate Street (west from Bank Street), Guildhall Street

LIVERPOOL

J AA Service Centre — Derby Square *tel 051-709 7252*

G ⓘ Tourist Information Centre — 187 St John's Precinct, 1st Floor, Elliot Street *tel 051-709 3631/8681*

Public buildings and places of interest

K(1) Anglican Cathedral This notable red sandstone Cathedral with a 331-ft tower was commenced in 1904. Its modern Gothic style is strongly marked by the individuality of its architect Sir Giles Gilbert Scott. It is still incomplete. ¼m S via Rodney Street.

J(2) Bluecoat Chambers Well-restored Queen Anne-style buildings of 1716.

C(3) College of Technology

F(4) Council Offices and Information Bureau

I(5) Cunard Building A well-known waterfront landmark.

I(6) Dock Board Offices

L(7) Metropolitan Cathedral (RC) This very impressive modern cathedral of conical shape was designed by Sir Frederick Gibberd and consecrated in 1967. It possesses a central pinnacled lantern tower with stained glass by John Piper and Patrick Reyntians.

L(8) Philharmonic Hall

E(9) Royal Liver Building Nearly 300ft in height, surmounted by two examples of the 'liver' a mythical bird, from which, by tradition the city takes its name.

G(10) St George's Hall A notable building of 1838-54, possibly the finest Greco-Roman style building in Europe, designed by H L Elmes and containing seven courts of law, a main hall with seating capacity for 1,750 and a small concert hall.

G(11) St John's Beacon A 450ft-high tower, Liverpool's highest building, with a restaurant and observation platform.

F(12) Town Hall Built 1749-54 to a design by John Wood the Elder, with enlargements of 1789-92 by James Wyatt and the addition of the portico and council chamber in 1811 and the large ballroom in 1820.

H(13) University Many of the colleges date from the 19thC but the University became a separate institution in 1903. The main site of over thirty modern buildings close to the centre of the town dates from 1949.

G(14) Walker Art Gallery, Merseyside County Museum and the City Libraries The art gallery contains the largest collection of European paintings in Britain outside of London, with works dating from the 14thC to the present day. The museum houses archaeology, ethnography, ceramics and applied arts from the Mayer collection; a historic musical instruments collection; geological and shipping galleries; a natural history display based on the Ainsdale National Nature Reserve; an aquarium; a new gallery of transport of the Merseyside region; displays illustrating the history of timekeeping and space exploration; and a planetarium.

The Library is one of the oldest and largest public libraries in England with a bookstock of over two million including the Brown Library with commercial, technical, arts and recreation, philosophical and religious and local history collections; the Hornby Library of fine and rare books, manuscripts, prints and autograph letters; and International Library.

Hospitals

A David Lewis Northern Hospital, Leeds Street *tel 051-236 6491*

L Hahnemann Hospital, 42 Hope Street *tel 051-709 8474*

H Liverpool Dental Hospital, Pembroke Place *tel 051-709 0281*

L Liverpool Ear, Nose and Throat Infirmary, Myrtle Street *tel 051-709 0741*

L Liverpool Maternity Hospital, Oxford Street *tel 051-709 5511*

H Liverpool Royal Infirmary, Pembroke Place *tel 051-709 5511*

L Royal Liverpool Children's Hospital, Myrtle Street *tel 051-709 0821*

E St Paul's Eye Hospital, Old Hall Street *tel 051-236 7794*

Sport and Recreation

E Liverpool Stadium, St Paul's Square

Theatres and Cinemas

G ABC Cinema, Lime Street *tel 051-709 1150*

G Empire Theatre, Lime Street *tel 051-709 1555*

L Everyman Theatre, Hope Street *tel 051-709 4776*

G Futurist Cinema, Lime Street *tel 051-709 3186*

K Neptune Theatre, Hanover Street *tel 051-709 7844*

G Odeon 1, 2, 3 & 4, London Road *tel 051-709 0717*

G Playhouse Theatre, William Square *tel 051-709 8363*

L(8) Royal Liverpool Philharmonic Society, Philharmonic Hall, Hope Street *tel 051-709 3789* (see also public buildings and places of interest)

G Scala Cinema, Lime Street *tel 051-709 1084*

K Studios 1, 2 & 3, Mount Pleasant Brownlow Hill *tel 051-709 8806*

Department Stores

Army and Navy Stores, 47 Ranelagh Street
Bekayswear, 190 St John's Market
Blackler's Stores Ltd, Elliot Street
Cape Clothing Ltd, 12 Williamson Street
Cost Crusha Centre Ltd, 93 London Road
G & H Stores, 81 Kirkdale Road
Gimbles, Great Charlotte Street
Henderson William and Sons Ltd, 9 Church Street
Hughes T J and Co Ltd, Audley House, London Road
Lee George Henry and Co Ltd, 20 Basnett Street
Lewis's Ltd, Ranelagh Street
Marks and Spencer Ltd, Compton House, Church Street
Millets Outfitters, Lord Street
Owen Owen Ltd, Clayton Square
Oxleys Department Store Ltd, 22 Fleet Street
Early closing day Wednesday

Markets

H   **Monument Place Market** (Thursday and Saturday)

G   **St John's Market**, St John's Centre (Daily)

Advertisers

E   **Mercantile Credit**

G   **THF** St George's Hotel

G   **Centre** Liverpool Centre Hotel

DISTRICT PLAN

P   **AA Road Service Centre (44)** — Car Park, Gomer Street, Birkenhead *tel* 051-647 7252

P   **Tourist Information Centre** — Reference Department, Central Wirral Area Library, Borough Road, Birkenhead *tel* 051-652 6106

Public buildings and places of interest

Q(15) **Birkenhead Town Hall and Information Bureau**

G(16) **Bootle Museum and Art Gallery** Small museum noted for its fine collection of English pottery and porcelain. Also monthly changing art exhibitions.

I(17) **Croxteth Hall** An 18th-C and later hall in a large park.

S(18) **Harthill Botanical Gardens**, Calderstones Park. A large and comprehensive collection of hardy and tropical plants, noted for its hot houses, in particular its Orchid House.

J(19) **Knowsley Safari Park** Situated in the grounds of a 17th- to 19th-C mansion, with lions, cheetahs, elephants, zebra, etc, roaming freely in natural surroundings. Also dolphinarium.

V(20) **Lady Lever Art Gallery**, Port Sunlight. Displays pictures by famous English masters in addition to collections of sculpture, Chinese porcelain, Wedgewood wares and English furniture.

Q(21) **Priory Ruins**, Birkenhead. These remains date from the 12thC.

K(22) **St James' Church**, Birkenhead. A modern church with a richly-decorated lecturn.

Q(23) **St Mary's Church**, Birkenhead. This was built in 1821.

X(24) **Speke Hall (NT)** A magnificent 'black and white' half-timbered hall, completed in 1610 with interior courtyard, Great Hall, 16th- and 17th-C plasterwork and the Mortlake tapestries.

R(25) **Sudley Art Gallery** An early 19th-C merchant's house containing a large collection of works including paintings by Reynolds, Gainsborough, Wilkie, Mulready, Romney, Holman Hunt, Turner and Bonington. Also some 19th-C French paintings, British sculpture, pottery and costume.

K(26) **Wallasey Town Hall and Information Bureauu**

P(27) **Williamson Art Gallery and Museum**, Birkenhead. Collections include an important English watercolours section, sculpture, decorative arts, ceramics, glass, silver and furniture. A local history and maritime museum adjoins.

Hospitals

C   **Aintree and Fazakerley Hospitals**, Longmoor Lane, Liverpool 9 *tel* 051-525 5980

N   **Alder Hey Children's Hospital**, Eaton Road, Liverpool *tel* 051-228 4811

P   **Ashton Hospital**, 26 Village Road, Oxton *tel* 051-652 3143

P   **Birkenhead Children's Hospital**, Woodchurch Road, Birkenhead *tel* 051-652 5401

P   **Birkenhead General Hospital**, Park Road North, Birkenhead *tel* 051-66134

G   **Bootle Hospital**, Derby Road, Liverpool *tel* 051-922 4541

N   **Broadgreen Hospital (General)**, Thomas Drive, Liverpool 14 *tel* 051-228 4878

X   **Garston Hospital**, Woolton Road

L   **John Bagot Hospital**, Netherfield Road North

G   **Liverpool Stanley Hospital**, Stanley Road *tel* 051-922 2161

M   **Mill Road Maternity Hospital**, Mill Road *tel* 051-263 2656

R   **Mossley Hill Hospital**, Park Avenue *tel* 051-724 2335

M   **Newsham General Hospital**, Belmont Road *tel* 051-263 7381

N   **Olive Mount Children's Hospital**, Old Mill Lane *tel* 051-722 2261

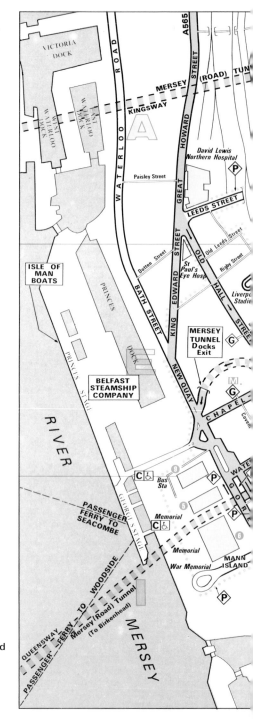

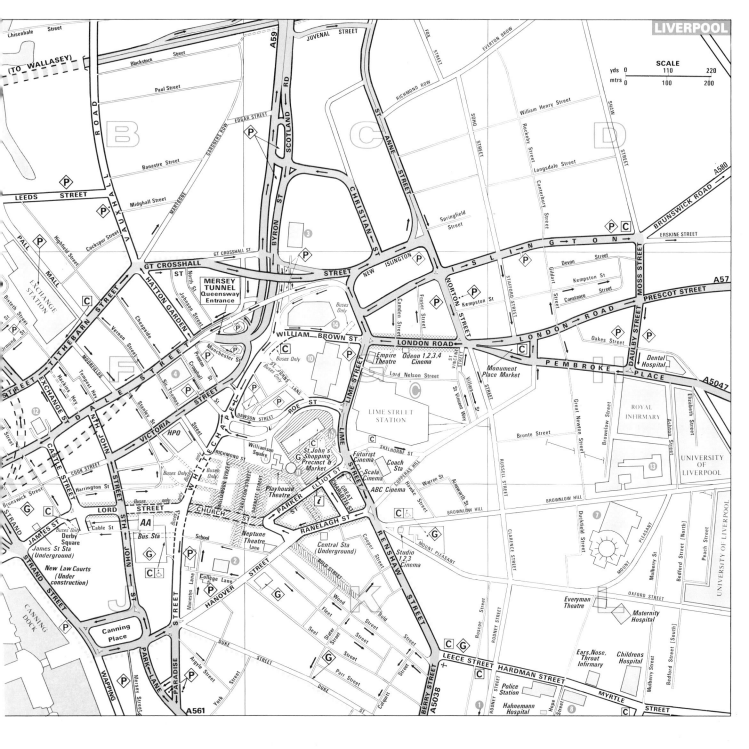

M   **Park Hospital**, Newsham Park *tel 051-263 9641*

R   **Princes Park Hospital**, 96 Upper Parliament Street *tel 051-709 7361*

N   **Rathbone Hospital**, Mill Lane *tel 051-228 4657*

Q   **Royal Southern Hospital**, Caryl Street *tel 051-709 6841*

P   **St Catherine's Hospital**, Church Road, Birkenhead *tel 051-652 2281*

K   **St James's Hospital**, Tollemache Road, Claughton *tel 051-652 3571*

R   **Sefton General Hospital**, Smithdown Road *tel 051-733 4020*

K   **Victoria Central Hospital**, Liscard Road, Wallasey *tel 051-638 7000*

K   **Wallasey Hospital for Women**, Claremount Road *tel 051-638 4224*

G   **Walton Hospital (General)**, Liverpool 9 *tel 051-525 3611*

M   **Women's Hospital**, Catherine Street *tel 051-709 5461*

Sport and Recreation

C   **Aintree Racecourse**

S   **Allerton Park Golf Course**, Allerton

P   **Birkenhead Park Rugby Union Football Club**, Park Road North

B   **Bootle Golf Club**, Dunnings Bridge Road

O   **Bowring Park Golf Course**, Roby Road

U   **Brackenwood Golf Club**, Brackenwood Park, Bracken Lane, Bebington

T   **Childwall Golf Club**, Naylors Road, Gateacre

H   **Everton Football Club**, Goodison Park

O   **Huyton Leisure Centre**, Roby Road, Huyton

O   **Huyton and Prescot Golf Club**, Hurst Park, Huyton Lane, Huyton

O   **Huyton Rugby League Football Club**, Endmoor Road, Huyton

D   **Kirkby Sports Centre**, Whitefield Road, Kirkby

D   **Kirkby Town Football Club**, Simonswood Lane, Kirkby

T   **Lee Park Golf Club**, Gateacre

W   **Liverpool Cricket Club**, Aigburth Road

H   **Liverpool Football Club**, Anfield Road

D   **Liverpool Municipal Golf Course**, Ingoe Lane, Kirkby, Liverpool

R   **Liverpool Rugby Union Football Club**, St Michael's, Church Road

F   **New Brighton Association Football Club**, Tower Stadium, New Brighton

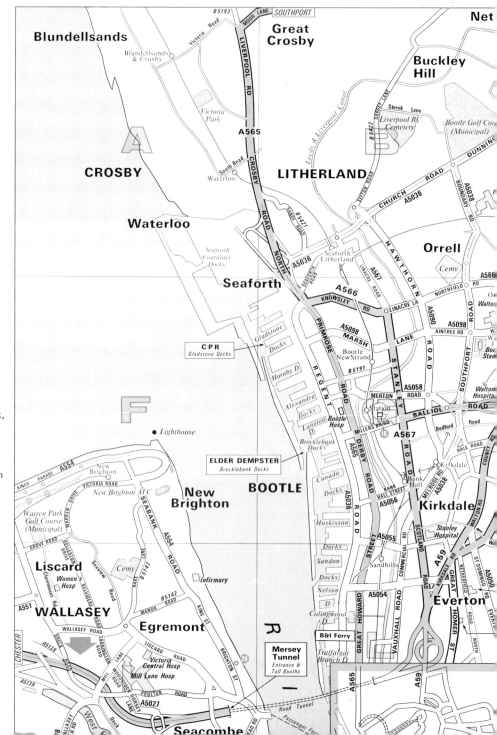

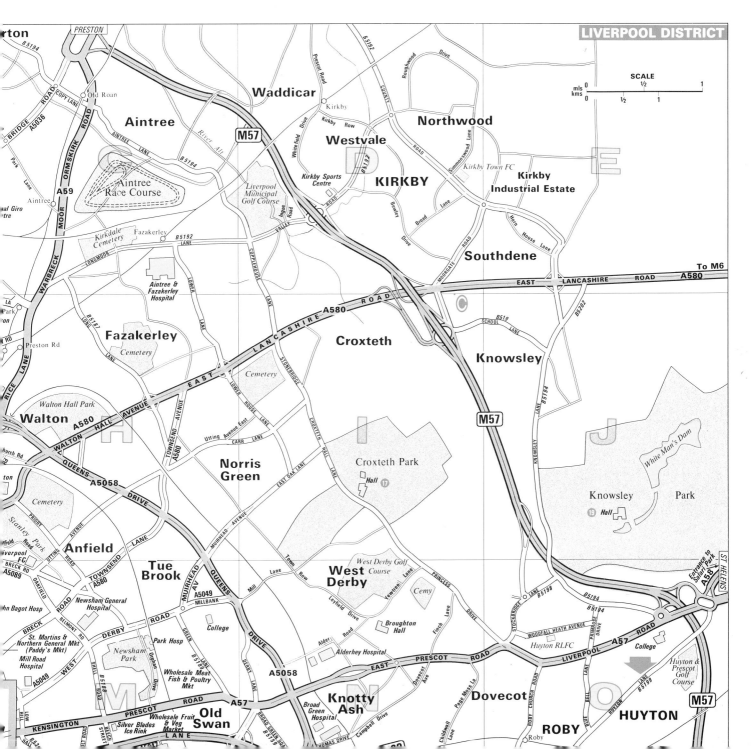

V	**Oval Sports Centre**, Old Chester Road, Bebington
V	**Port Sunlight Golf Club**, Spital Road, Bebington
U	**Prenton Golf Club**, Golf Links Road, Prenton, Birkenhead
M	**Silver Blades Ice Rink**, Prescot Road
P	**Tranmere Rovers Football Club**, Prenton Park, Birkenhead
F	**Warren Park Golf Links**, Grove Road, Wallasey
N	**West Derby Golf Club**, Yew Tree Lane
P	**Wirral Ladies Golf Club**, Bidston Road, Oxton, Birkenhead
Y	**Woolton Golf Club**, Doe Park, Woolton, Liverpool

Department Stores

Army and Navy General Stores, 160 Linacre Road

Beatties of Birkenhead, 92 Grange Road

Benmar Consultants Ltd, 98 Wallasey Village, Wallasey

Carney Miss S, 42 Fairfax Road, Wallasey

Hughes T J and Co Ltd, Grange Road, Birkenhead

Hughes T J and Co Ltd, New Strand, Bootle

Marks and Spencer Ltd, 212 Grange Road, Birkenhead

Marks and Spencer Ltd, 301 Liscard Road, Wallasey

Marks and Spencer Ltd, New Strand Shopping Precinct

Robb Brothers Ltd, Grange Road, Birkenhead

Rostance's Ltd, 13 Oxton Road, Claughton

Rostance's Ltd, 57 New Chester Road, New Ferry

Sturla Geo and Son Ltd, 165 Park Road

This 'N That, 222 Childwall Road

Wright Price, 11 Walton Vale

Markets

L	**North General** (Saturday) and **St Martin's Market** (Daily), Great Homer Street
M	**Wholesale Fruit, Vegetable and Flowers Market**, Prescot Road (Daily)
M	**Wholesale Meat, Poultry and Fish Market**, Prescot Road (Monday to Friday)

Advertisers

P	**Mercantile Credit**
Q	**Godfrey Davis**
I	**Crest** Liverpool Crest Motel

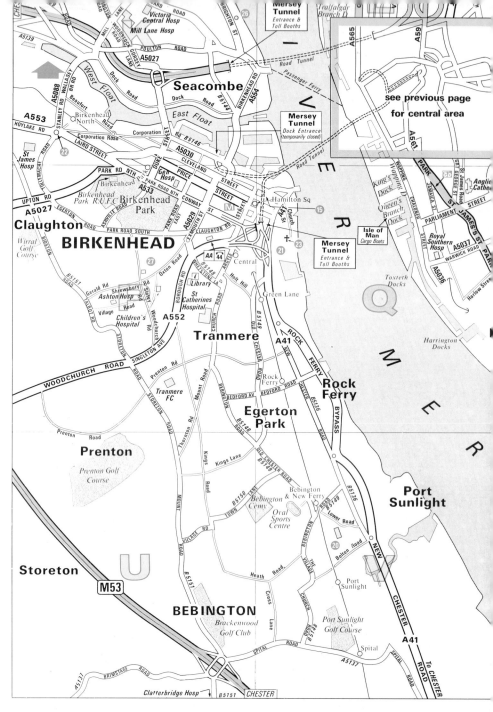

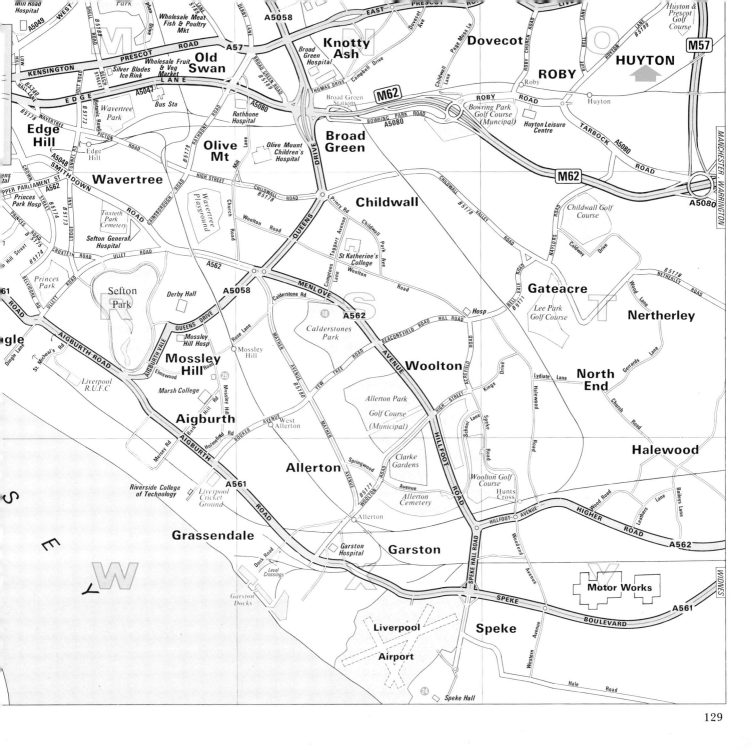

LLANDUDNO

E [i] **Tourist Information Centres** — Chapel Street *tel 76413*
B [i] Opposite Pier Gates, Promenade *tel 76572* (summer months only)

Public buildings and places of interest

E(1) **Doll Museum and Model Railway**
B(2) **Great Orme Cabin Lift** Longest passenger cable car in Britain, leading to Great Orme's Head.
A(3) **Great Orme Tramway** Over 60 years old and nearly a mile in length, this cable railway carries passengers to the summit of Great Orme (679ft) which dominates Llandudno.
B(4) **Happy Valley Rock Gardens**
D(5) **Haulfre Gardens** Interesting terraced gardens and aquarium.
I(6) **Rapallo House Museum and Art Gallery** A picture gallery and small museum with collection of china and glassware, an armoury, Roman relics and old Welsh kitchen. Also ornamental gardens.
E(7) **Town Hall**
St Tudno's Church, Great Orme's Head (A) Preserves some 13th-C coffin lids.

Hospitals

H **Llandudno General Hospital**, Maesdu, West Shore *tel 77471*

Sport and Recreation

D **Llandudno Cricket Club**, The Oval
H **Maesdu Golf Club**
G **North Wales Golf Club**, West Shore
E **Swimming Pool**, Mostyn Broadway

Theatres and Cinemas

F **Arcadia Theatre** (summer shows) *tel 76570*
D **Astra Entertainment Centre Cinema**, Gloddaeth Street *tel 76666*
F **Grand Theatre**, Mostyn Broadway *tel 77327*
B **Happy Valley Theatre**, (open-air summer shows)
E **Palladium Cinema**, Gloddaeth Street *tel 76244*
B **Pier Pavilion Theatre** *tel 75649*
E **Savoy Cinema**, Mostyn Street *tel 76394*

Department Stores

Clares Department Store, 97 Mostyn Street
Marks and Spencer Ltd, 61 Mostyn Street
Early closing day Wednesday (except summer)

Markets

E **Market Hall** (Daily except Wednesday afternoons)

Advertisers

B   **THF** Grand Hotel
E   **THF** Marine Hotel

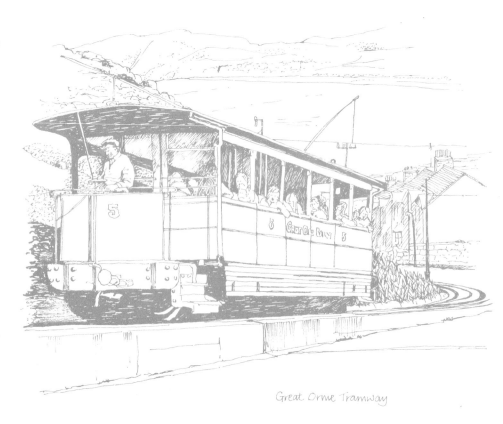

Great Orme Tramway

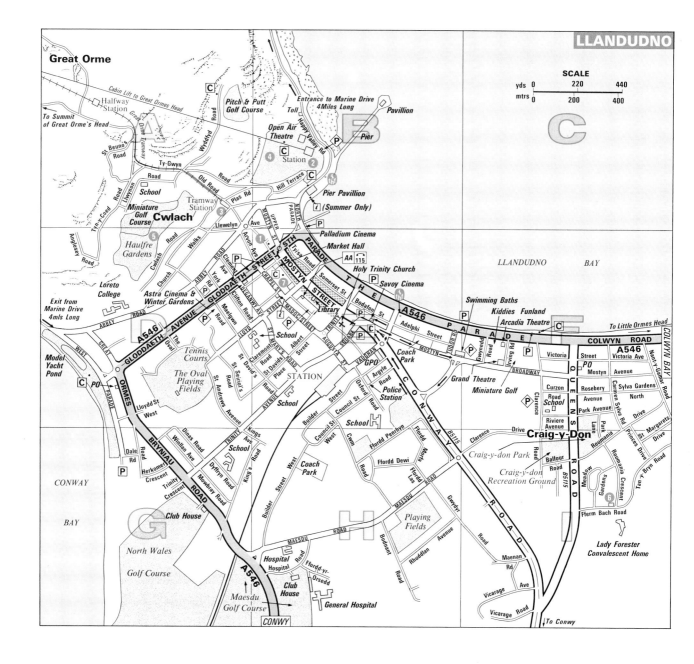

SCALE

yds 0   220   440

mtrs 0   200   400

Great Orme

Cabin Lift to Great Ormes Head

Halfway
Station

To Summit
of Great Orme's Head

Pitch & Putt
Golf Course

Entrance to Marine Drive
4 Miles Long

Toll

Pavillion

Open Air
Theatre

Happy Valley Rd

Pier

Station

St. Beuno's
Road

Ty-Gwyn

Old Road

Hill Terrace

Pier Pavillion

(Summer Only)

School

Plas Rd

Tramway
Station

Miniature
Golf
Course

Cwlach

Llewelyn

Ave

Palladium Cinema

Market Hall

AA 115

Holy Trinity Church

LLANDUDNO   BAY

Haulfre
Gardens

Walks

Savoy Cinema

Loreto
College

Astra Cinema &
Winter Gardens

Swimming Baths

Kiddies Funland

Arcadia Theatre

Exit from
Marine Drive
4 mls Long

Church

Library

School

COLWYN   ROAD

To Little Ormes Head

Model
Yacht
Pond

Tennis
Courts

School

STATION

Coach
Park

Grand Theatre

Miniature Golf

Victoria

Street

PO
Mostyn

A546

Victoria Ave

Avenue

Nant-y-Gamar Rd

COLWYN BAY

The Oval
Playing
Fields

School

Police
Station

BROADWAY

Curzon
Road
School

Roseberry

North

Carmen Sylva Rd

Sylva Gardens

Lloydd St
West

School

GPO

Argyle

Clarence

Park Avenue

Riviere
Avenue

Avenue

Princes Drive

St. Margarets

Drive

Dinas Road

School

Coach
Park

Council St
West

Ffordd Penrhyn

Craig-y-Don

Roumania Crescent

Tan-y-Bryn Road

CONWAY

Winllan Ave

Herkomer's
Crescent

Dale
Rd

Ffordd Dewi

Craig-y-don Park

Balfour
Road

Meadow

Gardens

BAY

Trinity
Crescent

Mowbray Road

Kings

Road

Playing
Fields

Craig-y-don
Recreation Ground

Fferm Bach Road

Club House

Rhuddlan
Road

Lady Forester
Convalescent Home

North Wales

Golf Course

Hospital

Hospital

General Hospital

Ffordd-yr-
Orsedd

Club
House

Maesdu
Golf Course

Maenan
Rd

Vicarage
Ave

CONWY

Vicarage   Road

To Conwy

LONDON (CENTRAL)

Public buildings and places of interest

N(1)   **Banqueting House** Built in 1619 to a design by Inigo Jones it contains painted ceilings by Rubens.

I(2)   **British Crafts Centre** Designed to promote and sell work by British craftsmen, the exhibits are changed regularly and cover a wide variety of British crafts.

D(3)   **British Museum** Founded in 1753 this vast museum is famous for ancient sculpture, prints, drawings and books.

P(4)   **British Museum of Natural History** The museum houses the national collection of animals and plants, both recent and fossil, and of rocks, minerals and meteorites.

P(5)   **Brompton Oratory** Roman Catholic Church in the Italian Renaissance style built in 1878 by Herbert Gribble.

R(6)   **Buckingham Palace** Built in 1703 it was remodelled by Nash in 1830 and the east front refaced in 1913 by Ashton Webb. A flag flies when the Queen is in residence. The changing of the guard takes place daily, outside.

D(7)   **Building Centre**

D(8)   **Courtauld Institute Galleries** Important collection of Impressionist and Old Master paintings.

N(9)   **Design Centre** Headquarters of the Design Council, the pictorial card index lists British quality goods, their price and where to buy them.

E(10)   **Dickens House** Dickens lived here 1837-39. The house contains many personal relics along with manuscripts and first editions.

J(11)   **HMS Discovery** Built in 1901 for Captain Scott's first expedition to the Antarctic. HMS *Discovery* is now used as a drill ship for the Royal Navy.

H(12)   **Embroiderers' Guild** A society to encourage the art of embroidery with a unique collection available for study.

E(13)   **Foundling Hospital** Pictures by Hogarth, Gainsborough and others, also sculpture and Handel relics.

P(14)   **Geological Museum** Exhibitions include The Story of the Earth, The Gemstone Collection, The Regional Geology of Great Britain and The Economic Minerals of the Earth.

S(15)   **Guards Museum** Small museum in Guards Chapel, Wellington Barracks.

N(16)   **Horse Guards** Built in 1753 from designs by William Kent. The ceremony of Mounting and Changing the Guard takes place daily.

T(17)   **Houses of Parliament** A mid-19th-C Gothic building. The House of Lords lies to the south of a central hall and the House of Commons to the north.

X(18)   **Industrial Health Safety Centre**

J(19)   **Inns of Court and Chancery**

S(20)   **Jewel Tower** 14th-C tower of the old Palace of Westminster.

T(21)   **Lambeth Palace** Official home of the Archbishops of Canterbury. The buildings date mainly from the 15th and 16th Cs.

M(22)   **Lancaster House** Built in the 19th C for the Duke of York, Lancaster House is now used as a centre for government hospitality.

J(23)   **London Silver Vaults**

B(24)   **Madame Tussauds** The wax exhibition came to England from Paris and settled in London in 1835. Exhibits include the Chamber of Horrors, historical figures and many famous and infamous people.

N(25)   **Marlborough House** Built by Sir Christopher Wren for the Duke of Marlborough. Inside are magnificent wall paintings depicting the Duke's famous battles.

M(26)   **Museum of Mankind** Ethnological and archaeological collections of pre-industrial societies from most parts of the world excluding Western Europe.

G(27)   **Music Box Gallery**

N(28)   **National Gallery** A collection of the chief European schools of painting from the 13th C to 1900.

N(29)   **National Portrait Gallery** National collection of portraits of the famous and infamous in British history, also sculptures, miniatures, engravings, photographs and cartoons.

J(30)   **Old Curiosity Shop** Now an antique shop, this Tudor house, built in 1567, was immortalised by Dickens in *The Old Curiosity Shop.*

D(31)   **Percival David Foundation of Chinese Art** Displays Chinese ceramics from the 10th to the 18th Cs.

N(32)   **Pipe Museum** Situated in Dunhill's tobacco shop.

B(33)   **Planetarium** The night skies are projected onto the inside of the dome to an accompanying commentary.

P(34)   **Polish Institute and Sikorski Museum**

D(35)   **Pollock's Toy Museum** Old toys, dolls and theatres are on display along with the oldest teddy bear in England.

C(36)   **Post Office Tower**

R(37)   **The Queen's Gallery** Changing exhibitions of pictures and works of art at Buckingham Palace.

J(38)   **Roman Bath** Restored in the 17th C.

M(39)   **Royal Academy of Arts** Founded by George III in 1768. The summer exhibition is of works by living artists, and loan exhibitions are held throughout the rest of the year.

J(40)   **Royal College of Surgeons**

V(41)   **Royal Hospital** Founded in 1682 by Charles II the Royal Hospital houses the Chelsea Pensioners, veteran and invalid soldiers. The Chelsea Flower Show is held in the hospital grounds every year.

R(42)   **Royal Mews** Many state coaches and carriages are on display including the Gold State Coach, the Irish State Coach and the Scottish State Coach.

N(43)   **St James Palace** Built by Henry VIII in 1530-6, with later additions by Wren.

N(44)   **St Martin in the Fields** The church was rebuilt in the early 18th C by Gibbs, a pupil of Wren. It has a fine steeple and a richly-decorated, galleried interior.

P(45)   **Science Museum** Many working models, actual locomotives and machinery etc cover all aspects of science and industrial and technological developments.

J(46)   **Sir John Soane's Museum** The home of Sir John Soane, built in 1812, contains his collections of antiques, sculpture, paintings, drawings and books.

X(47)   **Tate Gallery** Collections of British paintings from the16thC to the present day, also collections of foreign paintings and sculpture from 1880 to the present day.

P(48)   **Victoria and Albert Museum** Built as a result of the Great International Exhibition in 1851, the museum contains one of the world's greatest collections of fine and decorative arts.

G(49)   **Wallace Collection** The collection of works of art bequeathed to the nation by Lady Wallace in 1895 includes pictures by Rubens and Gainsborough and 18th-C French Art.

R(50)   **Wellington Museum** The London home of the 1st Duke of Wellington from 1817, Apsley House was presented to the nation by the 7th Duke in 1947.

S(51)   **Westminster Abbey** Founded in 1065 by Edward the Confessor, all the monarchs since William the Conqueror have been crowned here. The Statesmen's Aisle in the north transept commemorates the many English statesmen buried here.

R(52)   **Westminster Cathedral** Founded in 1896 and completed in 1903, the most notable features include the mosaics in Blessed Sacrament Chapel and a bronze panel of St Teresa of Lisieux.

T(53)   **Westminster Hall** Built 1097-99 by William Rufus, it is the oldest remaining part of Westminster Palace.

EXHIBITION AND CONCERT HALLS

H	**Aeolian Hall**
S	**Caxton Hall**
S	**Central Hall**
E	**Conway Hall**
O	**Hayward Gallery**
J	**Kingsway Hall**
J	**Lyceum** (Mecca Dancing)
O	**Purcell Room** including Queen Elizabeth Hall
P	**Royal Albert Hall**
P	**Royal College of Music**
O	**Royal Festival Hall**
X	**Royal Horticultural Halls**
B	**Rudolf Steiner Hall**
K	**Serpentine Gallery**
B	**Seymour Hall**
H	**Wigmore Hall**

Hospitals

U	**Brompton Hospital,** Fulham Road, SW3 tel 01-352 8121
U	**Chelsea Hospital for Women,** Dovehouse Street, SW3 tel 01-352 6446
G	**Fitzroy Nuffield Hospital,** 10-12 Bryanston Square, W1 tel 01-723 1288
S	**Grey Coat Hospital,** Greycoat Place, SW1 tel 01-834 8380
X	**Grosvenor Hospital for Women,** Vincent Square, SW1 tel 01-834 2862
E	**Hospital for Sick Children,** Great Ormond Street, WC1 tel 01-405 9200
E	**Italian Hospital,** Queen Square, WC1 tel 01-831 6961
C	**London Foot Hospital,** 33 Fitzroy Square, W1 tel 01-636 0602
C/D	**Middlesex Hospital,** Mortimer Street, W1 tel 01-636 8333
J	**Moorfields Eye Hospital,** High Holborn, WC1 tel 01-836 6611
C	**National Heart Hospital,** Westmoreland Street, W1 tel 01-486 0824
E	**National Hospital for Nervous Diseases,** Queen Square, WC1 tel 01-486 0824
A	**Paddington Green Children's Hospital,** Paddington Green, W2 tel 01-723 1081
N	**Royal Dental Hospital,** 32 Leicester Square, WC2 tel 01-930 8831
E	**Royal London Homoeopathic Hospital,** Gt Ormond Street, WC1 tel 01-837 3091
U	**Royal Marsden Hospital,** Fulham Road, London SW3 tel 01-352 8171
C	**Royal National Orthopaedic Hospital,** 234 Great Portland Street, W1 tel 01-387 5070
O	**Royal Waterloo Hospital,** Waterloo Road, SE1 tel 01-928 7421
Q	**St George's Hospital,** Hyde Park Corner, SW1 tel 01-235 4343
I	**St John's Hospital for Diseases of the Skin,** Lisle Street, Leicester Square, WC2 tel 01-437 8383
U	**St Luke's Hospital,** Sydney Street, SW3 tel 01-353 7311
F	**St Mary's Hospital,** Praed Street, W2 tel 01-262 1280
J	**St Paul's Hospital,** Endell Street, WC2 tel 01-836 9611
J	**St Peter's Hospital,** Henrietta Street, WC2 tel 01-836 9347
T	**St Thomas' Hospital,** Lambeth Palace Road, SE1 tel 01-928 9292
B	**Samaritan Hospital for Women,** Marylebone Road, NW1 tel 01-402 4211
I	**Shaftesbury Hospital,** Shaftesbury Avenue, WC2 tel 01-836 2711
D	**University College Hospital,** Gower Street, WC1 tel 01-387 9300

University College Hospital Group:

D	**Royal Ear Hospital,** Huntley Street, WC1 tel 01-387 9300
D	**Dental Hospital,** Mortimer Market, WC1 tel 01-387 0351
D	**Maternity Hospital,** Huntley Street, WC1 tel 01-387 9300
D	**Private Wing,** Grafton Way, WC1 tel 01-387 9300
B	**Western Opthalmic Hospital,** Marylebone Road, NW1 tel 01-402 5101
X	**Westminster Children's Hospital,** Vincent Square, SW1 tel 01-834 2581
X	**Westminster Hospital,** Dean Ryle Street, Horseferry Road, SW1 tel 01-834 7849

Theatres and Cinemas

I	**ABC 1 & 2,** 135 Shaftesbury Avenue, WC2 tel 01-836 8861
O	**Adelphi Theatre,** Strand, WC2 tel 01-836 7611
I	**Albery Theatre,** St Martins Lane, WC2 tel 01-836 3878
J	**Aldwych Theatre,** Aldwych, WC2 tel 01-836 6404
I	**Ambassadors Theatre,** West Street, WC2 tel 01-836 1171
I	**Apollo Theatre,** Shaftesbury Avenue, W1 tel 01-437 2663
I	**Astoria Theatre,** 157 Charing Cross Road, WC2 tel 01-580 9562
D	**Berkeley Cinema,** 30 Tottenham Court Road, W1 tel 01-636 8150
W	**Biograph Cinema,** 47 Wilton Road, SW1 tel 01-834 1624
I	**Cambridge Theatre,** Earlham Street, WC2 tel 01-836 6056
N	**Carlton Theatre,** Haymarket, SW1 tel 01-930 3711
I	**Casino Theatre,** Old Compton Street, W1 tel 01-437 6877
N	**Cinecenta 1, 2, 3 & 4 Cinema,** Hugenot Hse, Panton Street, SW1 tel 01-930 0631
I	**Classic Cinema,** Glasshouse Street, Piccadilly, W1 tel 01-437 2380
A	**Classic Cinema,** 5a Praed Street, W1 tel 01-723 5716
R	**Classic Cinema,** 52 Victoria Street, SW1 tel 01-834 6588

I   Classic Moulin Cinema, 43 Great Windmill Street, W1 tel 01-437 1653

I   Classic Royal Cinema, Charing Cross Road, WC2 tel 01-930 6915

I   Classic Windmill Cinema, Great Windmill Street, W1 tel 01-437 6312

A   Cockpit Theatre, Gateforth Street, NW8 tel 01-402 5081

N   Coliseum Theatre, St Martin's Lane, WC2 tel 01-836 3161

I   Columbia Theatre, 93 Shaftesbury Avenue, W1 tel 01-734 5414

N   Comedy Theatre, Panton Street, SW1 tel 01-930 2578

I   Compton Club, 60 Old Compton Street, W1 tel 01-437 4555

D   Continentale Cinema, 36 Tottenham Court Road, W1 tel 01-636 4193

N   Criterion Theatre, Piccadilly, W1 tel 01-930 3216

M   Curzon Cinema, Curzon Street, W1 tel 01-499 3737

I   Dominion Theatre, Tottenham Court Road, W1 tel 01-580 9562

J   Drury Lane Theatre, Catherine Street, WC2 tel 01-836 3687

J   Duchess Theatre, Catherine Street, WC2 tel 01-836 8243

N   Duke of York's Theatre, St Martin's Lane, WC2 tel 01-836 5122

I   Empire Theatre, Leicester Square, WC2 tel 01-437 1234

J   Fortune Theatre, Russell Street, WC2 tel 01-836 2238

G   Gala-Royal Cinema, Marble Arch, W2 tel 01-262 2345

N   Garrick Theatre, Charing Cross Road, WC2 tel 01-836 4601

I   Globe Theatre, Shaftesbury Avenue, W1 tel 01-437 1592

N   Haymarket Theatre, Haymarket, SW1 tel 01-930 9832

N   Her Majesty's Theatre, Haymarket, SW1 tel 01-930 6606

N   Institute of Contemporary Arts, Nash House, The Mall, SW1 tel 01-930 6393

I   Jacey Cartoon Theatre, Leicester Square, WC2 tel 01-437 2001

N   Jacey Film Theatre, Piccadilly, W1 tel 01-734 1449

I   Jacey News Theatre, Charing Cross Road, WC2 tel 01-437 4815

N   Jacey News Theatre, Trafalgar Square, WC2 tel 01-930 1143

E   Jeannetta Cochrane Theatre, Theobalds Road, WC1 tel 01-242 7040

N   Leicester Square Theatre, Leicester Square, WC2 tel 01-930 5252

I   The Little Theatre Club, Garrick Yard, St Martin's Lane, WC2 tel 01-240 0660

N   London Pavilion, 3 Piccadilly, W1 tel 01-437 2982

I   Lyric Theatre, Shaftesbury Avenue, W1 tel 01-437 3686

M   Mayfair Theatre, Stratton Street, W1 tel 01-629 3036

R   Metropole Cinema, 160 Victoria Street, SW1 tel 01-834 5500

O   National Film Theatre, South Bank, SE1 tel 01-928 3232

O   National Theatre, Upper Ground, South Bank, SE1 tel 01-928 2033

I   New Arts Theatre Club, 6 Great Newport Street, WC2 tel 01-836 7541

J   New London Theatre, Drury Lane, WC2 tel 01-405 0072

R   New Victoria, 17 Wilton Road, SW1 tel 01-834 0671

U   Odeon Theatre, Kings Road, SW3 tel 01-352 5858

N   Odeon Theatre, Leicester Square, WC2 tel 01-930 6111

G   Odeon Theatre, Marble Arch, 10 Edgware Road, W2 tel 01-262 8949

J   Odeon Theatre, St Martin's Lane, WC2 tel 01-836 0691

D   Open Space Theatre, 32 Tottenham Court Road, W1 tel 01-580 4970

I   Palace Theatre, Shaftesbury Avenue, W1 tel 01-437 6834

H   Palladium Theatre, 8 Argyll Street, W1 tel 01-437 7373

N   Paramount Theatre, 17 Regent Street, SW1 tel 01-839 6494

I   Phoenix Theatre, Charing Cross Road, WC2 tel 01-836 8611

I   Piccadilly Theatre, Denman Street, W1 tel 01-437 4506

O   Players Theatre (Club), 173 Hungerford Arches, Villiers Street, WC2 tel 01-839 1134

I   Prince Charles Cinema, Leicester Place, WC2 tel 01-437 7003

N   Prince of Wales Theatre, Coventry Street, W1 tel 01-930 8681

I   Queens Theatre, 51 Shaftesbury Avenue, W1 tel 01-734 1166

M   Regent Theatre, 307 Upper Regent Street, W1 tel 01-580 1744

I   Rialto Cinema, 3 Coventry Street, W1 tel 01-437 3488

I   Ritz Cinema, Leicester Square, WC2 tel 01-437 1234

U   Royal Court Theatre, Sloane Square, SW1 tel 01-730 1745

J   Royal Opera House, Covent Garden, WC2 tel 01-240 1066

J   Royalty Theatre, Portugal Street, WC2 tel 01-405 8004

I   St Martin's Theatre, West Street, WC2 tel 01-836 1443

O   Savoy Theatre, Strand, WC2 tel 01-836 8888

I   Shaftesbury Theatre, Shaftesbury Avenue, WC2 tel 01-836 6596

C/H   The Soho Poly, Theatre Club 16 Ridinghouse Street, W1 tel 01-636 9050

J   Strand Theatre, Aldwych, WC2 tel 01-836 2660

H   Studio 1 & 2 Cinemas, 225 Oxford Street, W1 tel 01-437 3300

I   Talk of the Town, Cranbourn Street, WC2 tel 01-734 5395 or Hippodrome Corner, WC2 tel 01-734 5051

B   Times Centa Cinema, Chiltern Court, Baker Street, NW1 tel 01-935 9772

D   Vanbrugh Theatre, Malet Street WC1 tel 01-580 7982

J/O   Vaudeville Theatre, Strand, WC2 tel 01-836 9987

R   Victoria Palace, Victoria Street, SW1 tel 01-834 1317

I   Warner Rendezvous, Cranbourn Street, WC2 tel 01-439 0791

I   Warner West End 1, 2 & 3, Cranbourn Street, WC2 tel 01-439 0791

R   Westminster Theatre, 12 Palace Street, SW1 tel 01-930 6692

I   Windmill Theatre, Great Windmill Street, W1 tel 01-437 6312

I   Wyndham's Theatre, Charing Cross Road, WC2 tel 01-836 3028

Department Stores

Army and Navy Stores Ltd, 105 Victoria Street, SW1

Bourne and Hollingsworth Ltd, 116-128 Oxford Street, W1

Civil Service Stores, 423-427 Strand
Debenhams Ltd, Oxford Street, W1
Dickens and Jones Ltd, 224-244 Regent Street, W1
Fortnum and Mason Ltd, 181 Piccadilly, W1
Gamages, 164-182 Oxford Street, W1
Harrods Ltd, 87-135 Brompton Road, Knightsbridge, SW1
Harvey Nichols and Co Ltd, 109-125 Sloane Street, Knightsbridge, SW1
John Lewis and Co, 278-306 Oxford Street, W1
Marks and Spencer Ltd, 173 Oxford Street, W1
Marks and Spencer Ltd, 458 Oxford Street, Marble Arch, W1
Marshall and Snelgrove, Oxford Street, W1
Peter Jones, Sloane Square, SW1
Selfridges, 400 Oxford Street, W1
Swan and Edgar, 49 Regent Street, W1
Early closing day — most large stores open six days a week. Shops in the West End are open until 7.30pm on Thursday; shops in Knightsbridge, Sloane Square and King's Road are open until 7.30pm on Wednesday. A few large stores do not open on Saturday afternoon.

Markets

I	**Berwick Street,** Soho, W1 (fruit and vegetables) (Monday to Saturday, Thursday morning only)	
I	**Earlham Street,** Holborn, WC2 (general and antiques) (Monday to Saturday)	
D	**Goodge Place,** W1 (general) (Monday to Saturday)	
J	**Jubilee Market,** Covent Garden, WC2 (general, fruit and vegetables) (Monday to Friday)	
T	**Lower Marsh,** The Cut, SE1 (general) (Monday to Saturday, Thursday morning only)	
I	**Rupert Street,** W1 (fruit and vegetables) (Monday to Saturday)	
X	**Tachbrook Street,** SW1 (general) (Monday to Saturday)	

Advertisers

	Centre Hotels
D	**Bedford Corner Hotel,** Bayley Street WC1
D	**Bloomsbury Centre Hotel,** Coram Street, WC1
I	**Ivanhoe Hotel,** Bloomsbury Street, WC1
I	**Kenilworth Hotel,** Great Russell Street, WC1
C	**Regent Centre Hotel,** Carburton Street, W1
S	**St James Hotel,** Buckingham Gate SW1
	Godfrey Davis Car Rental
B	Marylebone Road, NW1
W	Davis House, Wilton Road, SW1
J	**Mercantile Credit,** Great Queen Street, WC2
	Trust House-Forte Hotels
M	**Browns Hotel,** Dover Street, W1
N	**Cavendish Hotel,** Jermyn Street, SW1
L	**Grosvenor House Hotel,** Park Lane, W1
Q	**Hyde Park Hotel,** Knightsbridge, SW1
N	**Quaglino's,** Bury Street, W1
E	**Russell Hotel,** Russell Square, WC1
C	**St Georges Hotel,** Langham Place, W1
J	**Waldorf Hotel,** Aldwych, WC2

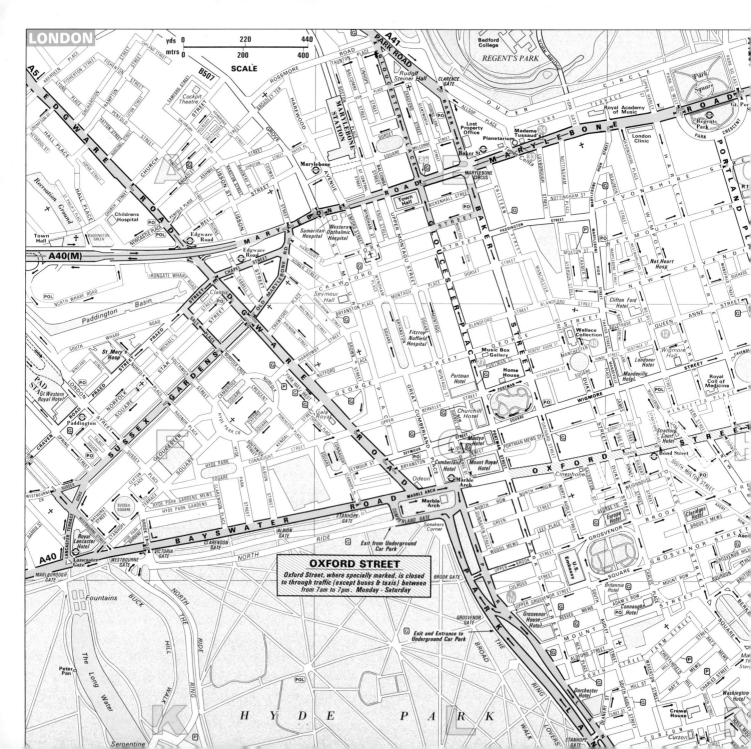

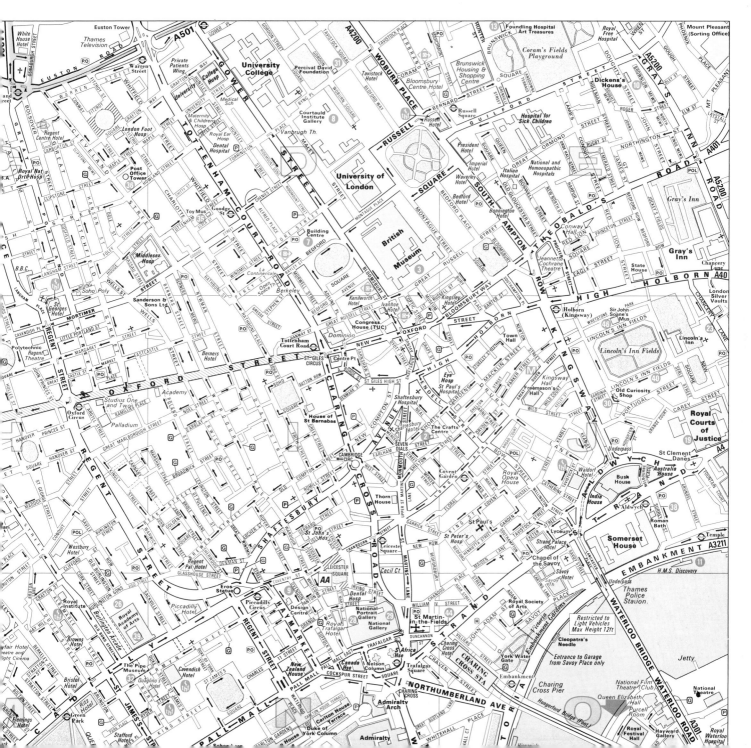

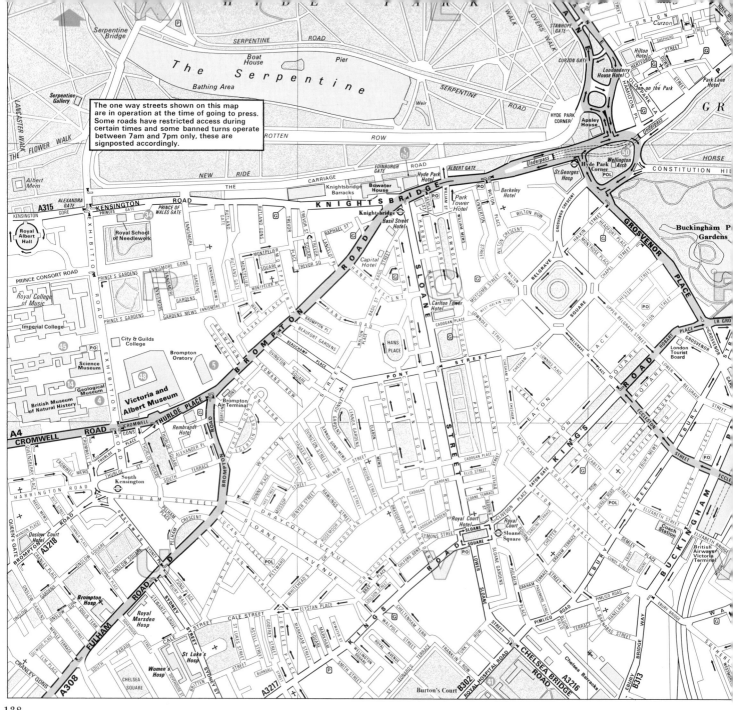

The one way streets shown on this map are in operation at the time of going to press. Some roads have restricted access during certain times and some banned turns operate between 7am and 7pm only, these are signposted accordingly.

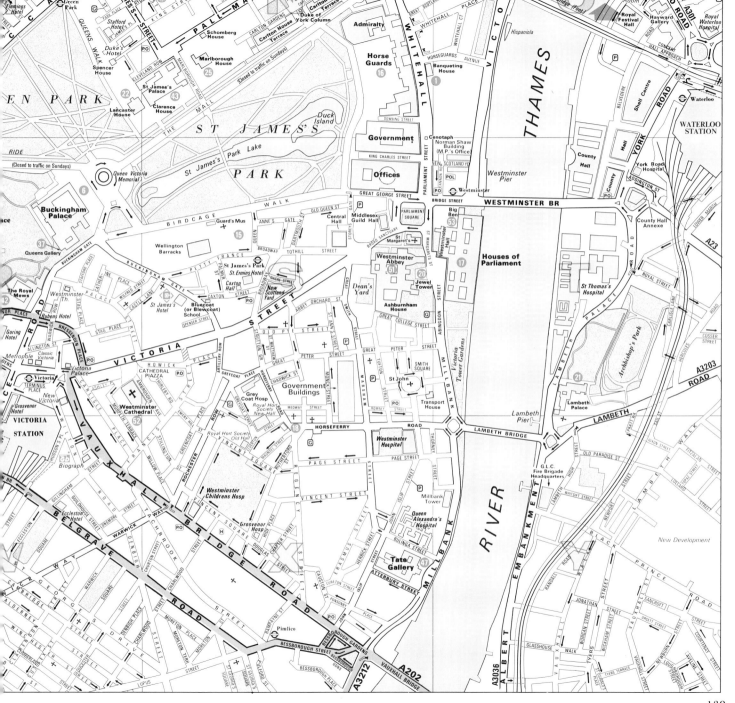

MANCHESTER

CENTRAL PLAN

F   **AA Service Centre** – St Ann's House, St Ann's Place *tel 061-485 6155* 24-hour Breakdown Service *tel 061-485 6299*

G 🛈   **Tourist Information Centres** – County Hall Extension, Piccadilly Gardens *tel 061-247 3111*

F(17)   **Town Hall** *tel 061-236 3377* (see also public buildings and places of interest)

Public buildings and places of interest

F(1)   **Art Gallery** Housed in building of 1824 by Sir Charles Barry, and contains large collection of paintings, silver, ceramics etc.

B(2)   **Cathedral** Until 1847 the parish church, this chiefly 15th-C structure is in Perpendicular style. It features some outstanding woodwork, particularly in the Choir and is the widest medieval church in Britain.

F(3)   **Cenotaph and Garden of Remembrance**

F(4)   **Central Library** This was designed in 1934 in the form of a rotunda and is England's largest municipal library. In the basement is the Library Theatre.

B(5)   **Chetham's Hospital** A mainly 15th-C building, but with parts dating back to Norman times and modern additions, now an independent grammar school. The free library founded 1653 claims to be the oldest in England.

E(6)   **City Exhibition Hall**

F(7)   **Cross Street Chapel** Originally built in 1697 this is the oldest nonconformist place of worship in Manchester.

F(8)   **Free Trade Hall** A fine building rebuilt in 1951 after severe bomb damage but retaining facade of 1856. This is the home of the Halle Orchestra.

F(9)   **John Ryland's University Library** Opened in 1899, the library houses a valuable collection of rare books, manuscripts and early bibles.

E(10)   **Liverpool Road Station (AM)** (not open). This was the Manchester terminus of the famous Liverpool and Manchester railway opened in 1830.

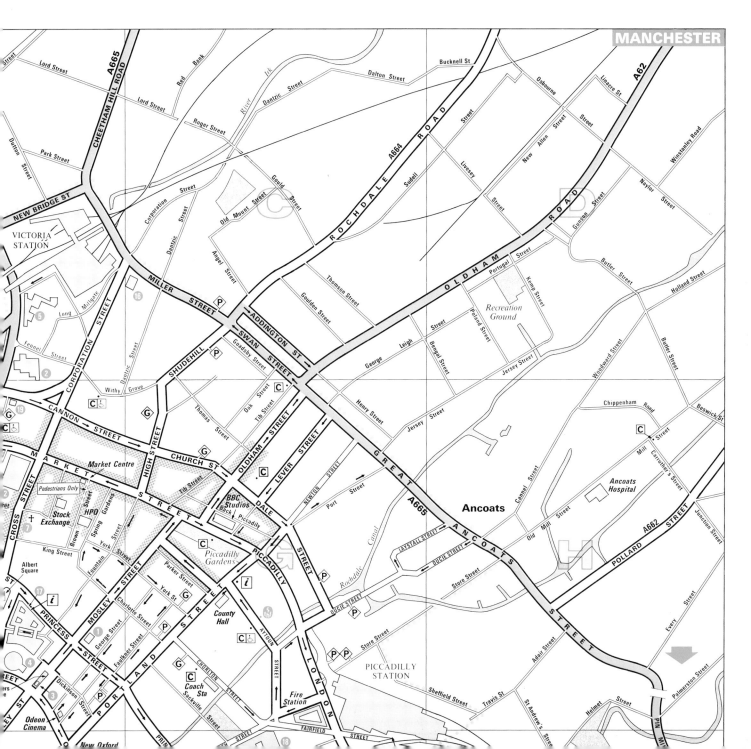

MANCHESTER

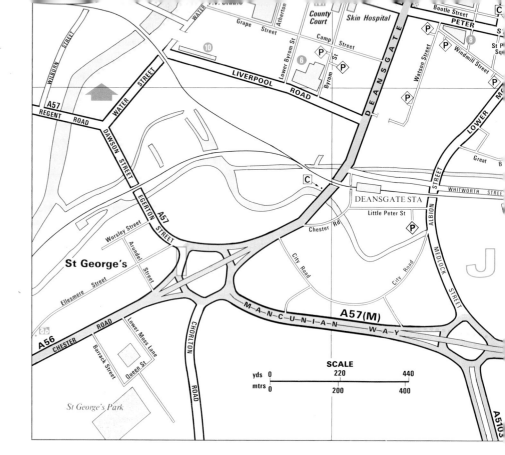

K(11) **North Western Museum of Science and Technology** Exhibits include steam and internal combustion engines, machine tools, electrical exhibits, paper-making, printing, and textile machinery.

F(12) **Royal Exchange** This includes the new Royal Exchange Theatre.

F(13) **St Anne's Church** An early 18th-C church in which de Quincey, the writer, was baptised. Notable items are a Queen Anne altar table and a fine oil painting of the *Descent from the Cross*.

E(14) **St John's Cathedral (RC)** Situated at Salford, this cathedral was rebuilt in 1848.

F(15) **St Mary's Church (RC)** Known as the 'Hidden Gem' because of its fine altar and hidden location.

C(16) **The New Century Hall**

F(17) **Town Hall** A building of 1877 in neo-Gothic style, with 280ft clock tower, on which the figures are represented by Lancashire roses and fleur-de-lis. The Council Chamber is housed in the Town Hall extension of 1938.

K(18) **University of Manchester Institute of Science and Technology**

F(19) **'Wellington' Inn** A picturesque half-timbered structure of the 14thC.

Hospitals

H **Ancoats Hospital**, Mill Street *tel 061-205 2204*

F **Manchester and Salford Skin Hospital**, Quay Street *tel 061-834 4346*

E **Salford Royal Hospital**, Chapel Street *tel 061-834 8656*

Sport and Recreation

L **Ardwick Sports Centre**, Hyde Road

A **Blackfriars Baths**, Richmond Street

Theatres and Cinemas

L **ABC Cinema**, Ardwick Green *tel 061-237 1141*

F **ABC Cinema**, Deansgate *tel 061-832 2112*

F(4) **Library Theatre** *tel 061-236 7406* (see also public buildings and places of interest)

J **New Oxford Theatre**, Oxford Street *tel 061-236 8266*

F **Odeon Film Centre**, Oxford Street *tel 061-236 8264*

F **Opera House**, Quay Street *tel 061-834 1787*

K **Royal Northern College of Music**, Oxford Road *tel 061-273 6283*

J **Palace Theatre**, Oxford Street *tel 061-236 0184*

F(12) **Sixty-Nine Theatre Co Ltd**, Royal Exchange, St Ann's Square *tel 061-832 4877* (see also public buildings and places of interest)

J **Studios 1-5**, Oxford Road *tel 061-236 2437*

F **Studios 6-9**, Deansgate House, Deansgate *tel 061-834 3580*

J **Tatler Cinema Club**, Oxford Road *tel 061-236 6015*

Department Stores

Arndale Centre, Market Street and Corporation Street
Debenhams, Market Street
Kendal Milne, Deansgate
Lewis's, Mosley Street and Market Street
Marks and Spencer Ltd, Market Street and Corporation Street
Early closing day Wednesday

Markets

F **Market Centre**, Market Street

Advertisers

E **Mercantile Credit**

I **Godfrey Davis**

G **THF** Grand Hotel

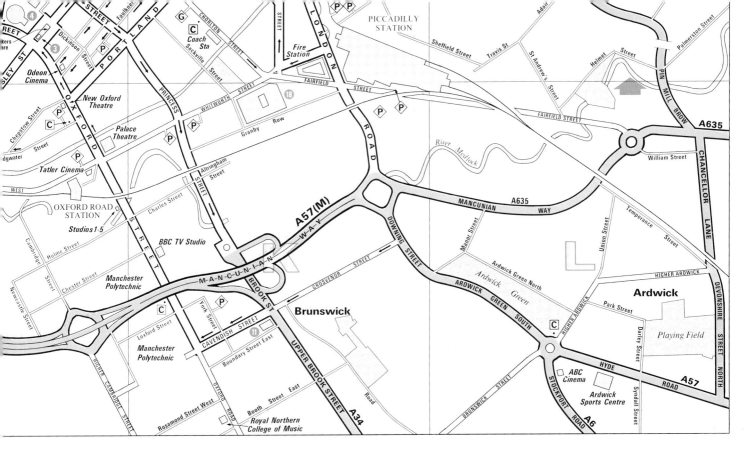

DISTRICT PLAN
Public buildings and places of interest

L(20) Belle Vue Leisure Park Zoological Gardens Covering some 68 acres, with lions and tigers, Great Ape House, Tropical house with hippos and tapirs, aviaries, aquarium and reptilium. Adjoining the zoo is a banqueting, exhibition and entertainment centre.

K(21) Manchester Museum, The University. Contains exhibits of geology, natural history, archaeology, coins, stamps, aquarium and vivarium.

E(22) Monks Hall Museum 16th-C building with later additions, with permanent collection of Nasmyth machinery, paintings, ceramics and local bygones. Also temporary exhibitions.

J(23) Ordsall Hall Museum Partly half-timbered manor house with later brick-built wing (1639), with Tudor Great Hall, Star Chamber with 14th-C features, Victorian farmhouse kitchen and social history displays.

K(24) Platt Hall Georgian Mansion of 1764, housing Gallery of English Costume.

C(25) Queen's Park Gallery Houses a permanent collection of pictures and sculpture and a museum of the Manchester Regiment and 14th/20th King's Hussars.

F(26) Salford Museum and Art Gallery Main features are a reproduction of a late 19th-C street, typical of a northern industrial town and the L S Lowry collection of paintings.

E(27) Salford Science Museum Of greatest interest is the replica of a coal-mine.

F(28) Salford University

L(29) Slade Hall, Rusholme. A timber-framed house dating from the late 16thC with some 19th-C alterations.

K(30) Whitworth Art Gallery The collections include oil paintings, British and European watercolours, drawings, prints, textiles, tapestries and embroideries.

K(31) University

Foxdenton Hall, Chadderton. A 17th-C hall in Renaissance-style which was restored in 1965. 6m NE via Oldham Road A62 (D) and Rochdale Road A663.

Heaton Hall A Georgian house designed by James Wyatt in 1772 with contemporary furnishings, the Assheton Bennett Collection of 17th- and 18th-C Dutch and Flemish paintings and an organ of 1790. In Heaton Park 3½m N via Bury Road A665 (B)

Wythenshawe Hall A restored 16th- to 19th-C half-timbered manor house with 17th-C furniture, paintings, Royal Lancastrian pottery and prints. In Wythenshawe Park (Wythenshawe Road B5167), 5m S via Princess Road A5103 (N)

Hospitals

D **Booth Hall Children's Hospital,** Charlestown Road, Manchester 9 *tel* 061-740 8174

O **Christie Hospital and Holt Radium Institute,** Wilmslow Road, Manchester 20 *tel* 061-445 8123

C **Crumpsall Hospital,** Crumpsall, Manchester 8 *tel* 061-740 1444

K **Dental Hospital of Manchester and Turner Dental School,** Bridgeford Street, Manchester 15 *tel* 061-273 5252

P **Duchess of York Hospital for Babies,** Burnage Lane, Manchester 19 *tel* 061-224 1427

E **Hope Hospital,** Eccles Old Road, Manchester 6 *tel* 061-789 5252

E **Ladywell Hospital,** Eccles New Road, Manchester 5 *tel* 061-789 2753

K **Manchester Royal Infirmary,** Oxford Road, Manchester 13 *tel* 061-273 3300

G **Manchester Victoria Memorial Jewish Hospital,** Elizabeth Street, Manchester 8 *tel* 061-834 0704

Wythenshawe Hall

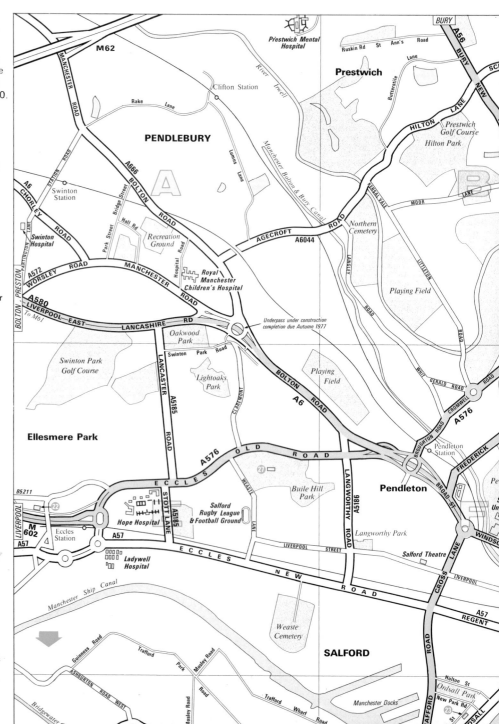

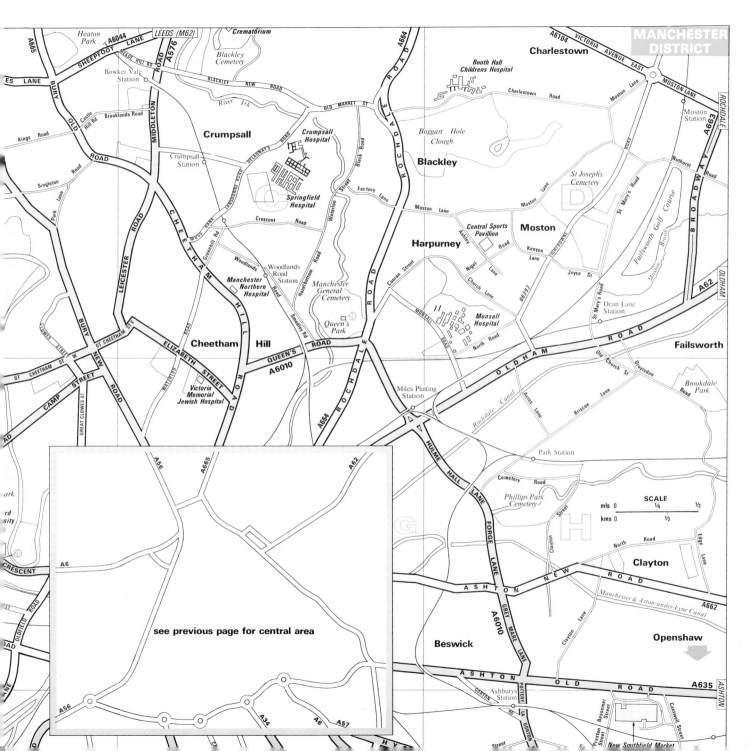

C **Manchester Northern Hospital,** Cheetham
Hill Road, Manchester 8 *tel 061-740 2244*

D **Monsall Hospital,** Monsall Road,
Manchester 10 *tel 061-205 2254*

A **Prestwich Mental Hospital,** Bury New
Road, Manchester *tel 061-773 9121*

A **Royal Manchester Children's Hospital,**
Pendlebury, Manchester *tel 061-794 4696*

J **St Joseph's Hospital,** Carlton Road,
Manchester 16 *tel 061-226 2231*

K **St Mary's Hospital,** Whitworth Park,
Manchester 13 *tel 061-224 9633*

C **Springfield Hospital,** Crumpsall,
Manchester 8 *tel 061-740 1444*

J **Stretford Memorial Hospital,** Seymour
Grove, Manchester 16 *tel 061-881 5353*

A **Swinton Hospital,** 196 Partington Lane,
Swinton *tel 061-794 1947*

O **Withington Hospital,** Nell Lane,
Manchester 20 *tel 061-445 8111*

Sport and Recreation

M **Ashton-on-Mersey Golf Course,** Church
Lane, Sale

L **Belle Vue Greyhound Stadium**

L **Belle Vue Speedway**

D **Central Sports Pavilion,** Ashley Lane

N **Chorlton Golf Course,** Barlow Hall

D **Failsworth Golf Course,** Nuthurst Road,
New Moston

P **Heaton Moor Golf Course,** Heaton Moor,
Stockport

P **Houldsworth Golf Course,** Longford Road
West

J **Lancashire County and Manchester Cricket
Club,** Old Trafford

K **Manchester City Football Club,** Maine
Road

J **Manchester United Football Club,** Old
Trafford

B **Prestwich Golf Course,** Hilton Lane

N **Sale Golf Course,** Old Hall Road

E **Salford Football Club,** Willows Road

E **Salford Rugby Football Club,** Willows
Road

J **Stretford Sports Centre,** Talbot Road

E **Swinton Park Golf Course,** East
Lancashire Road

J **White City Greyhound Stadium**

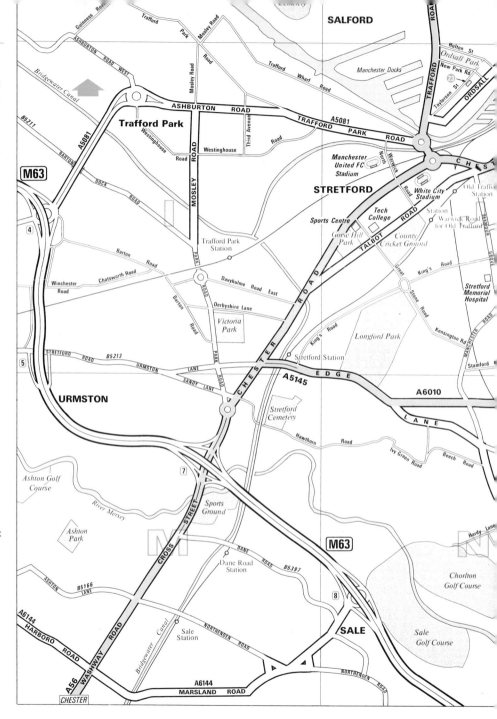

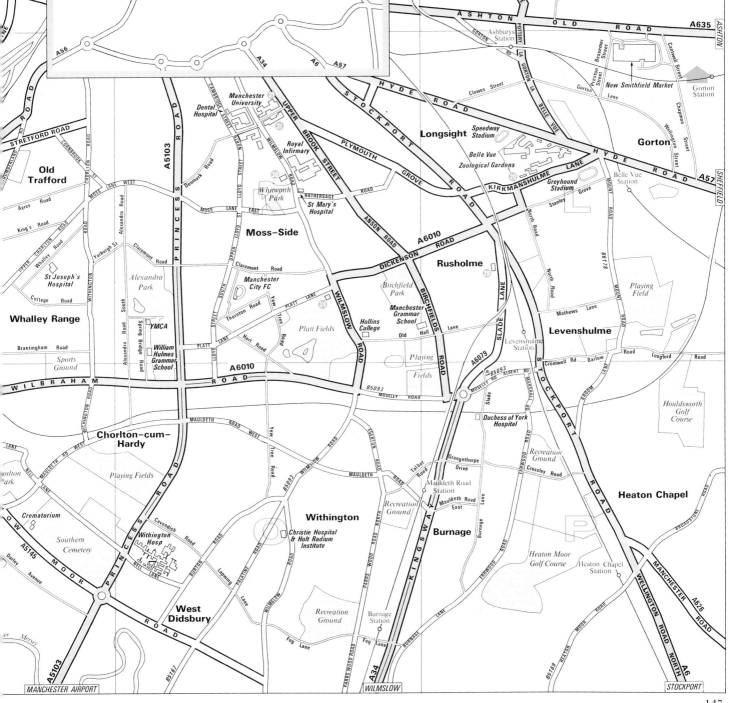

C	**AA Road Service Centre (107)** — Wilson Street *tel 46832*
G(5) [i]	**Tourist Information Centre** — 125 Albert Road *tel 45750* (see also public buildings and places of interest)

Public buildings and places of interest

J(1)	**Art Gallery** Contains a steadily growing collection of paintings including some good, contemporary British paintings. Also programme of monthly changing exhibitions.
C(2)	**Cathedral (RC)** The Cathedral is the see of a Roman Catholic bishop and contains a fine, canopied pulpit.
N(3)	**Dorman Museum** Recently extended to become a small arts centre and containing permanent collections illustrating the geology, ecology and natural history of the region.
G(4)	**Teeside Polytechnic**
G(5)	**Town Hall, Municipal Buildings and Tourist Information Centre**

Hospitals

M	**Middlesbrough General Hospital,** Ayresome Green Lane *tel 83133*
K	**Middlesbrough Maternity Hospital,** Park Road North *tel 45156*
F	**North Riding Infirmary,** Newport Road *tel 46002*
M	**West Lane Hospital** *tel 87736*

Sport and Recreation

O	**Albert Park** — Bowling Greens, Tennis Courts and Skating Rink
G	**Central Baths,** Gilkes Street
P	**Clairville Stadium (Athletics)**
N	**Middlesbrough Football Club,** Ayresome Park

Cleveland Park Stadium Stockton Road (Greyhound Racing and Speedway) 1½m SW via Newport Road A66 (I) and Stockton Road
Prissick Outdoor Sports Centre, Marton Road 2½m S via Marton Road A172 (P)

Theatres and Cinemas

G	**ABC Cinema,** Linthorpe Road *tel 47400*
G	**Odeon Cinema,** Corporation Road *tel 42888*

Department Stores

Baums Department Store, 89 Newport Road
Binns Ltd, 37 Linthorpe Road
Debenhams, The Corner, 1 Newport Road
Marks and Spencer Ltd, 25 Linthorpe Road
Upton E and Sons Ltd, 32 Southfield Road
Wright and Co Ltd, Tower House
Early closing day Wednesday

Markets

G	**The Arcade,** Grange Road (Saturday)

Advertisers

G	**Mercantile Credit**
H	**Godfrey Davis**

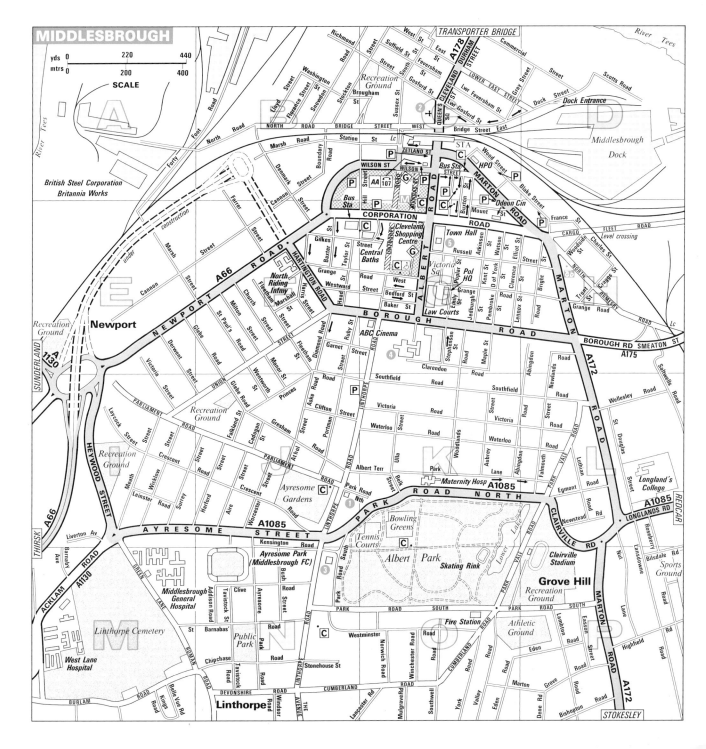

E **AA Service Centre** – 13 Princess Square *tel 610111*

E(3) **Tourist Information Centre** – City Information Service, Central Library, Princess Square *tel 610691* (see also public buildings and places of interest)

Public buildings and places of interest

H(1) **All Saints' Church** A rebuilt, 18th-C church.

H(2) **Black Gate** The 13th-C gatehouse now houses the Bagpipe Museum which displays over 100 sets of English, Irish, Scottish, European and Egyptian pipes.

E(3) **Central Library, Northern Arts Gallery and Tourist Information Centre**

G(4) **City Walls** Slight remains of the 14th-C city walls are still to be seen.

E(5) **Civic Centre**

D(6) **Eldon Square Sports Centre and Shopping Precinct**

H(7) **Guildhall and Merchants' Court** The Guildhall, dating from 1658, was recased in 1796. The adjoining Merchants' Court contains a 17th-C chimney piece.

B(8) **Hancock Museum** One of the finest natural history museums in England. Other collections include geological specimens and insects.

H(9) **John George Joicey Museum (Holy Jesus Hospital)** An almshouse founded in 1681 with displays of arms and armour, period rooms and local history.

E(10) **Laing Art Gallery and Museum** Armour, costumes, local history etc on display with British oil paintings from the 17thC onwards.

B(11) **Museum of Science and Engineering** Exhibits relate to the development of the transport, mining and ship-building industries in the north east.

H(12) **Plummer Tower Museum** The restored tower, part of the ancient city walls, is now a museum.

B(13) **Royal Grammar School**

D(14) **St Andrew's Church** A 13th- to 14th-C church, the oldest in the city. The font is 15th-C.

G(15) **St John's Church** This 13th- to 14th-C church has a fine 17th-C pulpit.

G(16) **St Mary's RC Cathedral** Designed by Pugin in 1844.

H(17) **St Nicholas' Cathedral** Dating mainly from the 14th and 15thCs this former parish church gained cathedral status in 1882. The crown spire, 194ft high is surmounted by an open lantern on flying buttresses. Inside, the knave and choir are 14th-C.

H(18) **The Keep (Castle)** The 12th-C keep of the castle is now a museum.

H(19) **Trinity House** An early 18th-C chapel and hall is the main feature of interest.

B(20) **University** In the Quadrangle, the Museum of Antiquities displays Roman remains and the Hatton Gallery contains mainly 14th- to 18th-C European paintings. The Greek Museum contains a collection of pottery, painted vases, bronzes and armour and weapons, and the Mining Museum has miscellaneous mining relics on display.

Hospitals

B **Fleming Memorial Hospital,** Burdon Terrace, Jesmond *tel 813257*

B **Princess Mary Maternity Hospital,** Great North Road *tel 811312*

The Tyne bridges

A **Royal Victoria Infirmary,** Queen Victoria Road *tel 25131*

Newcastle General Hospital, Westgate Road *tel 38811* 1¼m W via Westgate Road A69 (D)

Sport and Recreation

D **Newcastle United FC,** St James Park

E **Northumberland Baths,** Northumberland Road

C **Northumberland County Cricket Club,** Osborne Avenue

North Durham Cricket Ground, Prince Consort Road, Gateshead ¾m S via A1 (H)

Theatres and Cinemas

E **ABC Cinema,** Haymarket *tel 23345*

G **ABC 1 & 2,** Westgate Road *tel 23232*

E **Odeon Cinema,** Pilgrim Street *tel 26718*

E **Queens Cinerama Theatre,** Northumberland Place *tel 27888*

G **Studios 1, 2, 3 & 4,** Waterloo Street *tel 610151*

H **Theatre Royal,** Grey Street *tel 22061*

E **Tyneside Film Theatre,** Pilgrim Street *tel 21507*

Department Stores

Binns Ltd, Market Street

Farnons Department Store, 12 Nun Street

Fenwick Ltd, Northumberland Street

Marks and Spencer Ltd, 83 Northumberland Street

Ramshaw and Robson & Co, 21 Benwell Grove

S Wenger, 30 Grainger Street

Woolco Department Store, Citadel East

Early closing day Monday and Wednesday

Markets

G **Bigg Market** (Tuesday, Thursday and Saturday) (general)

D **Grainger Market,** Grainger Street (Daily) (general)

D **Clayton Street** (Daily) (fish, plants and vegetables)

H **Quayside Market,** Quayside (Sunday mornings) (general)

Advertisers

C **Mercantile Credit**

E **Centre** Newcastle Centre Hotel

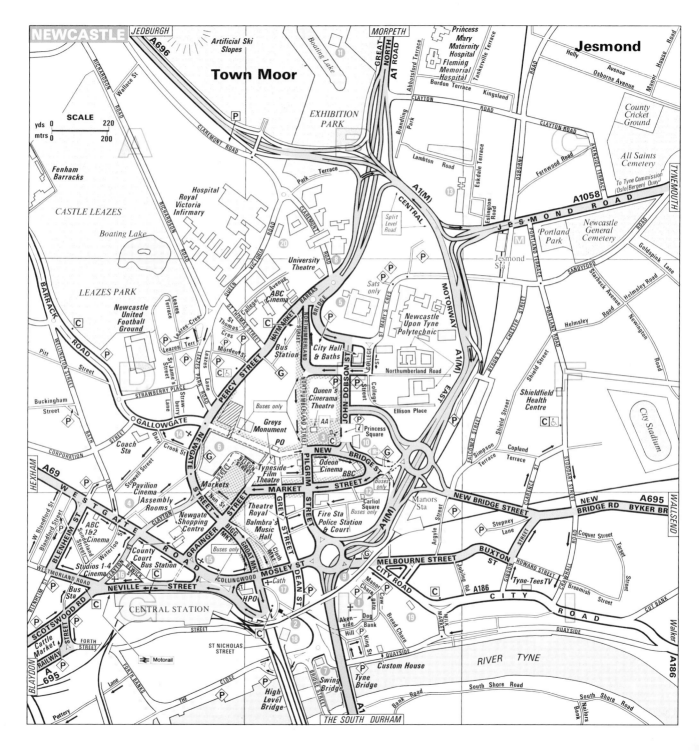

NEWQUAY

E [i] **Tourist Information Centre** — Morfa Hall, Cliff Road *tel 2119/2716*

Public buildings and places of interest

A(1) **Ancient Huer's Hut** Formerly used by fishermen watching for pilchard shoals.

E(2) **Municipal Offices and Public Library**

I(3) **Trenance Gardens, Zoo and Amusement Park** The gardens with their sheltered position are particularly favourable for the cultivation of uncommon flowers and shrubs and over 300 unusual varieties are contained here. The zoo, covering over 8 acres of landscaped grounds, has an interesting selection of animals, birds and reptiles. The park also contains pitch and putt, driving range, boating lake and miniature railway.

Trerice Manor (NT) A small Cornish manor house, rebuilt 1571-73 with an elaborate façade, displaying unusual curly gables. The interior includes some fine plaster ceilings and fireplaces. 3m SE via Henver Road A392 and A3058 (F)

Hospitals

I **Newquay and District Hospital**, St Thomas Road *tel 3883*

Sport and Recreation

I **Golf Driving Range**

H **Newquay Association Football Club**, Clevedon Road

D **Newquay Golf Club**

I **Pitch and Putt Golf Course**

F **Sports Centre** (Venue of Newquay Cricket Club and Newquay Hornets Rugby Football Club)

Theatres and Cinemas

F **Astor Cinema**, Narrowcliff *tel 2023*

E **Camelot Cinema**, The Crescent *tel 4222*

E **Cosy Nook Theatre**, Towan Parade *tel 3365*

E **Newquay Theatre** *tel 3379*

Department Stores

Dingle E and Co Ltd, 29 Bank Street
Early closing day Wednesday but most shops remain open during the summer months.

Trerice Manor

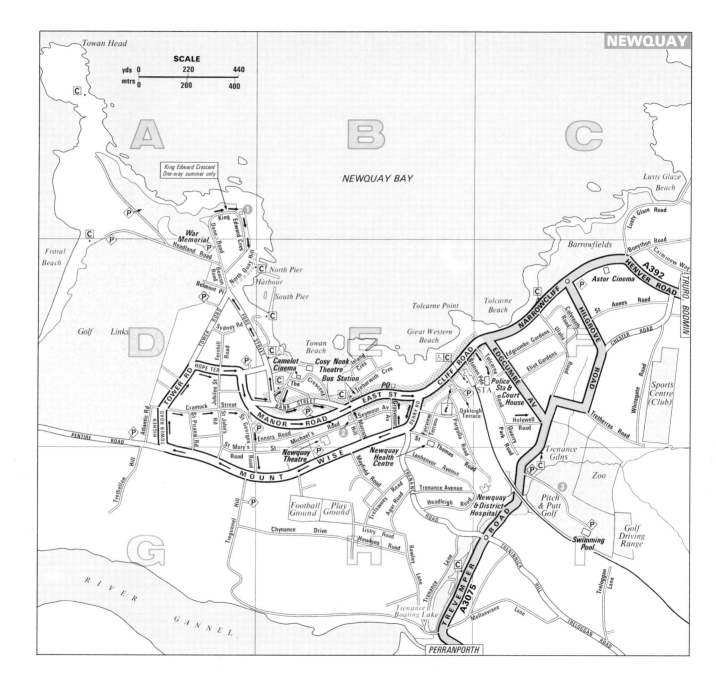

Towan Head

SCALE

yds 0   220   440

mtrs 0   200   400

A

B

C

NEWQUAY BAY

Lusty Glaze Beach

King Edward Crescent One-way summer only

War Memorial

King Edward Cres

Headland Road

Dane Road

North Quay Hill

Beacon Road

Fistral Beach

Belmont Pl

Harbour

North Pier

South Pier

Tolcarne Point

Tolcarne Beach

Barrowfields

Lusty Glaze Road

Bonython Road

Carminow Way

HENVER ROAD

A392

TRURO BODMIN

Golf Links

D

Sydney Rd

TOWER ROAD

Fernhill Road

HOPE TER

Crantock Street

St Prauls Rd

St John's Rd

St Georges Rd

Atlantic Rd

TOWER RD

HIGHER TOWER ROAD

Trethellan Hill

PENTIRE ROAD

Jubilee St

St Mary's Road

BANK STREET

MANOR ROAD

Ennors Road

St Michael's

Newquay Theatre

MOUNT

Tregunnel Hill

Camelot Cinema

Cosy Nook Theatre Bus Station

The Crescent

Towan Beach

Island Cres

Treharwith Cres

EAST ST

Seymour Av

Marcus Hill

WISE

Berry Rd

Fairview Terrace

Pargolla Road

Great Western Beach

E

CLIFF ROAD

EDGCUMBE AV

NARROWCLIFF

HILGROVE ROAD

Colkreath Road

Ulalia Road

Edgcumbe Gardens

Eliot Gardens

St Annes Road

CHESTER ROAD

Whitegate Road

Tretherras Road

Sports Centre (Club)

F

Astor Cinema

Station Rd

Police Sta & Court House

Oakleigh Terrace

Holywell Road

Quarry Park Road

Trenance Gdns

Zoo

Pitch & Putt Golf

Golf Driving Range

Swimming Pool

PO

St Thomas

Lanhenvor Avenue

Trenance Avenue

Headleigh Road

Newquay & District Hospital

TREVEMPER ROAD

A3075

Trevenson Road

TRENANCE ROAD

Mayfield Road

Trelawney Road

Agar Road

Newquay Health Centre

Football Ground

Play Ground

Chynance Drive

Listry Road

Hawkins Road

Rawley Lane

G

RIVER GANNEL

H

Trenance Lane

Trenance Boating Lake

Mellanvrane Lane

Mellanvrane Lane

TRELOGGAN ROAD

Treloggan Lane

Treninnick Hill

PERRANPORTH

153

NORTHAMPTON

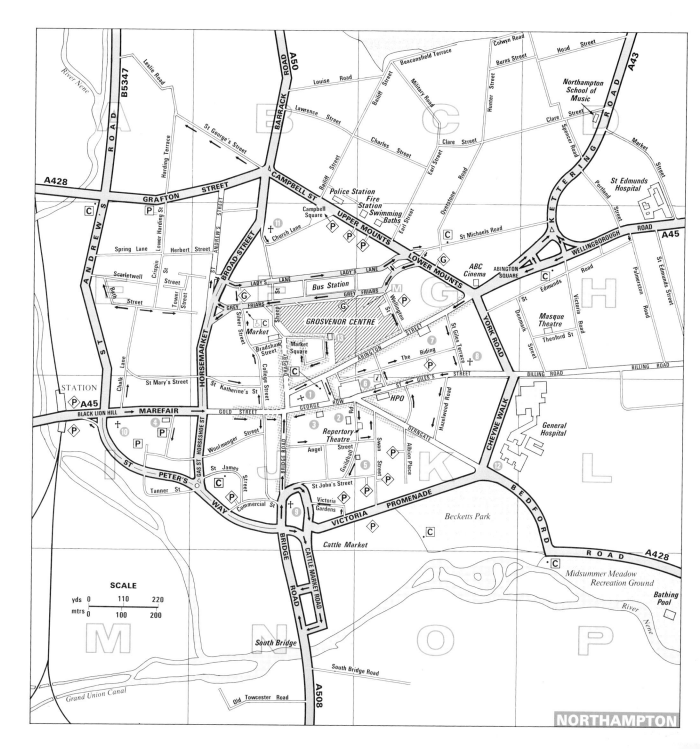

NORTHAMPTON

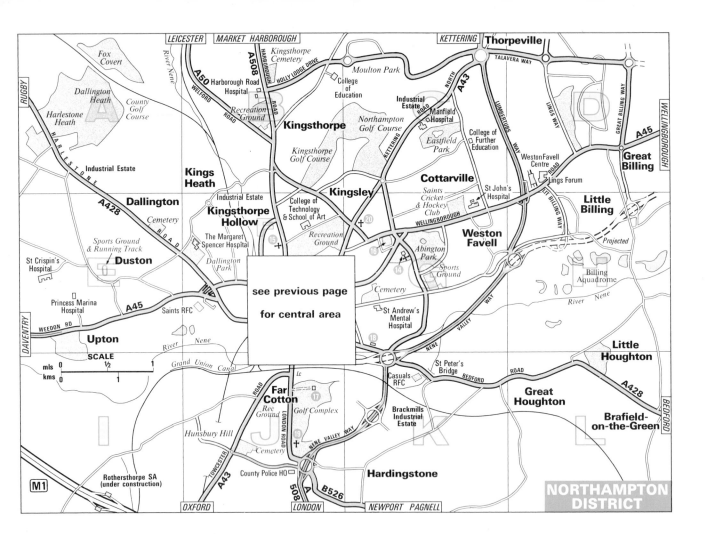

LEICESTER | MARKET HARBOROUGH | KETTERING | **Thorpeville**

Fox Covert

Dallington Heath

Harlestone Heath

RUGBY

A50

A508

Kingsthorpe Cemetery

HOLLY LODGE DRIVE

Moulton Park

College of Education

Industrial Estate

Manfield Hospital

TALAVERA WAY

GREAT BILLING WAY

WELLINGBOROUGH

County Golf Course

River Nene

HARBOROUGH ROAD

WELFORD ROAD

Harborough Road Hospital

Recreation Ground

Kingsthorpe

Northampton Golf Course

Kingsthorpe Golf Course

Eastfield Park

College of Further Education

LUMBERTUBS WAY

LINGS WAY

A45

Industrial Estate

Kings Heath

A428

Dallington

Cemetery

HARLESTONE ROAD

Industrial Estate

Kingsthorpe Hollow

The Margaret Spencer Hospital

Dallington Park

College of Technology & School of Art

Kingsley

KETTERING ROAD

15

20

WESTON FAVELL ROAD

Weston Favell Centre

Lings Forum

CITY BILLING WAY

Great Billing

Cottarville

Saints Cricket & Hockey Club

St John's Hospital

Weston Favell

Little Billing

Projected

Sports Ground & Running Track

St Crispin's Hospital

Duston

16

Recreation Ground

WELLINGBOROUGH

14

Abington Park

Sports Ground

Billing Aquadrome

Princess Marina Hospital

A45

Saints RFC

Cemetery

NENE VALLEY WAY

River Nene

Little Houghton

WEEDON RD

DAVENTRY

Upton

River Nene

Grand Union Canal

18

St Andrew's Mental Hospital

St Peter's Bridge

BEDFORD ROAD

A428

BEDFORD

see previous page
for central area

SCALE

mls 0 ½ 1

kms 0 1

Casuals RFC

Great Houghton

Brafield-on-the-Green

TOWCESTER ROAD

LONDON ROAD

lc

17

Golf Complex

Brackmills Industrial Estate

Far Cotton

Rec Ground

Hunsbury Hill

19

Cemetery

NENE VALLEY WAY

County Police HQ

M1

Rothersthorpe SA (under construction)

A43

A508

B526

Hardingstone

NORTHAMPTON DISTRICT

OXFORD | LONDON | NEWPORT PAGNELL

NORWICH

G[i]   **Tourist Information Centre** — Augustine Steward House, 14 Tombland *tel 20679*

Public buildings and places of interest

J(1)   **Assembly House** A restored Georgian building, now a centre for many of the city's arts and cultural societies, and including the Noverre cinema.

H(2)   **Bishop Bridge** This 13th-C bridge is the oldest in Norwich and one of the oldest in Britain. Visible upstream is the Cow Tower, a northern remnant of the city walls.

G(3)   **Bishop's Palace** A 12th- to 15th-C house.

P(4)   **Boom Towers** These are relics of the former city walls, and nearby on Carrow Hill are some more substantial remains of the 14th-C walls.

F(5)   **Bridewell Museum** Local industries and rural crafts contained in a 14th-C flint-faced house.

J(6)   **Castle and Gardens** The massive Norman castle keep, much restored, contains a museum and art gallery.

G(7)   **Cathedral** A Norman and later building, with a lofty decorated spire. The Norman nave, Saxon Bishop's throne, 15th-C choir stalls, beautiful cloisters and a wealth of carved roof bosses are all notable. In Life's Green is the grave of Nurse Edith Cavell, killed by the Germans in 1915.

J(8)   **Central Library and American War Memorial**

J(9)   **City Hall** An imposing modern edifice of 1938 and one of the best designed municipal buildings in England.

F(10) **Elm Hill** Perhaps the most picturesque street of old houses in the city. Includes the thatched 15th-C Briton's Arms.

G(11) **Erpingham Gate** An old gateway of 1420, leading to the Cathedral precincts.

G(12) **Ethelbert Gate** Built in 1272, with a chapel above the archway.

G(13) **Great Hospital** Founded in 1249 and incorporating the parish church of St Helen. Other buildings include the cloister and a house of 1752 by Thomas Ivory.

J(14) **Guildhall** A picturesque structure of chequered flints dating from 1407.

G(15) **King Edward VI Grammar School** Established in 1553. Among its most famous pupils was Admiral Lord Nelson.

F(16) **Maddermarket Theatre** A well-known reconstruction of an Elizabethan-style theatre housed in a former Roman Catholic chapel.

G(17) **Maid's Head** A hotel, dating back in part to the 15thC, which has an interesting interior including Norman, Tudor, Jacobean and Georgian work.

O(18) **Music House** The oldest dwelling-house in Norwich, part of which dates from the 12thC.

F(19) **Octagon Chapel** A fine building of 1756.

H(20) **Pull's Ferry** This is the former water-gate of the Cathedral precincts, but no ferry now operates.

F(21) **St Andrew's and Blackfriars' Hall** St Andrew's Hall dates from 1449 and is the most complete surviving example of a former Dominican Friary in England. Used for many years as a civic hall.

I(22) **St Giles' Church** An early-Perpendicular church showing a lofty tower.

I(23) **St John Baptist Church (RC)** A large, late-Victorian edifice, designed by the Brothers Scott, with some notable stained glass.

F(24) **St Peter Hungate Church** Carries the date of 1460 and has a hammerbeam roof. It is now a museum of Church art and craftsmanship.

J(25) **St Peter Mancroft Church** The largest of the city churches, with a fine 15th-C tower and much old glass.

J(26) **Shire Hall**

F(27) **Stranger's Hall** A notable 15th-C building, now used as a folk museum.

Assembly House.

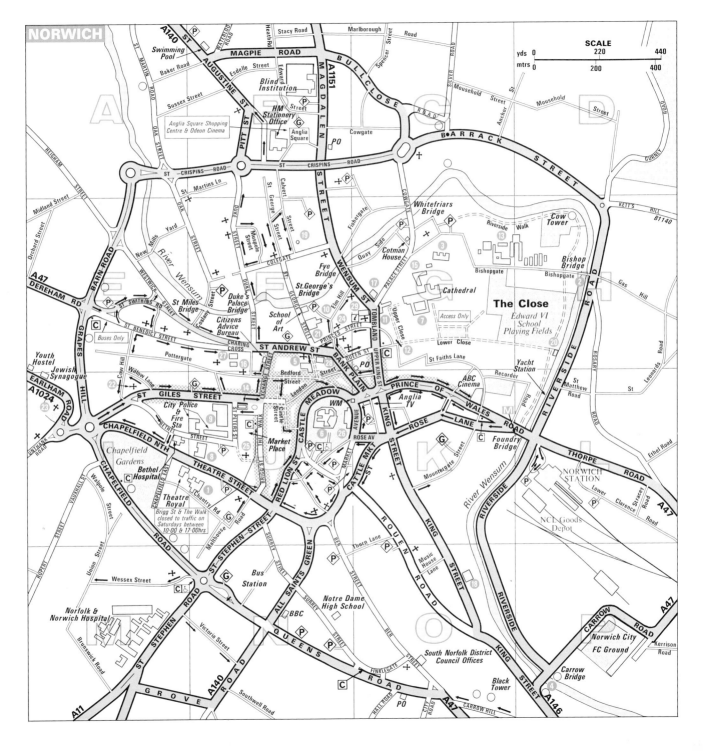

F(28)   **Suckling House and Stuart Hall** A 15th- to 16th-C merchant's house with a fine banqueting hall. The adjoining Stuart Hall is a modern assembly room.

G(29)   **Tombland Alley and Samson and Hercules House** The house displays quaint figures of 1549. Nearby stands the 16th-C house of Augustine Steward, who was a notable citizen of that time. The house now contains the Tourist Information Centre.

Hospitals

I   **Bethel Hospital,** Bethel Street *tel 24930*
M   **Norfolk and Norwich Hospital,** St Stephens Road *tel 28377*

Sport and Recreation

B   **City of Norwich Baths,** St Augustines
P   **Norwich City Football Club,** Carrow Road

Theatres and Cinemas

K   **ABC Cinema,** Prince of Wales Road *tel 23312*
F(16)   **Maddermarket Theatre,** St John's Alley *tel 20917* (see also public buildings and places of interest)
J(1)   **Noverre Cinema,** Assembly House, Theatre Street *tel 26402* (see also Assembly House under public buildings and places of interest)
B   **Odeon Cinema,** Anglia Square *tel 21903*
I   **Theatre Royal,** Theatre Street *tel 28205*

Department Stores

Bonds (Norwich) Ltd, All Saints Green
Butchers, GF Drapers Ltd, Swan Lane
Debenhams Ltd, Orford Place
Garlands, London Street
Jarrold and Sons Ltd, London Street
Marks and Spencer Ltd, Rampant Horse Street
Peter Robinson Shopping Centre, 15 The Haymarket
Early closing day Thursday. A few shops close all day.

Markets

Market Days Wednesday and Saturday
J   **The Provision Market,** Gentlemen's Walk (daily)

Advertisers

K   **Mercantile Credit**

DISTRICT PLAN

K   **AA Service Centre** — Fanum House, 126 Thorpe Road *tel 29401*

Public buildings and places of interest

G(30)   **Royal Norfolk Regiment Museum** Arms, armour, uniforms, medals etc of the Royal Norfolk Regiment from 1685 to the present day.
I   **University of East Anglia** Founded 1963.

Hospitals

A   **Hellesdon Hospital,** Drayton Road *tel 410611*
J   **Jenny Lind Hospital,** Department of Family Psychiatry, Unthank Road *tel 53270*
L   **St Andrew's Hospital,** Thorpe St Andrew *tel 35151*

E   **West Norwich Hospital,** Bowthorpe Road *tel 28377*
L   **Whitlingham Hospital,** Whitlingham *tel 28521*

Sport and Recreation

N   **Eaton Golf Club,** Newmarket Road
O   **Lakenham Baths,** Martineau Lane
K   **Lakenham Cricket Ground**
C   **Norwich Rugby Football Club,** Beeston Hyrne, North Walsham Road
A   **Royal Norwich Golf Club,** Hellesdon

Markets

Market days Wednesday and Saturday
N   **The Livestock Market,** Hall Road

Advertisers

N   **THF** The Post House
F   **Godfrey Davis**

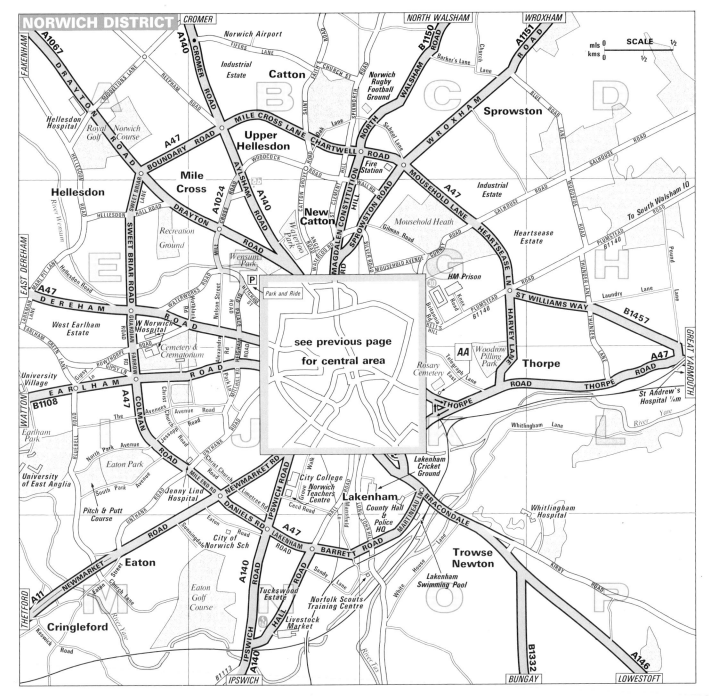

CROMER

NORTH WALSHAM

WROXHAM

SCALE

mls 0 ½
kms 0 ½

Norwich Airport

FIFERS LANE

Industrial Estate

Catton

Norwich Rugby Football Ground

Sprowston

FAKENHAM

A1067

DRAYTON ROAD

A140

CROMER ROAD

BELPHAM ROAD

MIDDLETONS LANE

Hellesdon Hospital

Royal Golf

Norwich Course

A47

BOUNDARY ROAD

MILE CROSS LANE

CHARTWELL ROAD

Upper Hellesdon

Mile Cross

WOODCOCK

A1024

AYLSHAM ROAD

A140

Hellesdon

River Wensum

HELLESDON HALL ROAD

SWEET BRIAR ROAD

SWEET BRIAR LANE

DRAYTON ROAD

Recreation Ground

New Catton

Waterloo Park

NORTH WALSHAM ROAD

CHURCH ST

SAINT

SPIXWORTH

OAK LANE

SCHOOL LANE

Fire Station

SPROWSTON ROAD

WROXHAM ROAD

B1150

A1151 ROAD

Church Lane

Barker's Lane

BLUE BOAR LANE

SALHOUSE ROAD

Industrial Estate

MOUSEHOLD LANE

A47

Mousehold Heath

Heartsease Estate

To South Walsham 10

B1140

EAST DEREHAM

A47

DEREHAM ROAD

MARL PIT LANE

Hellesdon Road

CATTON GROVE ROAD

CONSTITUTION HILL

MAGDALEN RD

ST CLEMENT HILL

WALL RD

SILVER RD

Gilman Road

MOUSEHOLD AVENUE

CURWEN ROAD

HM Prison

Britannia RD

KETT'S HILL

PLUMSTEAD ROAD

B1140

HEARTSEASE LN

ST WILLIAMS WAY

HARVEY LANE

THUNDER LANE

PLUMSTEAD ROAD

Laundry Lane

B1457

GREAT YARMOUTH

West Earlham Estate

GUARDIAN ROAD

W Norwich Hospital

WATERWORKS ROAD

Hotblack Rd

Nelson Street

OLD PALACE ROAD

Wensum Park

P

Park and Ride

see previous page for central area

30

AA

Telegraph Lane East

Woodrow Pilling Park

Rosary Cemetery

Thorpe

THORPE ROAD

A47

THORPE ROAD

St Andrew's Hospital ¼m

TARRMAN LANE

EARLHAM GREEN LANE

University Village

A47

EARLHAM ROAD

B1108

WATTON

Earlham Park

BUEBELL ROAD

University of East Anglia

GIPSY LN

GIPST LN

BOWTHORPE ROAD

FARROW ROAD

COLMAN ROAD

Cemetery & Crematorium

Alexandra Rd

Park Hill Rd

Avenues

Christ Church Rd

BELPHAM ROAD

Avenue Road

The

North Park Avenue

Jessopp Road

Eaton Park

South Park Avenue

Pitch & Putt Course

UNTHANK ROAD

Christ Church Road

MILE END RD

Jenny Lind Hospital

NEWMARKET ROAD

NEWMARKET RD

IPSWICH ROAD

Grove Walk

Cecil Road

City College

Norwich Teachers Centre

Mansfield

Lakenham

Whitlingham Lane

River Yare

Lakenham Cricket Ground

Whitlingham Hospital

County Hall & Police HQ

BRACONDALE

MARTINEAU LANE

Eaton

Road

Summingdale Rd

City of Norwich Sch

DANIELS RD

A47

LAKENHAM ROAD

BARRETT ROAD

Sandy Lane

White House Lane

Lakenham Swimming Pool

Trowse Newton

THETFORD

A11

NEWMARKET ROAD

Eaton

Eaton Street

Church Lane

Eaton

Cringleford

Keswick Road

Eaton Golf Course

A140

HALL ROAD

Tuckswood Estate

Livestock Market

Norfolk Scouts Training Centre

B1113

IPSWICH

A140

IPSWICH ROAD

River Tas

BUNGAY

B1332

LOWESTOFT

A146

KIRBY ROAD

River Yare

161

NOTTINGHAM

CENTRAL PLAN

G   **Tourist Information Centre** – 54 Milton Street *tel 40661*

Public buildings and places of interest

J(1)   **Albert Hall**

J(2)   **Albert Hall Institute**

B(3)   **Arboretum Park and Aviaries** Renowned for its dahlia border and other flowers in season.

N(4)   **Castle** The present castle consists of a 17th-C Italianate-style mansion, which forms a fine viewpoint, and houses a museum and art gallery. Displays include ceramics, silver, textiles, ethnography, archaeology, 17th- to 20th-C English and Dutch paintings, medieval alabasters, and modern paintings and sculpture. Also Regimental Museum of the Sherwood Foresters. Of the medieval castle only the late 13th-C gatehouse remains, which has been restored. Near the gateway is a group of statues representing Robin Hood and his Merry Men.

N(5)   **Castlegate Museum** An elegant row of Georgian terraced houses displaying costumes from 17thC to the present day, textiles, in particular lace, for which Nottingham is famed, and dolls.

J(6)   **Cathedral (RC)** This is an early work by Pugin, dating from 1842-44.

F(7)   **College of Art and Design**

K(8)   **Council House** A fine building of 1927-29, in Portland stone with façade displaying Greek and Roman influence and domed clock tower housing a loud bell known locally as 'Little John'.

A(9)   **Forest Recreation Ground** The Annual Goose Fair (amusements) is held here in the first week in October.

F(10)   **Guildhall**

G(11)   **Mechanics Institute**

G(12)   **Midland Design Centre**

J(13)   **Midland Group Gallery** Exhibitions of contemporary painting, sculpture, pottery and mixed media.

N(14)   **People's College**

J(15)   **Playhouse Theatre** A large modern theatre opened in 1963.

L(16)   **St Mary's Church** A large 15th-C structure, with a massive tower, Royal Arms of 1710, and some monuments.

N(17)   **St Nicholas' Church** A church of 1678 with additions of the 18thC.

K(18)   **St Peter's Church** A mainly 15th-C structure, retaining 13th-C work in the nave, and with rebuilt chancel of 1870. It features an organ of 1812.

K(19)   **Shire Hall** The central block was built to a design by James Gordon of 1770.

F(20)   **Theatre Royal**

J(21)   **The Royal Children Inn** The sign is made from the shoulder bone of a whale.

F(22)   **Trent Polytechnic (Newton Buildings)**

L(23)   **Victoria Baths and Exhibition Hall**

K(24)   **Willoughby House** A house built c1730.

J(25)   **Ye Olde Salutation Inn** A well-preserved and picturesque building of the 13thC.

N(26)   **Ye Olde Trip to Jerusalem Inn** This inn bears the date 1189, and is claimed to be the oldest inn in the country.

Hospitals

J   **Eye Hospital,** The Ropewalk *tel 46161*

J   **General Hospital,** Park Row *tel 46161*

B   **Women's Hospital,** Peel Street *tel 40591*

Sport and Recreation

L   **Humber Tenpin Bowling Alley,** Barker Gate

L   **Ice Stadium,** Lower Parliament Street

L(23)   **Victoria Baths,** Victoria Leisure Centre, Sneinton (see also public buildings and places of interest)

Theatres and Cinemas

J   **ABC Cinema,** Chapel Bar *tel 45260/46894*

J   **Odeon Film Centre,** Angel Row *tel 47766*

L(16)   **Playhouse Theatre,** Goldsmith Road *tel 45671* (see also public buildings and places of interest)

F(20)   **Theatre Royal** *tel 42328* (see also public buildings and places of interest)

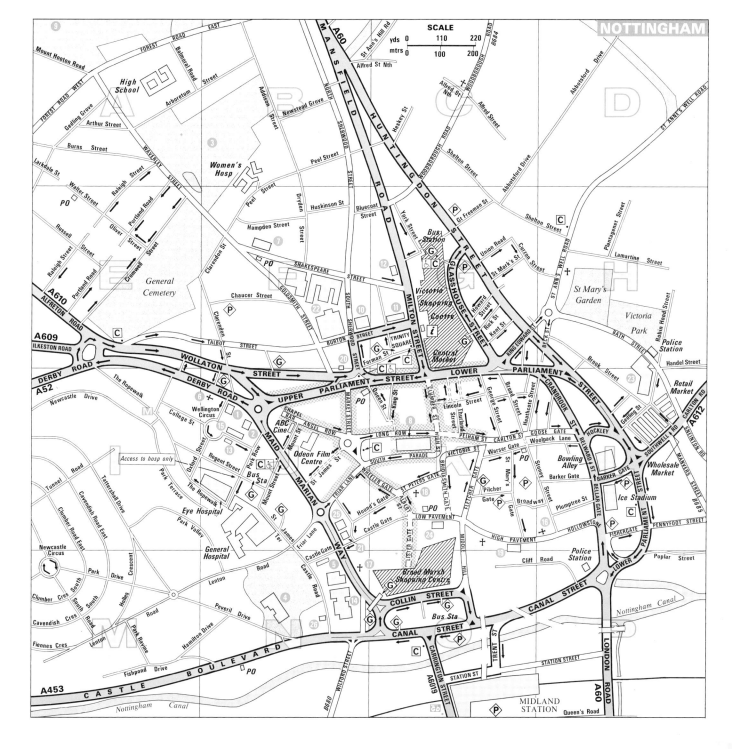

NOTTINGHAM

Department Stores

Debenhams Ltd, Long Row and Market Street
Farmer Henry and Co Ltd, Music House, 57 Long Row
Greater Nottingham Co-operative Society Ltd, Arndale Centre, Broad Marsh
Jessop and Son Ltd, Victoria Centre
Marks and Spencer Ltd, 5 Albert Street
Pearson Brothers (Nottingham) Ltd, Long Row
Tobys J H Ltd, 12 Friar Lane
Wigfall Henry and Son Ltd, Newcastle Chambers, Angel Row
Early closing day Thursday

Markets

G   **Central Market,** Victoria Centre (Daily-but main market days Monday, Wednesday, Friday and Saturday)
L   **Sneinton Open-air Retail Market,** Bath Street (Monday and Saturday mornings)
L   **Sneinton Wholesale Markets,** Bath Street (Monday to Friday 05.00-13.00 hrs; Saturday 05.00-13.30hrs)

Advertisers

I   **Mercantile Credit**
O   **Godfrey Davis**

DISTRICT PLAN

J   **AA Service Centre** — Fanum House, 484 Derby Road *tel 77751*

Public buildings and places of interest

I(27)   **Wollaton Hall** An imposing Elizabethan mansion dating from 1580-88, situated in a large park and housing a natural history museum. The courtyard buildings house a museum of Nottingham's industries, in particular lace-making, hosiery, pharmacy and printing.
J(28)   **University** Founded in 1881 it moved to its present site in 1928, and was granted its own charter in 1948. Many impressive new buildings have been added in recent years.

Hospitals

C   **Basford Hospital,** Hucknall Road *tel 607161*
C   **Cedars Hospital,** Woodthorpe *tel 63343*
G   **Children's Hospital,** Chestnut Grove *tel 607214*
C   **City Hospital,** Hucknall Road *tel 63361*
H   **Coppice Hospital,** Mapperley *tel 68144*
C   **Firs Maternity Hospital,** Mansfield Road *tel 63271*
B   **Highbury Hospital,** Highbury Road, Bulwell *tel 271275*
D   **Mapperley Hospital** *tel 68144*
H   **St Anne's Hospital,** Thorneywood Mount *tel 68144*

Sport and Recreation

C   **Carrington Lido,** Mansfield Road, Sherwood
J   **Highfields Open-air Swimming Pool,** University Boulevard
K   **Lenton Baths,** Willoughby Street
D   **Mapperley Golf Course**
G   **Noel Street Baths**
B   **Northern Baths,** Basford
L   **Nottingham Forest Football Club,** City Ground, Trent Bridge
L   **Nottingham Racecourse**
L   **Notts County Cricket Club,** Trent Bridge Ground
L   **Notts County Football Club,** Meadow Lane Ground
M   **Notts Rugby Football Club Ground,** Ireland Avenue, Beeston
G   **Radford Baths,** Boden Street
J   **Wollaton Park Golf Course**
Holme Pierrepont National Water Sports Centre, Adbolton Lane, Holme Pierrepont 3½m E via Radcliffe Road A52 (P)

Cinemas

K   **Savoy Cinema,** Derby Road *tel 42580*

Markets

L   **Cattle Market,** London Road (Monday to Saturday)

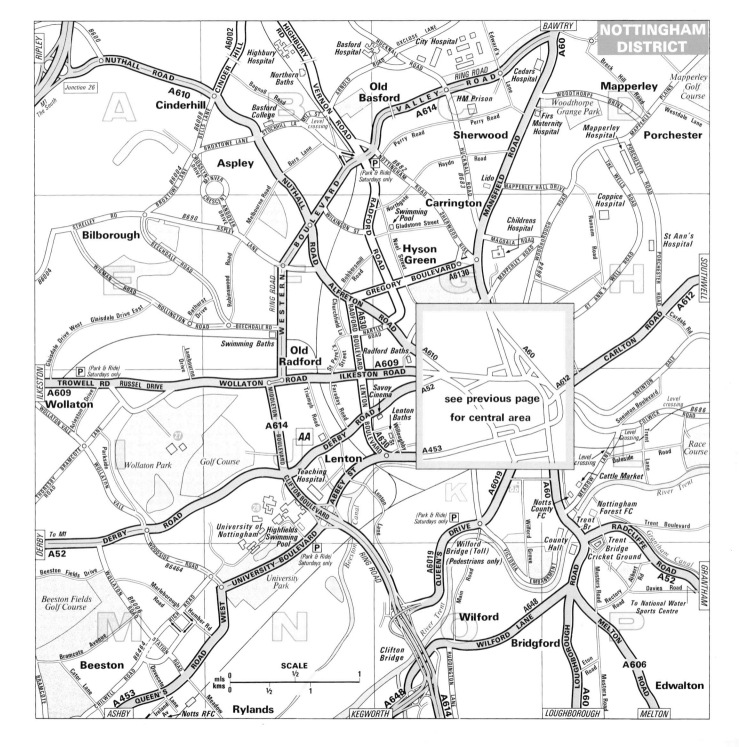

OXFORD

K   **AA Service Centre** – 133-4 High Street
tel 40286

J [i]   **Tourist Information Centre** – St Aldates
tel 48707

Public buildings and places of interest

COLLEGES

K(1)   **All Souls College (1437)**
J(2)   **Balliol College (1260-66)**
K(3)   **Brasenose College (1509)**
O(4)   **Christ Church (1525)**
K(5)   **Corpus Christi College (1516)**
K(6)   **Exeter College (1314)**
K(7)   **Hertford College (1874)**
J(8)   **Jesus College (1571)**
F(9)   **Keble College (1870)**
C(10)   **Linacre College (1962)**
K(11)   **Lincoln College (1427)**
L(12)   **Magdalen College (1448)**
G(13)   **Manchester College (1888)**
G(14)   **Mansfield College (1889)**
K(15)   **Merton College (1264)**
K(16)   **New College (1379)**
J(17)   **Nuffield College (1937)**
K(18)   **Oriel College (1324-26)**
N(19)   **Pembroke College (1624)**
K(20)   **Queen's College (1340)**
F(21)   **Regents Park College (1957)**
F(22)   **Ruskin College (1899)**
B(23)   **St Anne's College (1952)**
B(24)   **St Antony's College (1948)**
H(25)   **St Catherine's College (1962)**
L(26)   **St Edmund Hall (c1220)**
P(27)   **St Hilda's College (1893)**
F(28)   **St John's College (1555)**
J(29)   **St Peter's College (1929)**
F(30)   **Somerville (1879)**
F(31)   **Trinity College (1554-5)**
K(32)   **University College (1249)**
G(33)   **Wadham College (1610-13)**
I(34)   **Worcester College (1714)**

CHURCHES

K(35)   **All Saints Church** An imposing 18th-C structure noted for its panelled ceiling and fine tower.
O(36)   **Christ Church Cathedral** A Norman cathedral with later additions including the 13th-C cathedral spire. The cathedral was restored in the 1870's by Sir Gilbert Scott and the east wall was rebuilt.
K(37)   **St Mary's Church** The University Church of St Mary the Virgin has a fine spired 13th- to 14th-C tower and a porch of 1637 displaying twisted pillars. This has been the University Church since the 14thC.

OTHER PLACES OF INTEREST

F(38)   **Ashmolean Museum** One of the oldest museums in Europe, its treasures include Old Master and modern drawings, water-colours, prints and miniatures, and an extensive collection of coins.
K(39)   **Bodleian Library** Second only to the British Museum in the Commonwealth.
J(40)   **Carfax Tower** The 13th-C tower is all that remains from the former St Martin's Church.
J(41)   **City Library** Westgate Shopping Centre
J(42)   **County Hall**
K(43)   **Divinity School** Displays fine Perpendicular work, notably the arched roof with pendant bosses.
K(44)   **Indian Institute**
F(45)   **Martyrs' Memorial** Erected in 1841 by Sir Giles Gilbert Scott in memory of Cranmer, Ridley and Latimer burnt at the stake.
K(46)   **Museum of the History of Science** Collection of early scientific instruments etc.
J(47)   **Museum of Modern Art** Temporary exhibitions of contemporary British and International Art.
G(48)   **New Bodleian Library**
J(49)   **Oxford Castle** The Tower is all that remains of the chapel of the Norman Castle built in 1071.
K(50)   **Radcliffe Camera** Built by James Gibbs in 1739-49, with a remarkable view from the dome. It is now part of the Bodleian Library.
G(51)   **Rhodes House** Founded in 1926 for Rhodes Scholars from overseas.
K(52)   **Sheldonian Theatre** Designed by Wren and presented to the University in 1669. The Annual Commemoration is held here in late June. Opposite is the early 18th-C Clarendon building by Hawksmoor.

K(53)   **Town Hall,** Museum of Oxford. Main displays tell the story of Oxford through objects, photographs, models and sound.
G(54)   **University Museum** Built 1855-60 to house the natural science collections. The Pitt-Rivers anthropological collection is notable.

Hospitals

A   **The Oxford Eye Hospital,** Walton Street
tel 49891
B   **The Radcliffe Infirmary,** Woodstock Road
tel 49891

Sport and Recreation

C   **Oxford University Cricket Ground,** University Parks, Parks Road

Oriel College

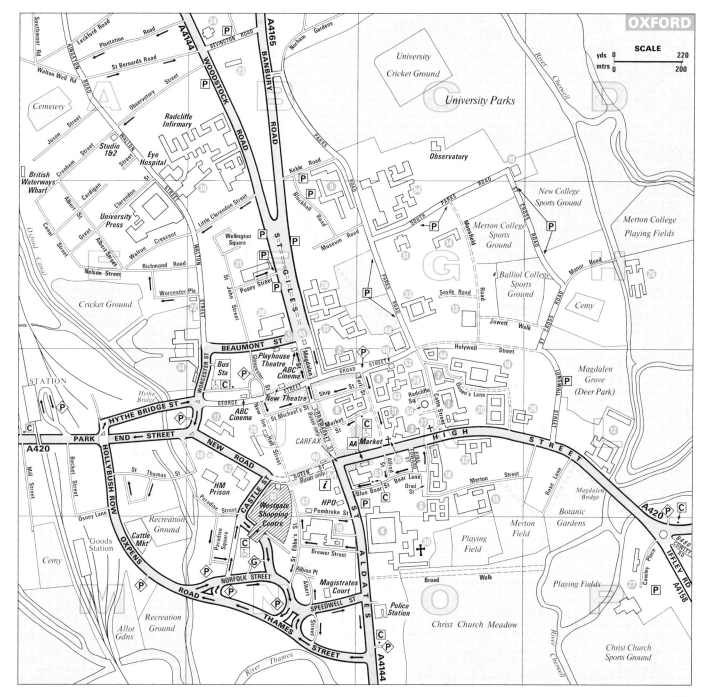

SCALE
yds 0   220
mtrs 0   200

Southmoor Rd
Leckford Road
Plantation Road
St Bernards Road
KINGSTON ROAD
Walton Well Rd
Observatory Street
A4144
BEVINGTON ROAD
WOODSTOCK ROAD
A4165 BANBURY ROAD
Norham Gardens

University Cricket Ground

University Parks

River Cherwell

Cemetery
Juxon Street
Cranham Street
Studio 1&2
Radcliffe Infirmary
Eye Hospital
Keble Road
Blackhall Road
Museum Road
PARKS ROAD

Observatory

SOUTH PARKS ROAD
Mansfield Road
ST CROSS ROAD

New College Sports Ground

Merton College Playing Fields

British Waterways Wharf
Albert St
Cardigan Street
Clarendon
University Press
Great Clarendon Street
WALTON STREET
Little Clarendon Street
Wellington Square
St John Street
Pusey Street
St GILES
Savile Road
Merton College Sports Ground

Balliol College Sports Ground

Manor Road
Cemy

Oxford Canal
Canal Street
Albert Street
Walton Crescent
Richmond Road
Nelson Street
Worcester Pla
WALTON STREET
Jowett Walk
Holywell Street

Cricket Ground

STATION
Hythe Bridge
WORCESTER ST
Bus Sta
Playhouse Theatre
ABC Cinema
Gloucester Street
Magdalen
BEAUMONT ST
Broad Street
Ship St
New Theatre
New Inn Hall Street
George Street
ABC Cinema
St Michael's St
Market St
CORNMARKET ST
Buses only
CARFAX
Market
AA Market
Radcliffe Sq
Catte Street
Queen's Lane
HIGH STREET
LONGWALL STREET

Magdalen Grove (Deer Park)

PARK END STREET
A420
HOLLYBUSH ROW
Becket Street
Mill Street
NEW ROAD
St Thomas St
HM Prison
Paradise Street
CASTLE ST
Westgate Shopping Centre
St Ebbe's St
Pembroke St
QUEEN ST
Buses only
HPO
Brewer Street
Albion Pl
Blue Boar St
Bear Lane
Oriel St
Alfred St
ST ALDATES
Merton Street
Rose Lane
Magdalen Bridge
A420
Botanic Gardens
IFFLEY RD A4158
B480 COWLEY RD

Goods Station
Cemy
Osney Lane
Recreation Ground
Paradise Square
OXPENS ROAD
NORFOLK STREET
Albert Street
Magistrates Court
SPEEDWELL ST
Police Station
Merton Field
Playing Field
Merton Field

Allot Gdns
Recreation Ground
THAMES STREET
River Thames
A4144
Christ Church Meadow
Broad Walk
Playing Fields
Christ Church Sports Ground
River Cherwell
Cowley Place

Theatres and Cinemas

J	**ABC 1, 2 and 3 Cinema,** George Street *tel 44607*
J	**ABC Cinema,** Magdalen Street *tel 43067*
J	**New Theatre,** George Street *tel 44544*
A	**Studio 1 and 2,** Walton Street *tel 54909*
J	**The Playhouse Theatre,** Beaumont Street *tel 47133*

Department Stores

H Boswell and Co Ltd, 1 Broad Street
Debenhams, Magdalen Street
Fenwicks of Bond Street, St Ebbes Westgate
Marks and Spencer Ltd, 18 Cornmarket Street
Selfridges Ltd, Westgate
Early closing day Thursday

Markets

M	**Cattle Market,** Oxpens Road, Wednesday (Cattle)
K	**Covered Market,** High Street, open every day except Thursday

Advertisers

J	**Mercantile Credit**
F	**THF** Randolph Hotel

DISTRICT PLAN

Public buildings and places of interest

COLLEGES

J(55)	Lady Margaret Hall (1878)
J(56)	St Hugh's College (1886)
J(57)	University Department of Education
M(58)	Westminster College (1899)
F(59)	Wolfson College (1966)

Hospitals

P	**The Churchill Hospital,** Headington *tel 64841*
O	**The Cowley Road Hospital,** Cowley Road *tel 64841*
K	**The John Radcliffe Hospital,** Nuffield Maternity Department *tel 64711*
S	**Littlemore Hospital (including Ashurst and Ley Clinics),** Littlemore *tel 778911*
L	**The Nuffield Orthopaedic Centre (including Mary Marlborough Lodge),** Headington *tel 64841*
L	**The Park Hospital for Children,** Headington *tel 45651*
O	**Rivermead Hospital,** Abingdon Road *tel 40321*
P	**The Slade Hospital,** Headington *tel 64841*
K	**The Warneford Hospital,** Headington *tel 45651*

Sport and Recreation

N	**Hinksey Pools,** Lake Street
O	**Long Bridges Bathing Place,** Thames tow-path from Folley Bridge
B	**North Oxford Golf Club,** Banbury Road
N	**Oxford City FC,** White House Road, Abingdon Road
N	**Oxford RFC,** Oxford Sports Club, Southern-by-pass
T	**Oxford Stadium,** Cowley — greyhound racing and speedway racing
K	**Oxford United FC,** Manor Ground, Osler Road, Headington
O	**Oxford University Association FC,** Iffley Road
O	**Oxford University RFC,** Iffley Road
O	**Oxford University Running Ground,** Iffley Road
P	**Southfield Golf Club,** Hill Top Road, Southfield
P	**Temple Cowley Swimming Baths,** Temple Road, Cowley
J	**Tumbling Bay Bathing Place,** Thames tow-path, Botley Road
E	**Wolvercote Bathing Place,** Port Meadow, Wolvercote

Markets

T	**Open Market,** Oxford Stadium, Cowley (open every day except Thursday)

Advertisers

A	**THF** Travelodge
I	**Godfrey Davis**

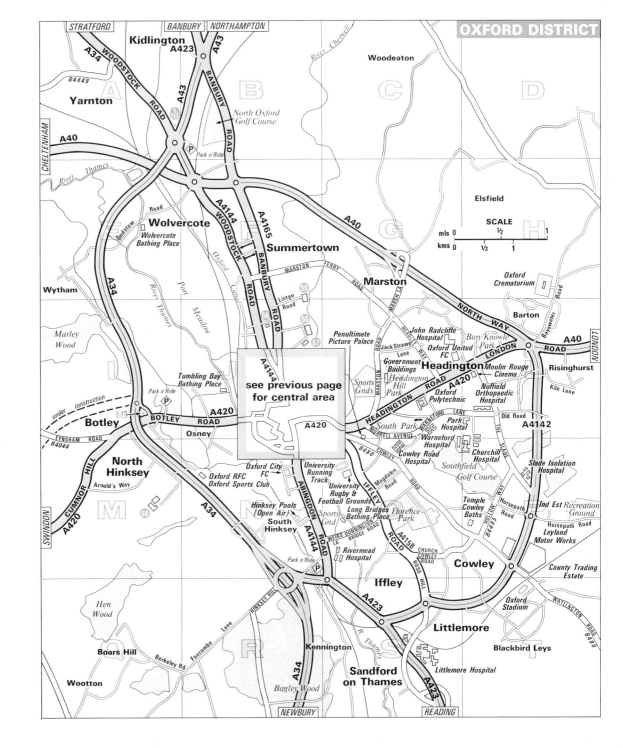

STRATFORD | BANBURY | NORTHAMPTON

Kidlington
A423
A43

A34 WOODSTOCK ROAD

B4449

Yarnton

A40 CHELTENHAM

North Oxford Golf Course

Park n' Ride

River Cherwell

Woodeaton

Elsfield

SCALE
mls 0   ½   1
kms 0   ½   1

River Thames
Road
Gosstow
Wolvercote
Wolvercote Bathing Place

A4144
A4165
A34
WOODSTOCK ROAD
BANBURY ROAD

Summertown

Oxford Canal

MARSTON
FERRY ROAD

Marston

MARSTON LA.

NORTH WAY

LONDON ROAD

Oxford Crematorium

Barton

A40 LONDON

Wytham

River Thames

Port Meadow

Linton Road
59
56
55

Penultimate Picture Palace

Marley Wood

Tumbling Bay Bathing Place

Park n' Ride

under construction

Botley
BOTLEY ROAD
A420
Osney

EYNSHAM ROAD
B4044

57

HEADLEY WAY
Jack Straws Lane
John Radcliffe Hospital
Oxford United FC

Government Buildings
Heddington Hill Park

Sports Gnds

HEADINGTON ROAD

MARSTON RD.

Bury Knowle Park

Headington
A420
Oxford Polytechnic

WARNEFORD LANE

South Park

MORRELL AVENUE

Moulin Rouge Cinema
Nuffield Orthopaedic Hospital
Old Road

Park Hospital
Warneford Hospital

Risinghurst
Kiln Lane
A40
A4142

THE SLADE

Bayswater Road

North Hinksey

CUMNOR HILL
Arnold's Way
A420 SWINDON

58

Oxford RFC
Oxford Sports Club

A34

Oxford City FC
University Running Track
University Rugby & Football Grounds

ABINGDON ROAD

COWLEY ROAD
B480

Cowley Road Hospital

Magdalen Road

Southfield Golf Course

Churchill Hospital

Slade Isolation Hospital

Ind Est Recreation Ground

Hinksey Pools (Open Air)
South Hinksey

Sports Gnd
WEIRS DONNINGTON LA.
DONNINGTON BRIDGE ROAD

Long Bridges Bathing Place

Florence Park

IFFLEY ROAD

Temple Cowley Baths

Horsepath Road

HOLLOW WAY

Horsepath Road
Leyland Motor Works

A4144
Rivermead Hospital

A158
CHURCH COWLEY ROAD

RISE HILL

Cowley

County Trading Estate

Hen Wood

Park n' Ride

Iffley
A423

R. Thames

Oxford Stadium

WATLINGTON ROAD
B480

Boars Hill

Berkeley Rd
Foscombe Lane
Hinksey Hill

Kennington
A34

Littlemore

Blackbird Leys

Littlemore Hospital

Wootton

Bagley Wood

Sandford on Thames
A423

NEWBURY | READING

see previous page for central area
A4144
A420

A420

Breakdown Service (09.00-18.00hrs) — *tel 23551*
N[i]   **Tourist Information Centre** — Perth
Tourist Association, Marshall Place
tel 22900/27108

Public buildings and places of interest

C(1)   **Balhousie Castle** Originally built in
1478, but restored in Scottish Baronial
style in the 17thC and extensively
added to in 1862. It now contains the
headquarters and regimental museum of
the famous Black Watch (The Royal
Highland Regiment).

T(2)   **Branklyn Gardens (NTS)** Although only
2 acres in area, it is considered to be
the finest garden of its size in
Britain, with a notable collection of
rhododendrons, shrubs and alpine plants.

I(3)   **City Hall**

I(4)   **Fair Maid's House** The home, during the
14thC, of Simon Glover, a noted
glovemaker, whose daughter Catherine
was the heroine of Sir Walter Scott's
Fair Maid of Perth. Now a centre for
Scottish crafts and antiques.

I(5)   **Museum and Art Gallery** The building has
a fine classical portico. The art
collection is mainly of the Scottish
school. The museum houses a fine
regional natural history collection,
and a guide to the city's life and
culture throughout history, including
early equipment used in the whisky
industry.

C(6)   **Old Academy** Now a school, it has a
façade of 1807.

I(7)   **Perth and Kinross District Council
Offices and Police Station**

I(8)   **St John's Church** A restored church in
Gothic style, dating from the mid 15thC,
with a fine carillon of bells which
chime every 15 minutes. John Knox
delivered a famous sermon here in 1559,
and several kings have attended services.
The north transept contains Sir Robert
Lorimer's War Memorial Chapel.

H(9)   **St Ninian's Episcopal Cathedral**

I(10)   **Sandeman Public Library**

I(11)   **Sheriff Courts** These stand on the site
of the former 16th-C Gowrie House,
where the conspiracy took place in 1660.

N(12)   **Sir Walter Scott's Statue**

I(13)   **Theatre**

Scone Palace and site of Royal City of Scone
Famous in Scottish history as a seat of
Government in Pictish times; home of the Stone
of Destiny until 1296, when it was removed to
Westminster Abbey; and crowning place of
Scottish kings until 1651. The present palace,
home of the Earl of Mansfield, was largely
rebuilt in 1803, and incorporates part of an
earlier palace of 1580. It contains a fine
collection of French furniture, porcelain, 16th-C
needlework, ivories and objets d'art. 2m N via
Isla Road A93 (D)

Hospitals

F   **City and County Royal Infirmary,**
Tullylumb *tel 23311*

O   **Hillside Hospital,** Barnhill *tel 22266*

H   **King James VI Hospital** tel 24660

E   **Murray Royal Hospital,** Muirhall Road
tel 24282

Fair Maid's House

Sport and Recreation

C   **Bell's Sports Centre,** Hay Street
P   **Craigie Hill Golf Course**
T   **King James VI Golf Course,** Moncrieffe
Island
D   **Perth Corporation Golf Course,** North
Inch
C   **Perth Corporation Swimming Baths,**
Dunkeld Road
B   **Perth Ice Rink and Tenpin Bowling,**
Dunkeld Road
D   **Perthshire Cricket Club,** North Inch
(pitch adjacent to Bell's Sports Centre)
B   **St Johnstone Football Club Ground,**
Muirton Park
Perth Hunt Racecourse, Scone Park 2m N via Isla
Road A93 (D)

Theatres and Cinemas

I   **Odeon Cinema,** Kinnoull Street *tel 24265*
I(13)   **Perth Theatre,** High Street *tel 21031*
(see also public buildings and places
of interest)
H   **Playhouse Cinema,** Murray Street
tel 23126

Department Stores

Caird A and Sons Ltd, 21 High Street
Co-operative, Scott Street
Lawsons Ltd, 198 South Street
McEwens of Perth, St John Street
Marks and Spencer Ltd, High Street
Early closing day Wednesday but some shops and
stores remain open during the summer months

Markets

Market Days Monday and Friday
H   **Auction Market,** Elbank Street
M   **Auction Market,** Glover Street

Advertisers

I   **Mercantile Credit**
G   **Godfrey Davis**
I   **THF** Royal George Hotel

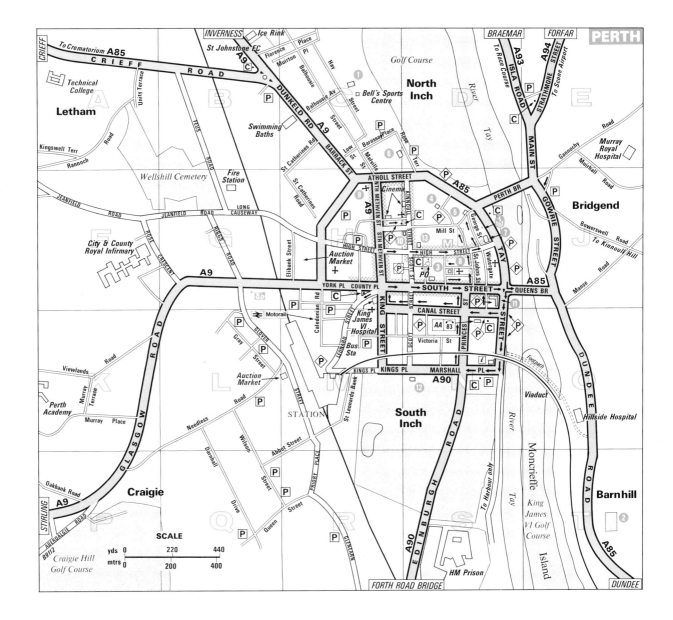

PERTH

Letham

Technical College

To Crematorium A85
CRIEFF ROAD
CRIEFF

Unity Terrace
Kingswell Terr
Rannoch
Road

Wellshill Cemetery

JEANFIELD ROAD
JEANFIELD ROAD

City & County Royal Infirmary

POST CRESCENT

TULLOS ROAD

A9

GLASGOW ROAD

Viewlands
Murray Terrace
Road

Perth Academy

Murray Place

STIRLING
A9
Oakbank Road
Craigie

ABERDALGIE ROAD
B9112

Craigie Hill Golf Course

SCALE
yds 0 — 220 — 440
mtrs 0 — 200 — 400

INVERNESS
Ice Rink
St Johnstone FC
Florence Place
Pl
Muirton
Hay
St
Balhousie Av
Barrack St
DUNKELD RD A9

Swimming Baths

Fire Station

LONG CAUSEWAY

Elibank Street

Motorail
Caledonian Rd

Gray Street
Glover Street

Auction Market

King's Road
STATION

Needless
Barnhill Road
Wilson Street
Queen Street
GLENFARG

Abbot Street
St Leonards
PRIORY PLACE

Bell's Sports Centre
North Inch
Golf Course
River Tay

Low St
Barossa Place
Melville
Rose Terr

St Catherines Rd
St Catherines Road

ATHOLL STREET
A85

Cinema
NTH METHVEN ST
STH METHVEN ST
A9
HIGH STREET
KINNOULL ST
SCOTT STREET
George St
Mill St
HIGH STREET
Watergate
St Johns St

Auction Market

York Pl County Pl
KING STREET
SCOTT STREET
SOUTH STREET
PRINCES ST
CANAL STREET
AA 83
Victoria St

King James VI Hospital
Bus Sta
LEONARD STREET

Kings Pl
KINGS PL
MARSHALL PL
A90
South Inch

Moncrieffe Island
King James VI Golf Course

EDINBURGH ROAD
A90

HM Prison

FORTH ROAD BRIDGE

BRAEMAR
A93
ISLA ROAD
FORFAR
A94
STRATHMORE STREET
To Race Course
To Scone Airport
MAIN ST

River Tay

PERTH BR
GOWRIE STREET
A85

Bridgend
Murray Royal Hospital
Gannochy Road
Murhall Road
Bowerswell Road
To Kinnoull Hill
Manse Road

QUEENS BR
DUNDEE ROAD

Viaduct
Hillside Hospital

Barnhill
A85

DUNDEE

171

PLYMOUTH

G	**AA Service Centre** – 10 Old Town Street *tel 69989*
J(7)	**Tourist Information Centre** – Civic
i	Centre *tel 68000 ext 2309/2409* (see also public buildings and places of interest)

Public buildings and places of interest

O(1)	**Aquarium and Marine Laboratory**
P(2)	**Barbican and Mayflower Memorial** The quay known as the Barbican, in Sutton Harbour, has inscribed tablets, one recalling the departure of the *Mayflower* in 1620.
E(3)	**Cathedral (RC)** A 19th-C building with a tall spire.
G(4)	**Central Library, City Museum and Art Gallery** Contains collections of paintings, including the Reynolds' family portraits and the Cottonian collection; ceramics; drawings; local and natural history; archaeology and model ships.
G(5)	**Charles Church** Dating from 1640-58, it was gutted during the last war and has been retained as a memorial to the city's civilian dead.
O(6)	**Citadel (AM)** Built by Charles II in 1666, it commands the old town and the approaches to the harbour. It is considered to be one of the finest fortifications of its kind in Britain. There is a magnificent entrance gateway, dated 1670 and the remaining buildings include the Guard House, the Governor's House and St Katherine's Chapel.
J(7)	**Civic Centre** An impressive building 200ft-high with a public viewing gallery giving excellent views across the city and Plymouth Sound. Regular art exhibitions are held here.
O(8)	**Elizabethan House** Located in the Elizabethan district of the old port (Sutton Harbour and the Barbican). This 16th-C merchant's house has been well restored as a museum of the period.
K(9)	**Guildhall** Built 1870-74, and re-opened in 1959 after extensive war damage.

It has a very prominent square tower and historical windows by F H Coventry.

K(10)	**Kathleen and Mays Schooner,** Guys Quay. The last of the wooden topsail trading schooners to trade from the West Coast. The Maritime Trust has restored her to the layout and rig which she had when launched in 1900. A display mounted by the National Maritime Museum is on view in the hold.
G(11)	**Plymouth Polytechnic**
K(12)	**St Andrew's Church and Prysten House** The fine 15th-C tower of the church escaped bomb damage during the last war. Nearby is Prysten (or the Priest's) house dating from 1490. It is the oldest house in the city.
N(13)	**Sir Francis Drake Statue**
N(14)	**Smeaton's Tower** The upper part of the lighthouse that once stood on the Eddystone Rock, 14m out to sea. The architect was the famous engineer Thomas Smeaton.
K(15)	**Wall Mural,** The Parade. A huge, colourful wall mural painted on the side of a house by a local artist.

Hospitals

D	**Plymouth General Hospital** (Freedom Fields) *tel 68080*
D	**Plymouth General Hospital** (Greenbank) *tel 68080*

Sport and Recreation

F	**Beaver Tenpin Bowling Ltd,** Mayflower Street
N	**Tinside Open-air Swimming Pool,** Hoe Road

Theatres and Cinemas

J	**ABC Cinema and Theatre** *tel 63300*
J	**Drake Cinema,** Derry's Cross *tel 68825*
N	**Hoe Theatre** *tel 68000*
I	**Odeon Cinema** *tel 61656*
J	**Athenaeum Theatre** *tel 266104*
L	**Studio Seven Cinema,** 36 Bretonside *tel 64450*

Plymouth Sound

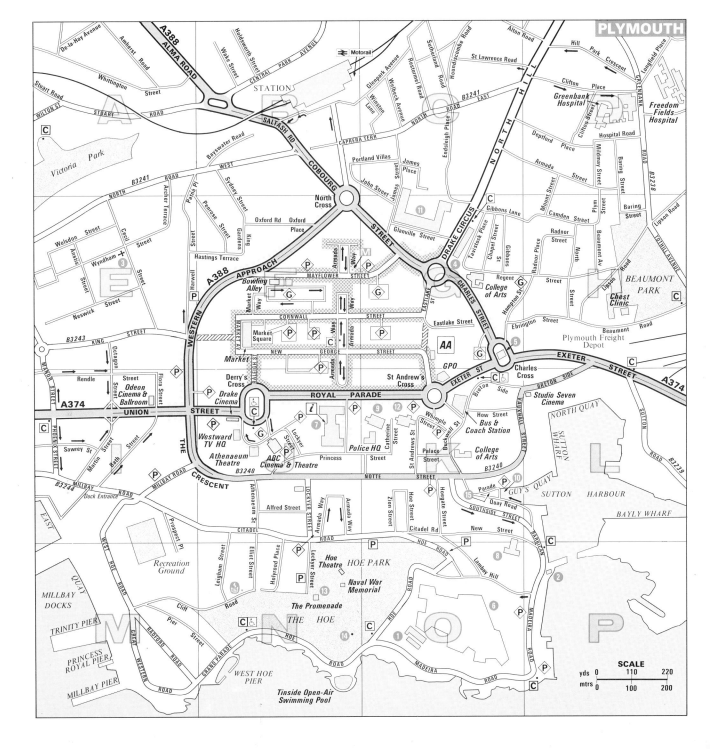

Department Stores

Alexandra Overalls Ltd, 152 Cornwall Street
Arcadia, 32 Eastlake Walk, Drake's Circus
Costers Ltd, New George Street
Dingle E and Co Ltd, 40 Royal Parade
Marks and Spencer Ltd, 29 Old Town Street
Early closing day Wednesday but most shops
remain open 6 days a week.

Markets

F   **Covered Market,** Market Avenue

Advertisers

F   **Mercantile Credit**
N   **THF** Mayflower Post House

DISTRICT PLAN
Public buildings and places of interest

N(16)   **Admiral's Hard,** Stonehouse. A landing
place in the Stonehouse Pool for the
passenger ferry to Cremyll (for Mount
Edgcumbe).

N(17)   **Drake's Island (NT)** A 7-acre island in
Plymouth Sound fortified for 500 years.
Defences strengthened by Drake, and
garrisoned up to the end of World War II.
Now developed as an adventure training
centre.

M(18)   **Mount Edgcumbe Park** A fine 16th-C
mansion, restored after bomb damage in
1941. It is set in a large deer park
with fine avenues and shrubberies
overlooking the Sound.

A(19)   **Royal Albert Bridge** Completed in 1859,
this railway bridge 110ft above river
level is probably the most famous of
all Brunel's works. It can be examined
closely from the adjacent road bridge
opened in 1961.

N(20)   **Royal William Victualling Yard** These
buildings at East Stonehouse are mainly
the work of John Rennie and incorporate
a statue of William IV.

L(21)   **Saltram House (NT)** A mid-18th-C
mansion incorporating the remains of
a Tudor house. The interior contains
two rooms designed by Robert Adam,
much fine period furniture and many
portraits by Sir Joshua Reynolds. It
is surrounded by a landscaped park.

F(22)   **Zoo,** Central Park. Contains varied
and ever-changing collection of
animals and birds, particularly so as
it is the quarantine centre for other
Chipperfield establishments.

Hospitals

K   **Mount Gould Hospital,** *tel 266286*
I   **Plymouth General Hospital,** Devonport
tel 53533
J   **Royal Naval Hospital,** Stonehouse *tel
53740*
F   **Scott Hospital** *tel 51363*

Sport and Recreation

J   **Central Park Swimming Pool**
J   **Devonport Services Rugby Football Club,**
Rectory Ground, Devonport

F   **Kitto Sports Centre,** Honicknowle Lane,
Honicknowle
F   **Mayflower Sports Centre,** Central Park
N   **Mount Wise Swimming Baths,** Mutton Cove
Devonport
F   **Plymouth Albion Rugby Football Club,**
Beacon Park
F   **Plymouth Argyle Football Club,**
Home Park, Central Park
F   **Plymouth Cricket Club,** Peverell Park
J   **United Services Cricket Ground,** Mount
Wise, Devonport

Cinemas

K   **Belgrave Cinema,** Belgrave Road, Mutley
tel 62423

Advertisers

H   **Godfrey Davis**

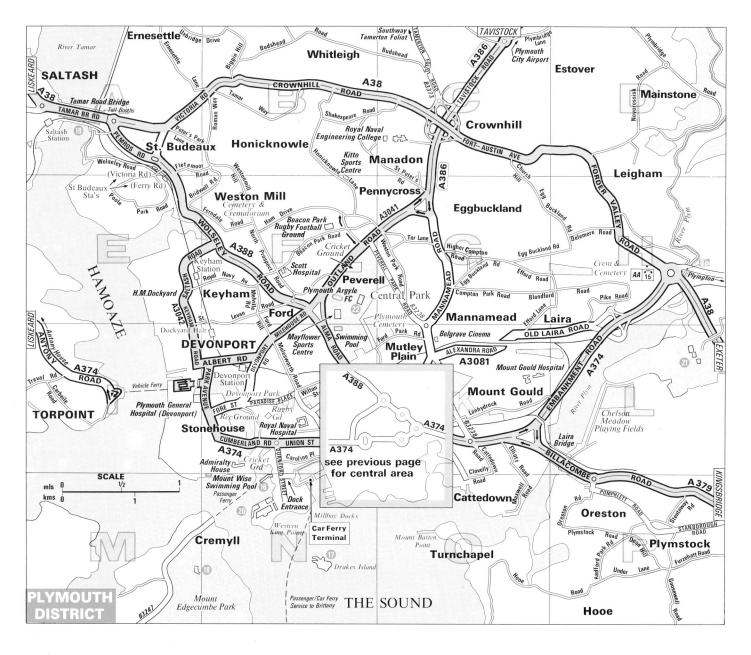

PORTSMOUTH

AA Road Service Centre (43) – *tel 67012*
At Portsbridge 3¾m N on A3 (B)

N [i] **Tourist Information Centres** – Castle Buildings, Clarence Esplanade, *tel 26722* (Regional)

F(8) **The Guildhall** *tel 21171 ext 52* (Local)

[i] (see also public buildings and places of interest)

Public buildings and places of interest

I(1) **Buckingham House** The Duke of Buckingham was murdered here in 1628.

I(2) **Cathedral** Incorporating the former Parish Church of St Thomas of Canterbury, founded in 1180 and still incomplete. The transepts and chancel are 12thC and the nave and tower were rebuilt in 1693.

F(3) **Cathedral (RC)**

B(4) **Charles Dickens' Birthplace Museum** The house where Charles Dickens was born in 1812, now displayed as a Georgian period house and containing many interesting Dickensian relics.

J(5) **City Museum and Art Gallery** Contains collections of English pottery, glass, furniture, sculpture and paintings. Also local history galleries and monthly temporary exhibitions.

O(6) **Cumberland House Museum** Exhibits include local natural history and geology and an aquarium of marine and freshwater fish.

I(7) **Garrison Church** A restored, partly-13th-C church.

F(8) **Guildhall** This imposing structure was burnt out during the Second World War, but was rebuilt in 1959.

A(9) **HMS Victory and Portsmouth Royal Naval Museum** Admiral Lord Nelson's famous flagship in the Battle of Trafalgar (1805), now preserved in dry dock. The adjacent museum contains many fine exhibits connected with Nelson, his officers and men; ship models, including the Victory, figureheads and a huge panorama of the Battle of Trafalgar.

I(10) **Lord Nelson Statue**

N(11) **Naval Memorial**

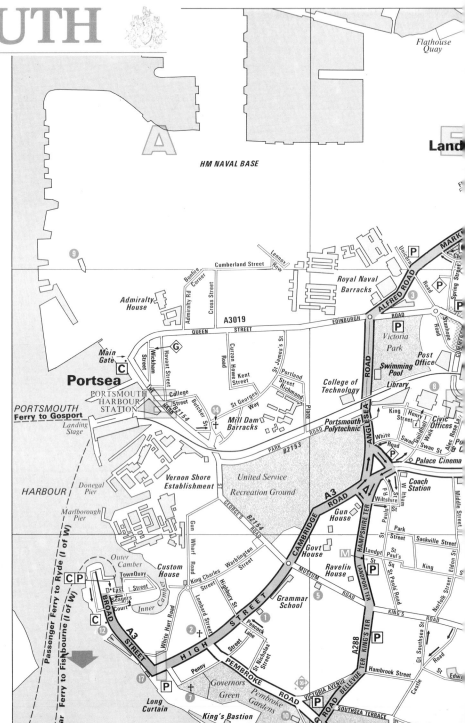

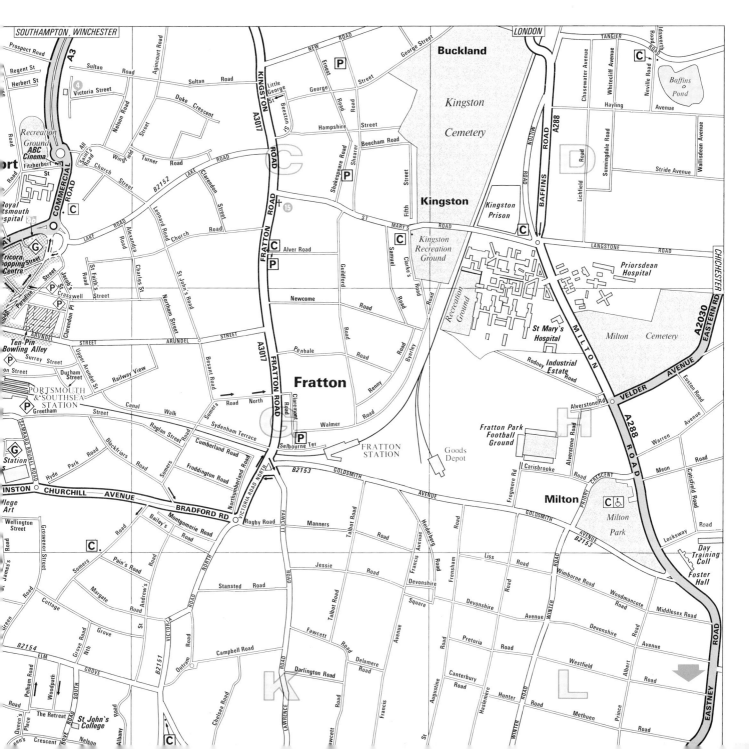

I(12) **Round Tower and Point Battery** An old tower dating back to 1417, and once part of an 18-gun battery defending the harbour.

L(13) **Royal Marines Museum,** Eastney Barracks. Displays the chronological history of the Royal Marines from 1644 to the present day and includes uniforms, badges and medals.

E(14) **St George's Church** A Georgian church, erected in 1754.

C(15) **St Mary's Church** In the churchyard is the 'Royal George' memorial of 1782.

N(16) **Southsea Castle Museum** A military and naval history museum, housed within Henry VIII's castle of 1539, including items salvaged from the wreck of Henry VIII's ship the *Mary Rose,* which sank in 1453.

I(17) **Square Tower** Dates from the time of Henry VIII and is surmounted by a bust of Charles I.

Eastney Beam Engine House Fine building housing Boulton and Watt reciprocal steam pumps installed 1887. Adjacent building of 1904 contains Crossley gas engines. 2½m E via Henderson Road (L)

Hospitals

B **Royal Portsmouth Hospital** *tel 22281*
H **St Mary's Hospital,** Milton Road – Artificial Limb and Appliance Centre *tel 29571;* General Practitioner Maternity Unit *tel 29695*

Sport and Recreation

F **Ambassador Tenpin Bowling Alley,** Arundel Street
H **Portsmouth Football Club,** Fratton Park, Southsea
E **United Services Sports Ground,** Burnaby Road (Cricket and Rugby)
F **Victoria Park Swimming Pool**
Portsmouth City Golf Course, Crookhorn Lane 4m E via Eastern Road A2030 (H)
Portsmouth Stadium, Target Road, Tipner (Greyhound Racing) 2½m N via A3 (B)

Theatres and Cinemas

B **ABC Cinema,** Commercial Road *tel 23538*
K **Kings Theatre,** Albert Road, Southsea *tel 28282*

F(8) **Guildhall Concert Hall** *tel 24355* (see also public buildings and places of interest)
K **Odeon Cinema,** Festing Road, Southsea *tel 32163*
F **Palace Cinema,** Guildhall Walk *tel 25029*

Department Stores

Debenhams, Palmerston Road, Southsea
Knight and Lee, Palmerston Road, Southsea
Landports Department Store, 134 Commercial Road

Marks and Spencer Ltd, 163 Commercial Road
Marks and Spencer Ltd, 41 London Road
Portsea Mutual Co-operative Society Ltd, Fratton Road
Early closing day Wednesday. Some shops in the Southsea area close all day Monday. Many stores remain open 6 days a week from May to September

Advertisers

J **Mercantile Credit**
B **Godfrey Davis**
I **Centre** Portsmouth Centre Hotel

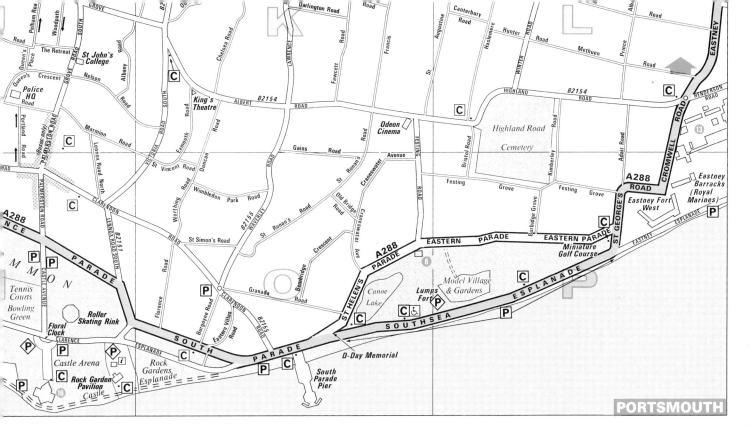

PORTSMOUTH

Boats in harbour

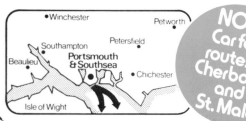

READING

I   **AA Service Centre** — 45 Oxford Road *tel 581122*

O (3)   **Tourist Information Centre** — Civic Offices, Civic Centre *tel 55911*
i

Public buildings and places of interest

J(1)   **Abbey Remains (AM)** The Benedictine abbey was founded in 1121 by Henry I, who was buried here in 1136. The abbey was one of the most important in the Kingdom in medieval times. After the dissolution in 1539 the abbey became a quarry for building materials.

J(2)   **Biscuit Factory** There are guided tours round the building.

O(3)   **Civic Offices and Tourist Information Centre** Adjacent to the Butts Shopping Centre.

Q(4)   **College of Technology**

I(5)   **Greyfriars Church** A flint church of the 14thC, with a fine west window.

X(6)   **Museum of English Rural Life, Whiteknights Park** A collection of highly interesting agricultural, domestic and craft exhibits, under the auspices of Reading University.

Q(7)   **Reading School**

J(8)   **St Laurence's Church** Dating from the 12thC, this church has a 111ft-high tower, a 16th-C font and interesting monuments.

I(9)   **St Mary's Church** Rebuilt in 1551, it contains a carved-oak gallery (1631) and a rebuilt organ which was at the Great London Exhibition of 1851.

J(10)   **Shire Hall, County Council Offices, Crown Court**

J(11)   **Town Hall, Museum, Art Gallery, Library and Information Centre** Collections of exhibits from the Roman town of Silchester. Also displays of the development of the Thames Valley.

X(12)   **University** The university, widely known for its Agricultural Faculty, received the Royal Charter in 1926, when located in the old buildings at London Road. Most of the university is now situated in the 600-acre Whiteknights Park.

Hospitals

G   **Battle Hospital,** 344 Oxford Road *tel 583666*

S   **Dellwood Maternity Home,** Leibenrood Road *tel 54266*

M   **Prospect Park Hospital,** Tilehurst *tel 54826*

Q   **Royal Berkshire Hospital,** 3 Craven Road *tel 85111*

Sport and Recreation

Q   **Arthur Hill Memorial Baths,** King's Road

H   **Central Swimming Baths,** Battle Street

U   **Coley Swimming Pool,** off Berkley Avenue

J   **King's Meadow Swimming Pool,** Caversham Lock

M   **Reading FC,** Elm Park, Norfolk Road

Calcot Park Golf Course, Calcot 3m W via Bath Road A4 (S)

Meadway Sports Centre, Dunsfold Road 3m W via Tilehurst Road and The Meadway (M)

Reading RUFC, Holme Park, Sonnings 3m E via London Road then B4446 (L)

Reading Stadium, Smallmead Road, 2m S via Basingstoke Road A33 (V)

Sonning Golf Course, Sonning 3½m E via London Road A4 (L)

Theatres and Cinemas

I   **ABC Cinema,** 25 Friar Street *tel 53931*

R   **ABC Cinema,** London Road, *tel 61465*

O   **Gaumont Cinema,** Oxford Road *tel 57887*

C   **Glendale Caversham Cinema,** 34 Church Street, Caversham *tel 471729*

I   **Odeon Theatre,** Cheapside *tel 57887*

P   **Studios 1 and 2,** 75 London Street *tel 51285*

Department Stores

The Co-operative, 18 Cheapside

Debenhams, Broad Street

Heelas, Broad Street

Knights, 100 Broad Street

Marks and Spencer Ltd, Broad Street

Early closing day — Some large stores close all day Monday, some small shops close half day Wednesday

Markets

I   **Great Knollys Street,** cattle (Monday)

O   **St Mary's Butts,** general (Saturday)

Advertisers

Q   **Mercantile Credit**

O   **Godfrey Davis**

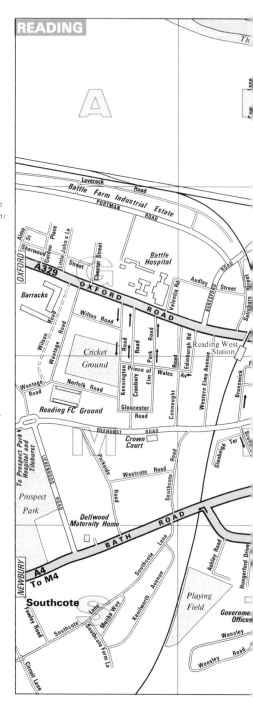

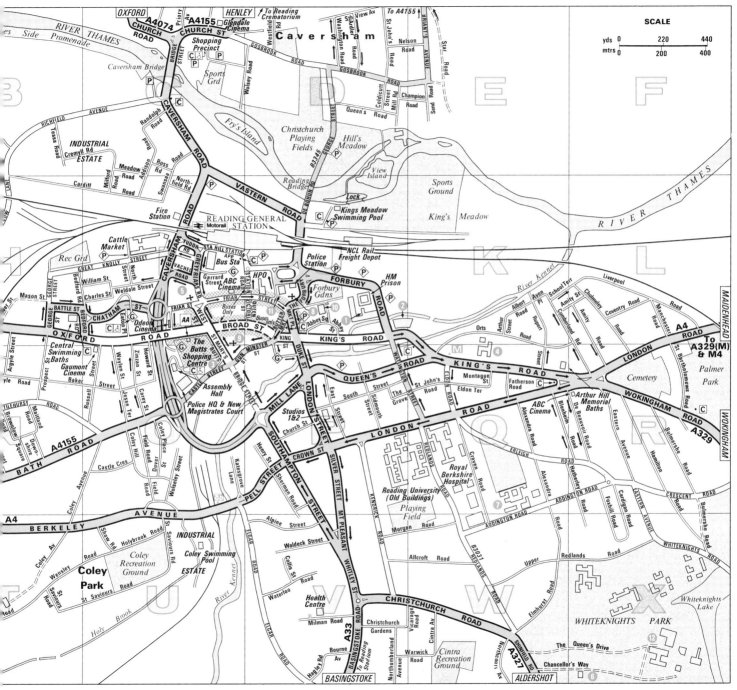

ROCHESTER & CHATHAM

A ⓘ **Tourist Information Centre** – 85 High Street (adjacent to Watts Charity Hospital) *tel Medway 43666*

Public buildings and places of interest

ROCHESTER

A(1) **Castle (AM)** The massive 104ft- high keep with its thick Kentish ragstone walls is one of the finest Norman military ruins in the country.

A(2) **Cathedral** Founded in 604, the present building dates from 1080. Among its notable features are the Norman West door, the 14th-C Decorated Chapter Room doorway, the large Early English crypt, and the 14th-C paintings on the choir walls.

E(3) **College of Art**

D(4) **Eastgate Museum** An Elizabethan house portrayed in Charles Dickens' *Edwin Drood* as the 'Nuns' House'. It now houses a museum of local and natural history including Dickensian items and relics of the Roman occupation. A portion of the Roman and Medieval walls stands nearby.

A(5) **Guildhall** An impressive red-brick building of 1687 standing on a series of Doric columns and surmounted by a copper weather vane of 1780 in the form of a full-rigged ship. The interior hall has fine panelling, an outstanding plaster ceiling and several interesting portraits.

D(6) **King's School** One of the oldest schools in England, founded in 604 and refounded by Henry VIII in 1542.

G(7) **Medway and Maidstone College of Technology**

A(8) **Old Corn Exchange** The unusual clock which projects from the 18th-C façade is referred to in two of Dickens' novels.

A(9) **Public Library and Information Bureau**

D(10) **Restoration House** Built 1587, and by tradition the place where Charles II stayed on his return to England for the Restoration in 1660. It houses some scale model steam locomotives.

D(11) **St Margaret's Church** Dates mainly from a rebuilding of 1823, but retains its fine 15th-C castellated tower.

A(12) **St Nicholas' Church** Dates originally from 1423, but rebuilt in 1624 and restored in 1862. Now partly used as Diocesan offices. It contains a curious octagonal font.

A(13) **Sailing Barge Cambria** One of the last of the famous Thames barges, now a floating museum.

A(14) **Watts Charity Hospital (Six Poor Travellers' House)** This building has Dickensian associations as the 'Seven Poor Travellers' Hostel'. Its foundation by Richard Watts dates from 1579, but the present building was erected in 1771.

Old Corn Exchange

CHATHAM

B(15) **HM Naval Dockyard** Guided tours are available, starting from the Pembroke Gate.

E(16) **St Bartholomew's Chapel** This is the chapel of the leper hospital founded in 1078, and is the oldest surviving building in the locality.

E(17) **St Mary's Parish Church** Parts of this church date from 1120.

E(18) **Sir John Hawkins' Hospital** Founded in 1592 and rebuilt in 1722.

F(19) **Gillingham Public Library and Information Bureau.**

Hospitals

I **All Saints Hospital**, Magpie Hall Road *tel Medway 41212*

I **Medway Hospital**, Windmill Road *tel Medway 46111*

E **St Bartholomews Hospital**, New Road *tel Medway 41511*

G **St Williams Hospital**, St Williams Way *tel Medway 44622*

Sport and Recreation

C **Black Lion Swimming Pool**, Brompton Road

C **County Cricket Ground**, Brompton Road

A **Open-air Swimming Pool**, The Esplanade, Rochester

C **Rugby Football**, United Services Ground, Brompton

Chatham Town Football Club, The Sports Ground, Maidstone Road 1m S via Maidstone Road A230 (H)

Greyhound Racing, Rochester Stadium, City Way 1¾m S via City Way A229 (G)

Theatres and Cinemas

F **ABC Cinema**, 385 High Street, Chatham *tel Medway 46756*

D **Odeon Cinema**, High Street, Rochester *tel Medway 43272*

Department Stores

ROCHESTER

Featherstone's Ltd, 375 High Street

CHATHAM

Bates Edward, 125 High Street
Harwood T C Ltd, 108 High Street
Marks and Spencer Ltd, 154 High Street
Early closing day Wednesday

Markets

A **Market**, Corporation Street, Rochester (Friday)

Note

The High Street Chatham, between Church Street and Railway Street, and between Railway Street and Manor Road is closed to traffic on Saturdays between 10.00 and 17.00hrs.

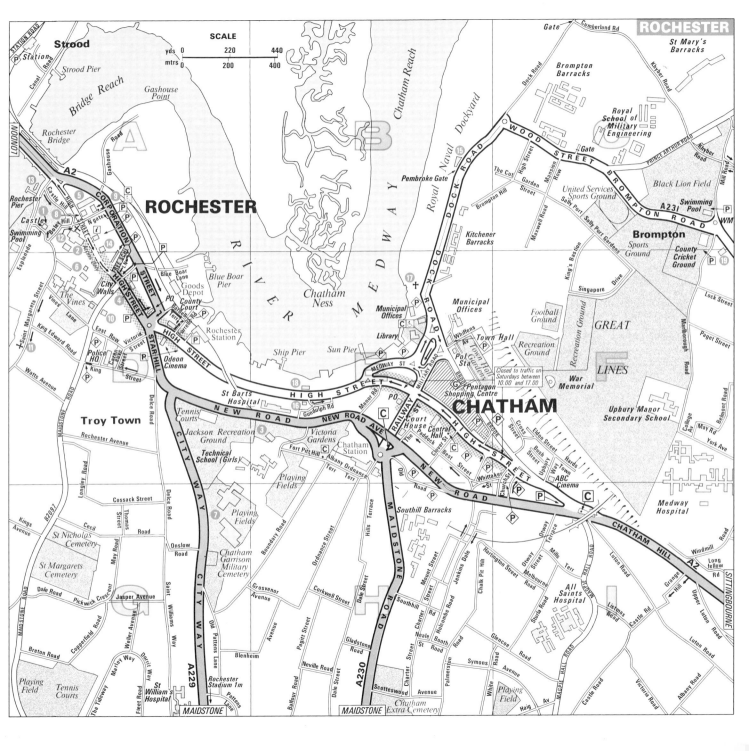

SALISBURY

G   **AA Road Service Centre (101)** — Central Car Park *tel 22246*

G⃞*i*   **Tourist Information Centre** — 10 Endless Street *tel 4956*

Public buildings and places of interest

K(1)   **Bishop's Palace** An old house, part of which dates back to the 13thC, which now houses the Cathedral Preparatory School.

K(2)   **Cathedral** Built over a period of 38 years from 1220, this Gothic-style Cathedral preserves a striking unity of design which was enhanced by the addition in 1334 of the decorated tower and spire (404ft). Also notable are the Cathedral cloisters, the largest in England; the chapter house; the medieval clock; and one of the three originals of the Magna Carta contained in the Cathedral Library.

K(3)   **Church House** A 15th-C house in Perpendicular style with garden frontage on the River Avon.

F(4)   **City Hall**

G(5)   **City Library** On the site of and retaining the façade of the Victorian corn exchange. Also housed here, on the first floor, are the Edwin Young Art Gallery and John Creasey Literary Museum.

G(6)   **Council House** A fine 18th-C building.

G(7)   **Guildhall** This dates back to 1795 and contains two courts of justice and a banqueting room.

K(8)   **Harnham Gate** One of the Cathedral Close gateways.

K(9)   **High Street Gate** A picturesque old gateway leading to the Cathedral precincts.

G(10)   **House of John A'Port and William Russell House** The former, built in 1425, is a fine example of 15th-C timber work both inside and out, and contains a 17th-C Jacobean oak-panelled room and fireplace. The latter, dating from 1306-1314, exposes two examples of wattle and daub infill. Today the two houses are the premises of Watson & Co's china shop.

G(11)   **John Halle's Hall** Preserved in the façade and foyer of the Odeon Cinema is this 15th-C banqueting hall, a splendid example of black and white timbering.

K(12)   **Joiners' Hall (NT)** Displays a timbered 16th-C façade.

K(13)   **King's Arms** An old inn with Civil War associations.

J(14)   **King's House** A late 14th-C house, one of the finest in the Cathedral Close, which is part of the College of Sarum St Michael.

K(15)   **Malmesbury House** A Queen Anne house dating in part from the 14thC, famous for its Baroque and Rococo plasterwork.

K(16)   **Mompesson House (NT)** A notable house of 1701 in the Cathedral Close, with splendid panelling, woodwork and plasterwork. Nearby is the old College of Matrons.

J(17)   **North Canonry** A 17th-C flint and stone house.

G(18)   **Poultry Cross** A cross dating from the 14thC.

K(19)   **St Ann's Gate** One of the Cathedral Close gateways.

G(20)   **St Edmund's Church** A Perpendicular structure, with a later tower of 1655, which is now used as an Arts Centre.

L(21)   **St Martin's Church** An early English to Perpendicular church, noted for its ribbed-timber roof, plaster panels and modern, painted glass.

K(22)   **St Nicholas Hospital** An old building, situated near Harnham Bridge and the River Avon.

G(23)   **St Thomas' Church** Early English to Perpendicular building, which is well known for its 15th-C 'doom' painting above the chancel arch.

K(24)   **Salisbury and South Wilts Museum** An exceptionally interesting museum of Wiltshire natural and social history, and archaeology, including models of Old Sarum and Stonehenge; pottery; costumes and crafts.

Old Sarum (AM) Originally an Iron Age camp, later a Roman fortress, and finally the site of a Norman castle and cathedral town. Foundations of the cathedral and castle can still be seen. 2m N via Castle Road A345 (C)

Wilton House A magnificent 16th- to 19th-C house, with 17th-C state apartments by Inigo Jones, including the famous 'Double Cube' Room; a world famous collection of paintings; furniture and sculpture and an exhibition of 7,000 miniature model soldiers. The grounds are noted for their giant cedars of Lebanon and the Palladian bridge of 1737. 3m W via Wilton Road and A36 (A)

Hospitals

N   **Harnwood Hospital**, Old Blandford Road *tel 4454*

O   **Newbridge Hospital**, Odstock Road *tel 5111*

O   **Odstock Hospital**, Odstock Road *tel 6262*

E   **Old Manor Hospital**, Wilton Road *tel 3216*

F   **Salisbury General Hospital**, Fisherton Street *tel 6212*

Sport and Recreation

C   **Salisbury Football Club**, Victoria Park, Castle Road

G   **Swimming Pool**, College Street

Salisbury Racecourse, Netherhampton 4½m W via Netherhampton Road A3094 and Netherhampton (I)

Theatres and Cinemas

G(11)   **Odeon Cinema**, New Canal *tel 22080* (see also John Halle's Hall under public buildings and places of interest)

F   **Playhouse Theatre**, Fisherton Street *tel 22104* (moving to new premises in the Central Car Park during 1977)

Department Stores

Blooms, New Canal
Debenhams, Blue Boar Row
Marks and Spencer Ltd, New Canal
Woodrows of Salisbury Ltd, 9 Queens Street
Wessex Co-operative, 7-15 Winchester Street
Early closing day Wednesday

Markets

B   **Cattle Market** (Tuesday)

G   **Market Place** (Tuesday and Saturday)

Advertisers

G   **Godfrey Davis**

K   **THF** White Hart Hotel

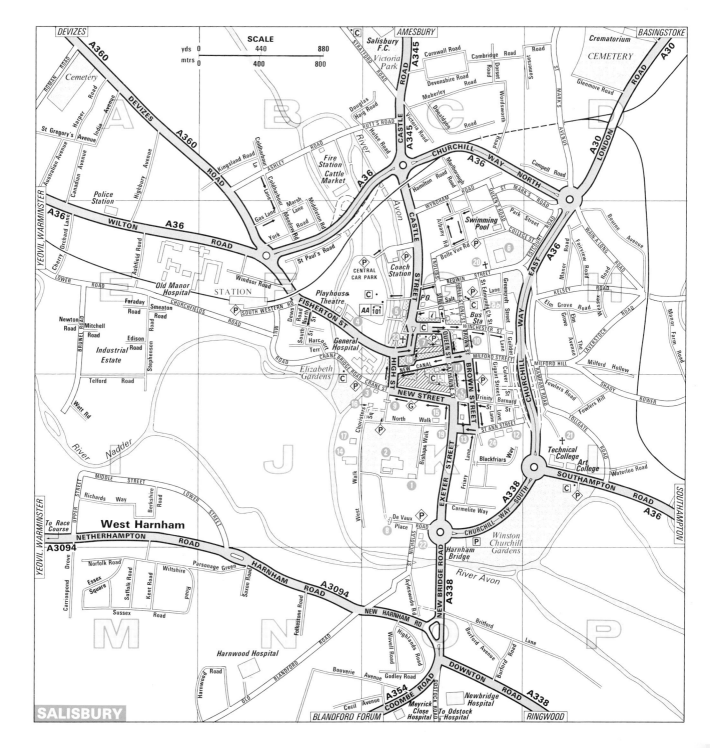

SCARBOROUGH

H   **AA Road Service Centre (74)** — West Pier *tel 60344*

K $\boxed{i}$ **Tourist Information Centre** — St Nicholas Cliff *tel 72261*

Public buildings and places of interest

K(1)   **Art Gallery** Contains a permanent collection by local artists and the Laughton collection (English school). Also frequent loan exhibitions.

H(2)   **Castle** Situated on a headland dividing the North and South Bays, the castle is notable for its 12th-C keep, the 13th-C barbican, and the long, curtain walls. In the castleyard are the remains of a 4th-C Roman signal station.

O(3)   **Italian and Holbeck Gardens**

K(4)   **Londesborough Lodge** A museum of bygones and Scarborough history.

B(5)   **Northstead Manor Gardens** Contains the Scarborough Zoo and Marineland, miniature railway (longest of its kind in Britain), an adventure playground and Open Air Theatre. Among the zoo's attractions are performing dolphins and sea lions and a display entitled 'Land of the Dinosaurs' with life-size models.

B(6)   **Planetarium** Housed in an interesting octagonal-shaped building with a hemispherical dome 17ft in diameter, onto which the night sky is projected.

K(7)   **Public Library and Library Theatre**

K(8)   **Rotunda Museum** Regional archaeology.

H(9)   **St Mary's Church** A Transitional-Norman and Early-English church, with old chantry chapels, and in the churchyard the grave of Anne Brontë.

H(10)   **Three Mariners** Once an inn, this old house dates from 1300. It now houses a fishermen's craft centre and museum.

K(11)   **Town Hall**

K(12)   **Wood End** A former home of the Sitwell family, situated in charming gardens, with a collection of first editions and portraits of this literary family. Also contained here are a natural history museum, a Yorkshire geological collection and an aquarium.

Hospitals

F   **St Mary's Hospital** *tel 76111*

G   **St Thomas Hospital**, Foreshore *tel 74347*

Sport and Recreation

B   **North Bay Swimming Pool**

A   **Northstead Indoor Swimming Pool**

B   **Scarborough Cricket Club Ground**, North Marine Road

L   **Scarborough Yacht Club**, Lighthouse Pier

P   **South Bay Swimming Pool**

Motor Cycle Racing, Olivers Mount Circuit 1¾m S via Filey Road A165 (O)

North Cliff Golf Club, 1¾m N via Columbus Ravine and Burniston Road A165 (A)

Scarborough Football Club, Athletic Ground, Seamer Road 1¼m SW via Westborough and Seamer Road A64 (M)

Scarborough Sports Centre, Filey Road 1m S via Filey Road A165 (O)

South Cliff Golf Club 1¾m S via Filey Road A165 (O)

Theatres and Cinemas

J   **Capitol Cinema**, Albermarle Crescent *tel 65708*

B   **Floral Hall**, Alexandra Gardens *tel 73039*

K   **Futurist Cinema**, Foreshore Road *tel 60644*

K(7)   **Library Theatre**, Vernon Road *tel 74279* (see also public buildings and places of interest)

J   **Odeon Cinema**, Westborough *tel 61725*

B(5)   **Open Air Theatre**, Northstead Manor Gardens (see also public buildings and places of interest)

O   **The Spa Theatre**, Spa Gardens *tel 65068*

Department Stores

Boyes W and Co Ltd, Queen Street
Debenhams Ltd, 31 Westborough
Marks and Spencer Ltd, 7 Newborough
Early closing day Monday or Wednesday

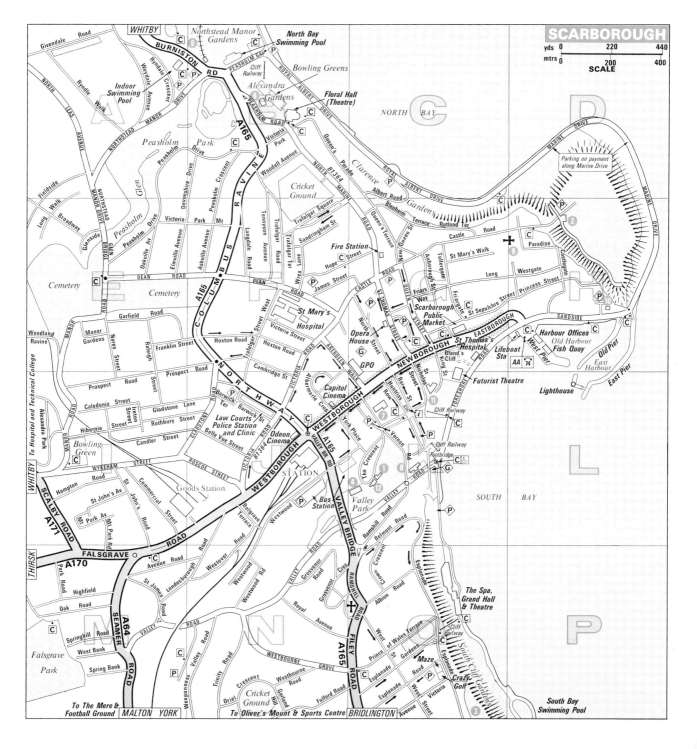

SHEFFIELD

CENTRAL PLAN

B　**AA Service Centre** — Fanum House, 2 Fargate *tel 28861*

G(7)　**Tourist Information Centre** — Civic
[i]　Information Service, Central Library, Surrey Street *tel 734768* (see also public buildings and places of interest)

Public buildings and places of interest

B(1)　**Cathedral** The cathedral church of Saint Peter and Saint Paul was formerly the parish church and dates from the 14th and 15thCs. The 16th-C Shrewsbury Chapel contains fine monuments. A new chapel was consecrated in 1948.

B(2)　**City Hall** Built from Darley Dale stone in 1932 it has six halls for meetings and concerts. Of note are the Oval Hall, seating over 2,600 people and the Memorial Hall, a memorial to the fallen of the First World War.

C(3)　**Crucible Theatre** A modern theatre built in 1971.

B(4)　**Cutlers' Hall** A Grecian-style building dating from 1832. It contains the Cutlers' Company collection of silver plate, with examples of craftsmanship dating from 1773. The historic Cutlers' Feast, dating from the early 17thC, is held here annually.

B(5)　**Former Girls' Charity School** An attractive pedimented house built in 1786.

B(6)　**Georgian houses in Paradise Square**

G(7)　**Graves Art Gallery, Central Library and Tourist Information Centre** The Central Library, dating from 1934, is one of the finest in the country and is officially approved as a repository for manorial records and other historical documents. The Graves Art Gallery, in the same building, has examples of Italian, English, and French painting, and collections of Chinese, Indian, Islamic and African Art.

G(8)　**Technical College**

F(9)　**Town Hall** Contains the Lord Mayor's Parlour, the Council Chamber, and administrative offices. It dates from 1897 and has a tower 193ft high and an impressive grand staircase.

A(10)　**University** Dating from 1905 the university has nine faculties. Recent development includes a 19-storey Arts Tower.

Hospitals

A　**Jessop Hospital**, Leavygreave Road *tel 29291*

F　**Royal Hospital**, West Street *tel 20063*

Sport and Recreation

D　**Hyde Park Stadium**, Manor Oaks Road — greyhound racing

G　**Sheaf Valley Indoor Swimming Baths**

J　**Sheffield United Association Football Club**, Bramall Lane

K　**Silver Blades Ice Rink**, Queens Road

Theatres and Cinemas

C　**ABC Cinema**, Angel Street *tel 24620*

K　**Alhambra Music Hall**, Queens Road *tel 70696*

C　**Cinecenta**, Pond Street *tel 77939*

F　**Cineplex**, Charter Square *tel 70778*

C　**Classic Cinema**, Fitzalan Square *tel 25624*

C(3)　**The Crucible Theatre**, Norfolk Street *tel 79922*

F　**Gaumont Twin Cinemas**, Barkers Pool *tel 77962*

G(7)　**Library Theatre**, Tudor Place *tel 734716*

Department Stores

John Atkinson, The Moor
Cole Brothers Ltd, Barkers Pool
Marks and Spencer Ltd, Fargate
Marks and Spencer Ltd, 76 The Moor
Pauldens Ltd, 2 The Moor
Schofields (Yorkshire) Ltd, Angel Street
Walsh's of Sheffield, 50 High Street
Wilson, Tupholme Ltd, 290 Pitsmoor Road
Early closing day — markets and small shops close on Thursday

Markets

C　**Castle Market**, Exchange Street, general (each weekday except Thursday)

J　**Open Markets**, The Setts and Moorfoot, general (Tuesday, Friday and Saturday)

C　**Sheaf Market**, Dixon Lane, general (each weekday except Thursday)

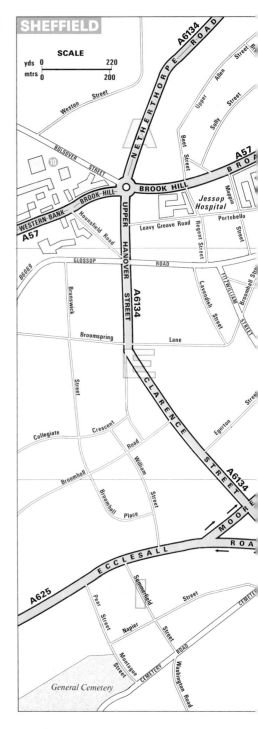

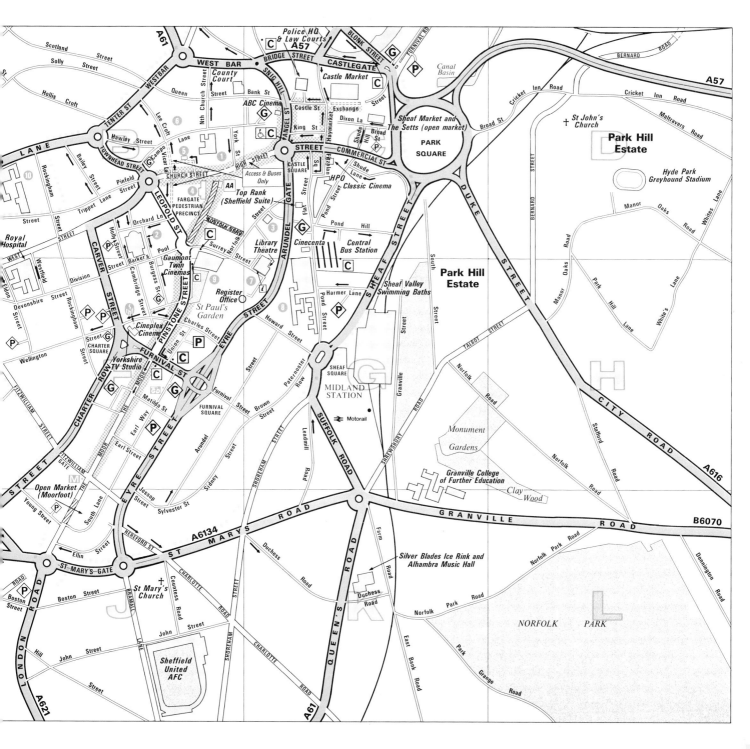

Advertisers

F   Mercantile Credit
F   Godfrey Davis
F   THF Grosvenor House

DISTRICT PLAN

Public buildings and places of interest

N(11)   **Bishops House** A picturesque, restored timber-framed yeoman's house of c1500.

I(12)   **Botanical Gardens** The well laid out gardens cover an area of 18 acres. There is also an aviary and an aquarium.

I(13)   **City Museum** A regional museum of geology, natural history, archaeology, and Sheffield area trades. The cutlery section is famous, including European and Sheffield work from the 16thC and the world's largest collection of Sheffield plate. Associated with the City Museum is Shepherd Wheel at Whiteley Wood, a preserved example of a Sheffield 'little mester's' water powered grinding shop. Adjacent is the Mappin Art Gallery which contains British paintings and sculpture from the 18th to 20thCs.

K(14)   **Manor Lodge** Part of Sheffield Castle, the Turret House was thought to have been built to house Mary, Queen of Scots, in the 14 years she was imprisoned in the castle.

Abbeydale Industrial Hamlet 4m SW via Abbeydale Road A621. Sited at Abbeydale is the Abbeydale Industrial Hamlet, an 18th- and early 19th-C steel and scythe works now open to the public and one of the first examples of industrial archaeology preservation. Nearby in Abbey Lane stand the ruins of Beauchief Abbey, founded in 1175. (M)

Hospitals

I   **Charles Clifford Dental Hospital,** Wellesley Road *tel 663251*
I   **Children's Hospital,** Western Bank *tel 71111*
E   **Commonside Hospital,** Commonside *tel 662557*
I   **Hallamshire Hospital,** Glossop Road *tel 26484*
A   **Middlewood Hospital** *tel 349491*
M   **Nether Edge Hospital** *tel 56371*
B   **Northern General Hospital** *tel 387009*

F   **Royal Infirmary,** Infirmary Road *tel 20977*
I   **Weston Park Hospital,** Whitham Road *tel 686071*
I   **Winter Street Hospital** *tel 28881*

Sport and Recreation

C   **Concorde Sports Centre,** Shire Green Lane
A   **Hillsborough Golf Club,** Worrall Road
N   **Lees Hall Golf Club,** Hemsworth Road, Norton
B   **Open Air Swimming Pool,** Longley Park, Crowder Road
E   **Owlerton Stadium,** Penistone Road — greyhound racing and speedway racing
A   **Sheffield Wednesday Football Club,** Hillsborough
H   **Tinsley Park Golf Course,** Tinsley

Department Stores

Hitchins Retail Store, 602 Attercliffe Road
Wades Departmental Stores Ltd, Manor House, Ecclesall Road South

Markets

K   **Abbatoir and Meat Market,** Cricket Inn Road
K   **Parkway Wholesale Fruit and Vegetable Market,** Markets Road

Advertisers

I   THF Hallam Tower Hotel

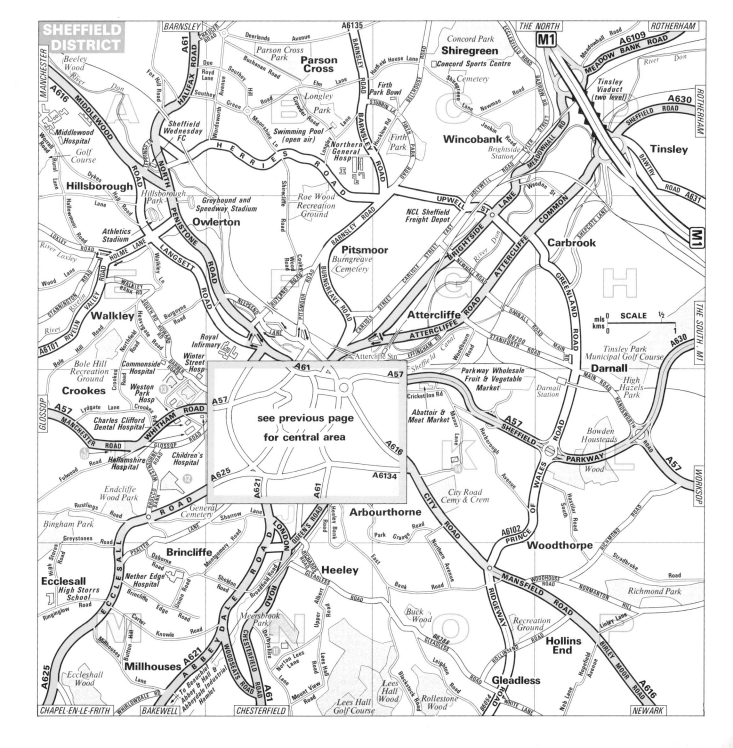

AA Road Service Centre (53) — Oteley Road *tel 53003.* 1¾m SE via A458 (0)

M(15) **Tourist Information Centre** — The
ⓘ Square *tel 52019* (see also public buildings and places of interest)

Public buildings and places of interest

O(1) **Abbey Church** A fine Norman and Perpendicular church containing monuments of interest including an effigy of the founder, Roger de Montgomery.

H(2) **Abbot's House** One of the finest of the old houses in the town.

H(3) **Bear Steps** Recently-restored, timber-framed, 14th-C cottages with shops and a meeting hall. The Hall has a mid-14th-C crown-post roof.

H(4) **Butcher Row** An attractive street of old houses continued in Fish Street.

D(5) **Castle** Partly-13th-C, but converted during the 18thC into a house, and now used as a Council Chamber.

B(6) **Charles Darwin's Birthplace** A house known as the Mount, where Darwin was born in 1809.

M(7) **Clive House (Museum)** A Georgian house of architectural interest, once occupied by Clive of India and now housing a collection of pottery and porcelain.

O(8) **Coleham Pumping Station** The building and its two beam engines are now preserved as a museum.

I(9) **Draper's Hall** One of Shrewsbury's old half-timbered houses.

H(10) **Grope Lane** A picturesque and particularly narrow little alley.

N(11) **Guildhall**

H(12) **Ireland's Mansion** A fine, half-timbered house of the late 16thC.

D(13) **Library**

B(14) **Millington Hospital** A range of fine brick-built almshouses dating from 1748.

M(15) **Music Hall and Tourist Information Centre**

D(16) **Old Council House Gateway** This fine, half-timbered gateway is of 17th-C date.

M(17) **Old Market Hall** A fine Elizabethan structure of 1595.

G(18) **Rowley's House** A notable, restored half-timbered house, now a museum of Roman remains excavated from Wroxeter.

H(19) **St Alkmund's Church** A church of 1795 with an earlier spire, 174ft high.

G(20) **St Chad's Church** Dates from 1792, the nave being in the form of a rotunda.

M(21) **St Julian's Church** Preserves an old tower, the remainder of the church dating mainly from 1750.

I(22) **St Mary's Church** A fine 12th- to 17th-C church, noted for its old Herkenrode glass, and a Jesse window.

AN HISTORIC TOWN IN A COUNTRY SETTING

FREE MINI-GUIDE or 30p for OFFICIAL GUIDE from DEPT 5 INFORMATION CENTRE

SHREWSBURY

A MARKET TOWN IN A COUNTRY SETTING

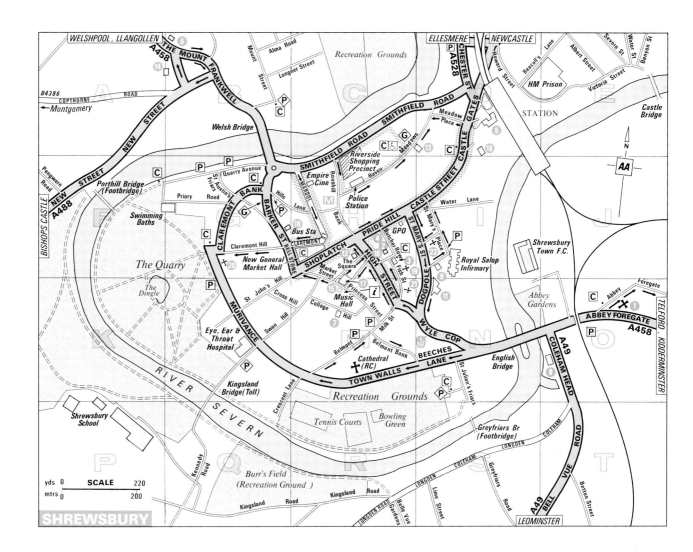

Hospitals

L   **Eye, Ear and Throat Hospital** *tel 55771*
I   **Royal Salop Infirmary** *tel 53931*

Sport and Recreation

G   **Shrewsbury Swimming Baths,** Priory Road
I   **Shrewsbury Town Football Club,** The Gay
Meadow

Theatres and Cinemas

H   **Empire Cinema,** Mardol *tel 62257*
M(15) **Music Hall** The Square *tel 52019*
(see also public buildings and places
of interest)

Department Stores

Marks and Spencer Ltd, 5 Castle Street
Owen Owen Ltd, Pride Hill
Rackhams (Harrods) Ltd, 37 High Street
Wades, Mardol Block, Market Hall

Markets

H   **General Market** (Monday to Saturday,
but main market days Wednesday and
Saturday)

Advertisers

H   **Mercantile Credit**
N   **THF** Lion Hotel

SOUTHAMPTON

CENTRAL PLAN

B   **AA Service Centre** – Fanum House, 11
The Avenue *tel 36811*

S   **AA Port Service Centre** – No. 9 Berth
(entrance via no. 2 gate, Canute Road),
Southampton Docks *tel 28304*

S i   **Tourist Information Centres** – Canute
Road (opposite Dock Gate 3) *tel 20438*
(National)

J i   **The Precinct,** Above Bar Street *tel*
23855 ext 615 (Local)

Public buildings and places of interest

N(1) **Arundel or Wind Whistle Tower (AM)**
One of the towers of the City Walls,
which dates from the Norman period.

N(2) **Bargate (AM)** Originally a Norman
construction, but with later additions
including the Edwardian drum towers.
The upper-storey contains the former
Guildhall, now a museum of local
interest which includes a fine D-day
embroidery recording Southampton's
involvement in World War Two.

N(3) **Catchcold Tower (AM)** At the North-
West corner of the City Walls.

J(4) **Cenotaph**

J(5) **Civic Centre, Guildhall, Library and
Art Gallery** A modern group of buildings
in Portland stone, built 1932-39 and
surmounted by a very prominent clock-
tower. The Art Gallery includes 18th-
to 20th-C British paintings, continental
Old Masters and modern French paintings.
Also temporary exhibitions.

J(6) **College of Art**

J(7) **College of Technology** Contains the
Mountbatten Theatre.

R(8) **God's House and God's Gate** God's House,
or Hospital, was founded in 1185, and
contains the restored Norman chapel of
St Julian. God's Gate c1300 adjoins the
God's House Tower.

R(9) **God's House Tower** Dating from the
early 15thC and part of the ancient
city walls, this tower now contains
an archaeological museum containing
local prehistoric, Roman, Saxon and
Medieval finds.

N(10) **Holy Rood Church** Only the 14th-C tower

of this church survived intact the
bombing of 1940. The ruins are now
preserved as a memorial to men of the
Merchant Navy who lost their lives
during the Second World War.

R(11) **Mayflower Park with Memorials** The
Pilgrim Fathers' Memorial, which stands
opposite the park on the Western
Esplanade recalls the sailing of the
Mayflower from the West Quay on 15
August 1620.

N(12) **Polymond Tower** One of the towers of the
City Walls which stands at the north-
east corner.

O(13) **St Mary's Church** Restored and re-
dedicated in 1956. It was the origin
of the song 'The Bell's of St Mary's'.

N(14) **St Michael's Church** The oldest church
in the city, with parts dating back to
1070. The tall, slender spire was added
in the 19thC and serves as a landmark
for ships in Southampton water.
Preserved here is a rare 12th-C black
marble Tournai font.

F(15) **Titanic Memorial** A memorial to the
engineers of the famous liner which
struck an iceberg in 1912.

N(16) **Tudor House Museum** A restored half-
timbered, 16th-C mansion containing
a fine oak-panelled banqueting hall
with minstrel's gallery, and exhibits
of antiquarian and historical interest
including furniture, decorative arts,
paintings of Southampton and musical
instruments. There is access through
the garden to a Norman Merchant's
house, dating from c1175.

N(17) **West Gate** Dating from the 13thC, it
led to the old West Quay, from where
the Mayflower sailed.

R(18) **Wool House Maritime Museum** A fine
example of a 14th-C warehouse, with
buttressed stone walls and old roof
timbering, containing an impressive
maritime museum including models of
great ships.

City Walls These date back to the 12thC but have
more recent additions. The best preserved
sections extend from the Arundel Tower
southwards to the Town Quay. The notable
arcaded sections of the wall are best seen near the
southern part of the Esplanade.

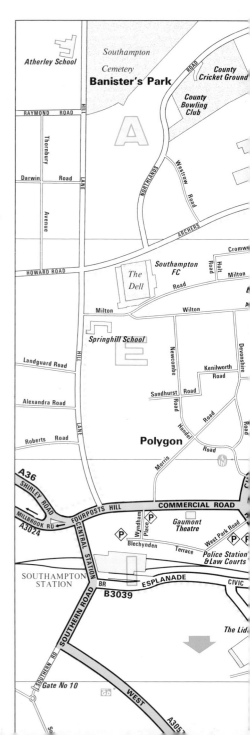

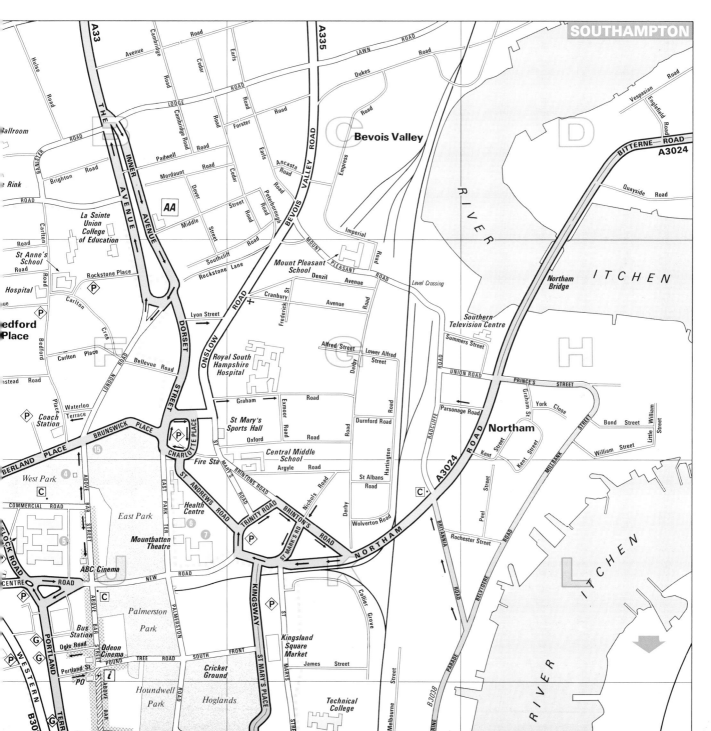

Hospitals

G   **Royal South Hants Hospital**, Fanshawe Street *tel 34288*

F   **Southampton Eye Hospital**, Wilton Avenue *tel 22208*

Sport and Recreation

N   **Central Baths**, Western Esplanade

A   **Hampshire County Cricket Club**, Northlands Road

I   **Lido**, Western Esplanade

F   **St Mary's Sports Hall**, St Mary's Road

E   **Southampton Football and Athletic Club**, The Dell, Milton Road

A   **Top Rank Ice Skating**, Banister Road

Theatres and Cinemas

J   **ABC Cinemas 1 and 2**, Forum Buildings, Above Bar Street *tel 23536*

I   **Gaumont Theatre (Cinema)**, Commercial Road *tel 29772*

J(5)   **Guildhall**, Civic Centre *tel 32601* (see also public buildings and places of interest)

J(7)   **Mountbatten Theatre**, College of Technology (see also public buildings and places of interest)

J   **Odeon Cinema**, Above Bar Street *tel 22243*

Department Stores

Co-operative Retail Services, Above Bar Street
Debenhams, Queens Buildings, Queensway
Marks and Spencer Ltd, Above Bar Street
Owen Owen Ltd, 173 High Street
Plummers, Above Bar Street
Tyrrell and Green Ltd, 138 Above Bar Street
Early closing day Wednesday, or all day closing Monday, but many shops remain open six days a week

Markets

K   **St Mary's Street Market**, Kingsland Square — mainly fruit and vegetables (Friday and Saturday)

Advertisers

N   **Mercantile Credit**

N   **THF** Dolphin Hotel

E   **THF** Polygon Hotel

R   **THF** Post House

M   **Godfrey Davis**

N   **Centre** Arundel Centre Inn

Civic Centre

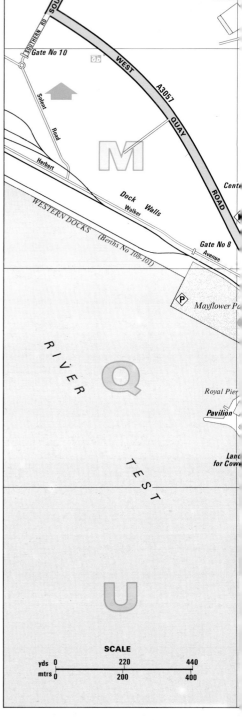

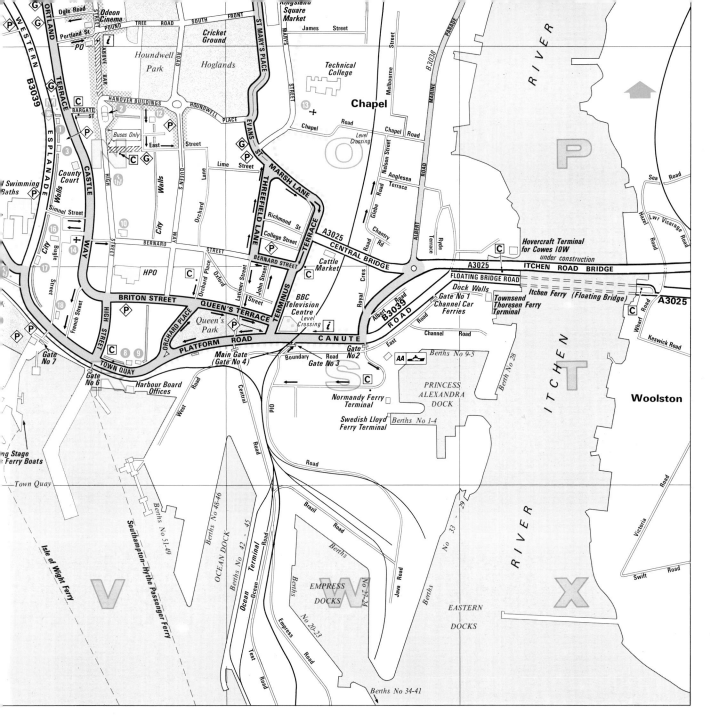

DISTRICT PLAN

Public buildings and places of interest

H(19) **Nuffield Theatre,** University of Southampton. This building was designed by Sir Basil Spence.

B(20) **Sports Centre** Covers approximately 270 acres and caters for a wide range of outdoor sports. It is considered to be one of the finest of its kind in the Commonwealth.

H(21) **University of Southampton** Dates from 1902 when it was the Hartley University College. It became a university by Royal Charter in 1952. Recent expansion includes many fine buildings designed by Sir Basil Spence.

H(22) **Zoological Gardens,** Southampton Common. Small but attractively laid out zoo, with comprehensive collection of animals and birds.

Hospitals

C **Fred Wooley House** (Royal South Hants Hospital Annexe), Winchester Road, Chilworth *tel 68524*

J **Moorgreen Hospital,** West End *tel West End 2258*

G **Southampton General Hospital,** Tremona Road *tel 777222*

G **Southampton Western Hospital,** Oakley Road, Millbrook *tel 771042*

Sport and Recreation

N **Bitterne Tenpin Bowling Alley,** Bitterne Road

C **Southampton Corporation Golf Course**

B(20) **Sports Centre** (see also public buildings and places of interest)

C **Stoneham Golf Club,** Bassett Green Road

N **Weston Cricket Ground,** Weston Lane, Woolston

Theatres and Cinemas

H(19) **Nuffield Theatre,** University Road *tel 555028* (see also public buildings and places of interest)

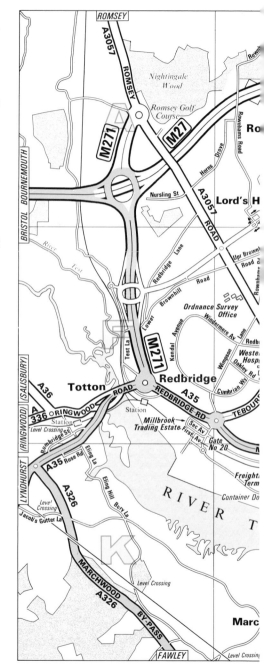

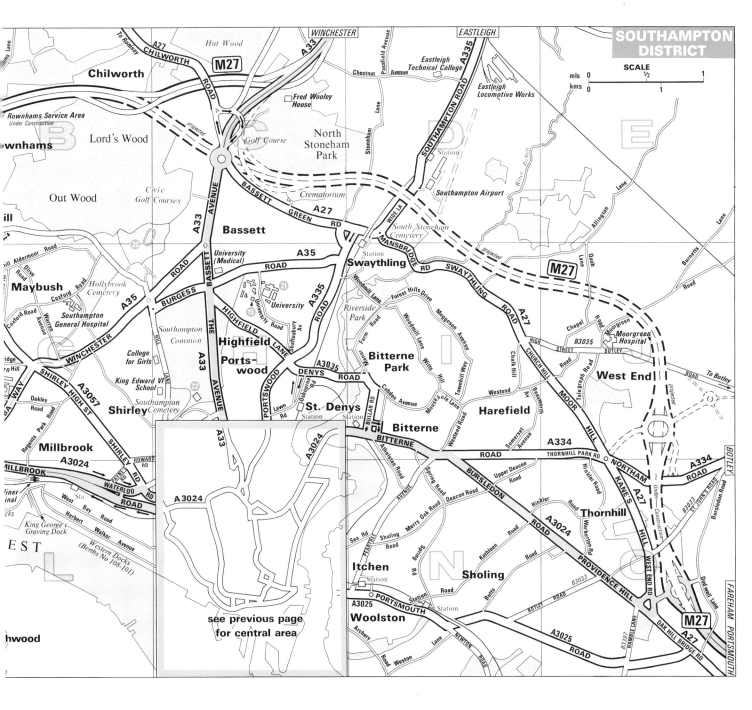

SOUTHAMPTON DISTRICT

SCALE

mls 0 ½ 1
kms 0 1

WINCHESTER
EASTLEIGH

To Romsey
A27 CHILWORTH ROAD
M27
Chilworth
Hut Wood
A33

Eastleigh Technical College
A335
Passfield Avenue
Chestnut Avenue

Eastleigh Locomotive Works

Rownhams Service Area Under Construction
Lord's Wood
Fred Wooley House
North Stoneham Park
Stoneham Lane
Station

wnhams

Out Wood
projected
Golf Course
Civic Golf Courses
Crematorium
A27
BASSETT GREEN RD
River Itchen

Southampton Airport

ll
20
A33 ROAD
A33 BASSETT AVENUE
Bassett
WIDE LA
South Stoneham Cemetery
MANSBRIDGE

M27
M27

Aldermoor Road
Olive Road
Hollybrook Cemetery
University (Medical)
A35
ROAD
Station
Swaythling
RD SWAYTHLING ROAD
A27

Maybush
Coxford Road
BURGESS ROAD
A35
University Road
19
University
21
Shaftesbury Av
A335 ROAD
Woodmill Lane
Forest Hills Drive
Chapel Road
B3035
Moorgreen Moorgreen Hospital

Coxford Road
Warren Avenue
Southampton General Hospital
College for Girls
Southampton Common
THE AVENUE
HIGHFIELD LANE
Highfield
Riverside Park
Farm Road
Woodmill Lane
Mousehole Lane
Magdalen Avenue
Chalk Hill
HIGH STREET
BOTLEY
Telegraph Road

dge
m Hill
WINCHESTER
A3057
SHIRLEY HIGH ST
A33 LANE
Portswood
Portswood
A3035
DENYS ROAD
Bitterne Park
Witts Hill
Townhill Way
Westend
CHURCH HILL
West End
To Botley
ROAD

WAY
Oakley Road
Regents Park Road
Shirley
King Edward VI School
Southampton Cemetery
22
Lawn Rd
Osbourne Rd
St. Denys Station
BULLAR RD
Cobden Avenue
Av
Beauworth
Av
Somerset Avenue
Westend
MOOR HILL
NORTHAM
A334 ROAD
BOTLEY

Millbrook
A3024
HOWARD RD
WATERLOO RD
PAYNES RD
SHIRLEY RD
A33
A3024
Athelstan Road
Bitterne
BITTERNE ROAD
Westend Road
THORNHILL PARK RD
A334
A27 WEST END RD
BOTLEY
FAREHAM PORTSMOUTH

MILLBROOK
A3024
West Bay Road
Herbert Walker Avenue
Sta
ROAD
A3024
see previous page for central area
Spring Road
BURSLEDON
Upper Deacon Road
Hinkler Road
KANE'S HILL
ST JOHN'S ROAD
Bursledon Road

iner inal
cks
King George V Graving Dock
Western Docks (Berths No 108-101)
AVENUE
PEARTREE
Sea Rd
Sholing Road
Merry Oak Road
Deacon Road
Hinkler Road
Warburton Rd
A3024
Thornhill
B3033
Dodwell Lane
Under Construction
M27

EST
L
Itchen
Station
Spring Rd
Butts
Kathleen Road
Sholing
PROVIDENCE HILL
B3033
OAK HILL BRIDGE RD

hwood
7
A3025 PORTSMOUTH
Woolston
Station
Archery Road
NEWTON ROAD
Weston Lane
BOTLEY ROAD
A3025 ROAD
HAMBLE LANE
B2397

201

Public buildings and places of interest

F(1) **Gower Memorial Statue** A statue of Shakespeare flanked by four of his characters.

E(2) **Grammar School and Guildhall** A 15th-C half-timbered range of buildings. The original Guildhall occupies the ground floor and the upper hall has been used by the Grammar School since the Guild was suppressed.

E(3) **Guild Chapel** A 13th- to 15th-C chapel built for the Guild of the Holy Cross which contains the remains of a series of wall paintings.

H(4) **Hall's Croft** A Tudor house with a walled garden, this was the former home of Shakespeare's daughter Susanna and her husband Dr John Hall.

E(5) **Harvard House** A half-timbered house dating from 1596, the former home of the mother of the founder of Harvard University in the USA, John Harvard.

H(6) **Holy Trinity Church** The Church contains the tomb of and a monument to Shakespeare. The Church itself has a number of interesting features.

E(7) **Judith Shakespeare House and Tourist Information Centre** The former home of Shakespeare's daughter, Judith Quiney.

E(8) **Louis Tussaud's** Shakespearian play scenes in wax.

E(9) **Mason Croft, Shakespeare Institute** An early- 18th-C brick building which was the home of the novelist, Marie Corelli and is now a study and lecture centre for the University of Birmingham.

E(10) **New Place Estate** Foundations of Shakespeare's house and a replica of an Elizabethan garden. Furniture and local history exhibits are displayed in the adjacent Nash's House.

E(11) **Royal Shakespeare Theatre**

E(12) **Royal Shakespeare Theatre Picture Gallery and Museum** The gallery contains portraits of Shakespeare, and famous Shakespearian actors and actresses, in addition to other theatrical relics.

B(13) **Shakespeare Centre** The headquarters of the Shakespeare Birthplace Trust which contains a specialised library and study centre.

E(14) **Shakespeare's Birthplace** A 16th-C half-timbered building which contains many relics connected with the poet's life, time and works.

B(15) **Stratford Motor Museum** A former Victorian church and school which displays cars and relics in period settings. The museum specialises in exotic sports, and grand touring cars.

E(16) **Town Hall** A dignified building dedicated to the memory of Shakespeare by the famous actor David Garrick in 1769.

Hall's Croft

Anne Hathaway's Cottage, Shottery. The thatched and timbered Elizabethan cottage, where Anne Hathaway, who became Shakespeare's wife, was born. 1½m W via Shottery Road or Footpath (D)

Mary Arden's House A picturesque half-timbered Tudor building which was the birthplace of Shakespeare's mother. A farming museum is housed in the barns. 3¾m NW via Birmingham Road A34 (A)

Hospitals

A **Stratford-upon-Avon General Hospital,** Alcester Road *tel 5831*

Sport and Recreation

F **Stratford-upon-Avon Boat Club,** The Boat House

I **Stratford-upon-Avon Cricket, Hockey and Squash Club**

C **Stratford-upon-Avon Swimming Pool**

D **Stratford-upon-Avon Town Football Club,** Alcester Road

Stratford-upon-Avon Golf Club. 1m NE via Tiddington Road B4086 (F)

Stratford-upon-Avon Racecourse, Luddington Road. ½m SW via Evesham Road A439 (G)

Stratford-upon-Avon Rugby Club, Pearcecroft, Loxley Road (F)

Theatres and Cinemas

E(11) **Royal Shakespeare Theatre** *tel 2271* (see also public buildings and places of interest)

D **Stratford-upon-Avon Picture House,** Greenhill Street *tel 2622*

E **The Other Place,** Southern Lane *tel 2565*

Department Stores

Debenhams, High Street
Winters, High Street
Early closing day Thursday

Markets

D **Cattle Market** (Tuesday and Friday)

E **General Market,** Rother Street (Friday)

Advertisers

E **THF** White Swan Hotel

E **THF** Shakespeare Hotel

F **THF** Alveston Manor

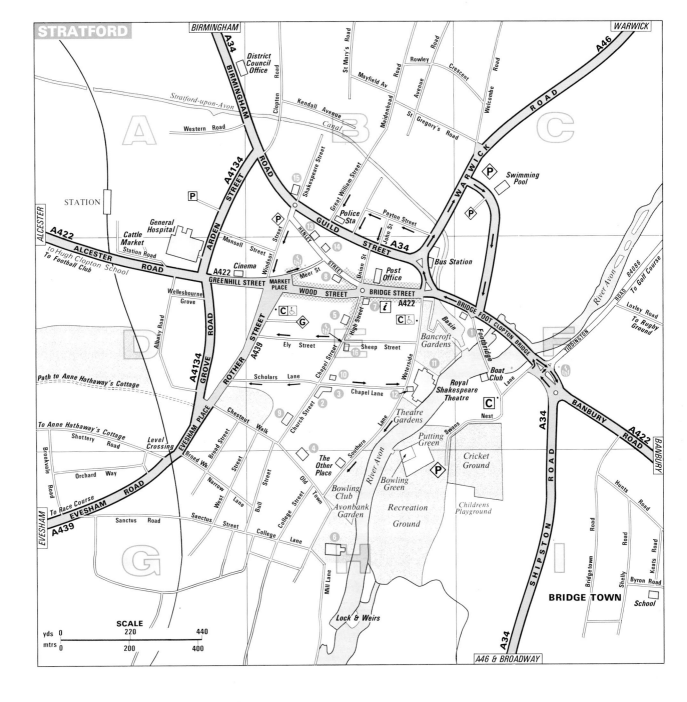

STRATFORD

BIRMINGHAM A34

WARWICK A46

District Council Office

Clopton Road

St Mary's Road

Rowley Road

Crescent

Welcombe Road

Stratford-upon-Avon Canal

Kendall Avenue

Mayfield Av

Maidenhead Road

Avenue

St Gregory's Road

Western Road

ALCESTER A422

STATION

ALCESTER ROAD

A422

to Hugh Clopton School
To Football Club

Cattle Market

General Hospital

Station Road

Mansell Street

Shakespeare Street

Great William Street

Police Sta

Payton Street

John St

A34

Swimming Pool

BIRMINGHAM ROAD

ARDEN STREET

A4134

Windsor Street

Hetley Street

GUILD STREET

Bus Station

WARWICK ROAD

A422 Cinema

GREENHILL STREET

Wellesbourne Grove

Albany Road

MARKET PLACE

Meer St

WOOD STREET

Union St

Post Office

BRIDGE STREET

A422

River Avon

B4086
To Golf Course

Loxley Road
To Rugby Ground

BRIDGE FOOT CLOPTON BRIDGE

Basin

Bancroft Gardens

Boat Club

TIDDINGTON

GROVE ROAD A4134

Path to Anne Hathaway's Cottage

ROTHER STREET A439

Ely Street

High Street

Chapel Street

Sheep Street

Nest

Waterside

Bancroft Gardens

Royal Shakespeare Theatre

To Anne Hathaway's Cottage

Shottery Road

Brookvale Road

To Race Course

EVESHAM PLACE

Level Crossing

Chestnut Walk

Broad Wk

Broad Street

Narrow Lane

West Lane

Bull Street

College Street

Old Town

Scholars Lane

Chapel Lane

Church Street

Southern Lane

The Other Place

Bowling Club

Avonbank Garden

River Avon

Theatre Gardens

Putting Green

Swans

Bowling Green

Recreation Ground

Cricket Ground

Childrens Playground

A34

BANBURY ROAD A422

BANBURY

EVESHAM ROAD A439

Orchard Way

Sanctus Road

Sanctus Street

College Lane

Mill Lane

Lock & Weirs

SHIPSTON ROAD A34

BRIDGE TOWN

Hunts Road

Bridge town Road

Shelly Road

Byron Road

Keats Road

School

A46 & BROADWAY

SCALE

yds 0   220   440
mtrs 0   200   400

B(8) Tourist Information Centre – St Peter's
Church, St Peter's Way (see also public
buildings and places of interest)

Public buildings and places of interest

E(1) Central Museum, Art Gallery and Library
Contains examples of local lustre-ware,
pottery, glassware, a collection of
15th- to 19th-C silver, models of
Sunderland-built ships, archaeology,
natural history, local history, period
rooms and 19th- to 20th-C paintings.

H(2) Civic Centre and Town Hall A modern
building of interesting design, opened
in 1970.

F(3) Holy Trinity Church This church dates
from the 18thC.

A(4) Monkwearmouth Station Museum One of
the best examples of Victorian railway
architecture, designed by Thomas Moore
of Sunderland in 1848. Re-opened as a
land transport museum in 1971, it
contains a restored Victorian booking
office complete with figures of clerks
and passengers, and a collection
relating to the social and industrial
history of Sunderland.

D(5) National Museum of Music Hall Empire
Theatre. Contains a small, reconstructed
Edwardian music hall together with an
array of posters, playbills, costumes
etc.

D(6) Recreational Centre Features of this
new building will include an ice rink,
indoor bowling green and fun pool with
artificial waves.

D(7) St Michael's Church Largely a
rebuilding of the 19th- and 20th-Cs
in a modified Perpendicular style, but
preserves fragments of stonework,
dating back to the 13thC including an
effigy in the south aisle.

**B(8) St Peter's Church and Tourist
Information Centre** Originally part of
a monastic foundation of AD674, of which
only the Saxon tower (60ft) and West
Wall remain. The remainder of the
church was rebuilt in the 19thC. The
octagonal chapter house was built in
1974 to mark the 13th centenary and

contains tourist information and a
display illustrating the history of
the church.

Fulwell Windmill This famous landmark, now fully
restored, is the only complete windmill in the
North East. 1¾m N via Newcastle Road A19 (A)

Grindon Library Museum Grindon Lane.
Edwardian period rooms and shop interiors.
2¾m W via Chester Road A183(D)

Hylton Castle (AM) The well-preserved shell of a
15th-C tower-house castle. 2½m W via Southwick
Road B1289 (A) then the Sunderland Airport
Road A1290

Ryhope Engines Museum Housed in the Ryhope
Pumping Station, one of the finest industrial
monuments of mid-Victorian times, are two
restored beam engines and a museum illustrating
varied aspects of water supply and use. Open
weekends only. 3m S via Ryhope Road A19 (H)

Seaburn Ocean Park and Amusement Centre
2m NE via Dame Dorothy Street and Whitburn
Road A183 (B)

Fulwell Windmill

Hospitals

D Royal Infirmary, New Durham
Road tel 56256
Children's Hospital, New Durham Road tel 56256
1½m SW via New Durham Road A690 (G)
Eye Infirmary, Queen Alexandra Road tel 60811
1½m S via Ryhope Road A19 (H) then Sea View
Road and Queen Alexandra Road
General Hospital, Chester Road tel 56256
1¼m W via Chester Road A183 (D)
Orthopaedic and Accident Hospital, Newcastle
Road tel 70031 1m N via Newcastle Road A19 (A)

Sport and Recreation

D(6) Recreational Centre, (see also public
buildings and places of interest)
D Swimming Pool, High Street West
Mecca Bowling Centre, Newcastle Road ¾m N via
Newcastle Road A19 (A)
Sunderland Association Football Club, Roker Park
Ground 1¼m N via Roker Avenue (B) Gladstone
Street and Roker Park Road
Sunderland Cricket and Rugby Football Club,
Ashbrooke Ground 1¼m S via Tunstall Road
Swimming Pool, Newcastle Road ¾m N via
Newcastle Road A19 (A)

Theatres and Cinemas

D ABC Cinema, Holmeside tel 74148
D(5) Empire (Civic) Theatre, High Street
West tel 73274 (see also public
buildings and places of interest)
D Odeon Theatre (Cinema), Holmeside
tel 74881
E Studios 1 and 2, Sans Street tel 76317

Department Stores

Binns Ltd, Fawcett Street
Joplings Ltd, John Street
Marks and Spencer Ltd, 77 High Street West
Thompson W C Ltd, Liverpool House, High
Street West
Early closing day Wednesday

Markets

D Covered Market, Shopping Centre (daily)

Advertisers

E Mercantile Credit

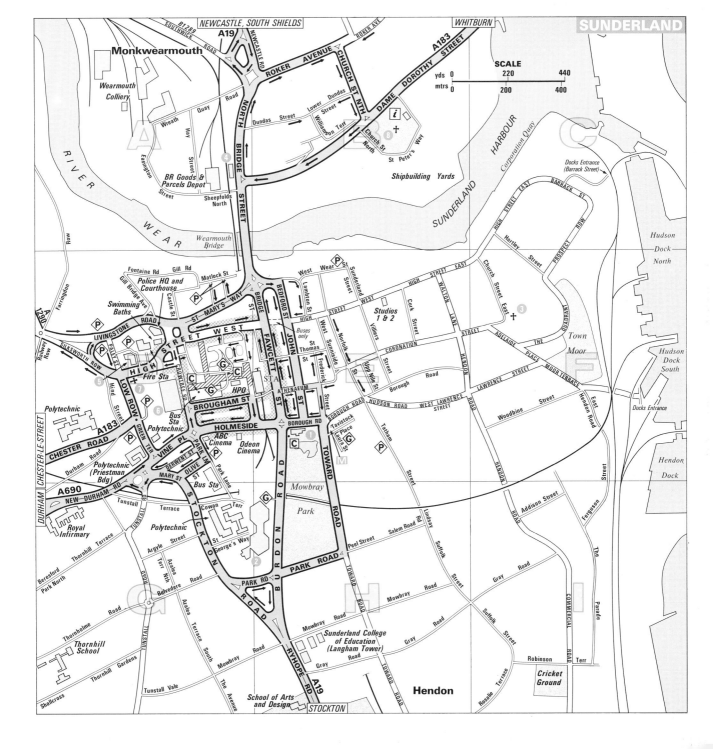

SWANSEA

K AA Road Service Centre (111) — Greenfield Street Car Park *tel 55598*
J(3) Tourist Information Centre — Civic Centre *tel 50821* (see also public buildings and places of interest)

Public buildings and places of interest

H(1) **Castle** There are slight remains of this 14th-C castle or fortified manor house.
H(2) **Central Library**
J(3) **Civic Centre** A handsome white building, housing the Guildhall, Law Courts and Brangwyn Hall used for concerts and dances, and noted for the 20-ft high British Empire Panels painted by the Welsh artist Frank Brangwyn RA.
H(4) **Glynn Vivian Art Gallery** Contains notable collections of Continental and local Swansea and Nantgarw pottery and porcelain; Old masters of the British, French and Italian schools; and contemporary British works of art.
J(5) **Patti Pavilion** Dances and varied seasonal entertainments take place here.
L(6) **Royal Institution of South Wales Museum** Founded in 1875 with exhibits including local antiquarian and archaeological finds; Swansea and Nantgarw china; a reconstruction of a 19th-C Gower kitchen; and industrial exhibits including machinery from local steel, copper and aluminium plants and a small steam locomotive.
K(7) **St Mary's Church** The largest church in Swansea, rebuilt in 1847, and restored again after severe war damage in 1941. It possesses unique carvings and some fine stained glass.
I **Univesity College of Swanseas**

Hospitals

C **Mount Pleasant Hospital** *tel 55882*

Sport and Recreation

K **Swansea City Association Football Club,** Vetch Field
I **Swansea Rugby Football and County Cricket Club,** St Helen's Ground
J **Victoria Swimming Baths**

Blackpill Municipal Golf Course. 2¼m W via Mumbles Road A4067 (I)
Swansea Greyhound Stadium, Ystrad Road, Fforesach. 3¾m NW via Carmarthen Road A483 (D) and Ystrad Road A470

Theatres and Cinemas

G **Albert Hall Cinema,** Craddock Street *tel 54576*
G **Carlton Cinema,** Oxford Street *tel 54596*
H **Castle Cinema,** Worcester Place *tel 53433*
K **Grand Theatre,** Singleton Street *tel 55141*
G **Odeon Cinema,** The Kingsway *tel 52351*

Department Stores

Co-operative, Oxford Street
David Evans and Co (Swansea) Ltd, Princess Way
Marks and Spencer Ltd, Oxford Street
Early closing day Thursday

Markets

G **Covered Market,** Oxford Street (Saturday)

Advertisers

G **Mercantile Credit**
G **THF** Dragon Hotel

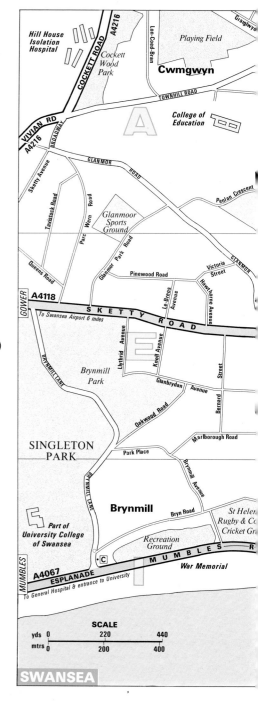

206

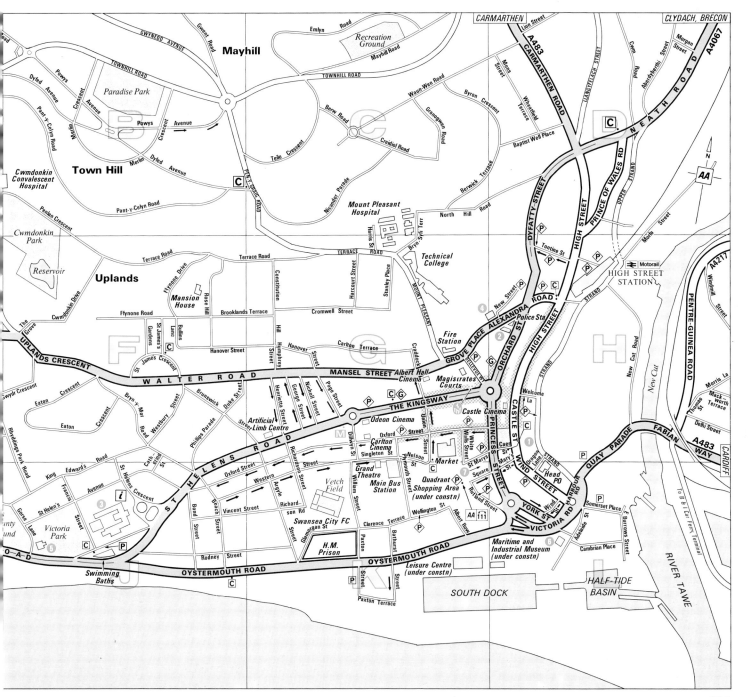

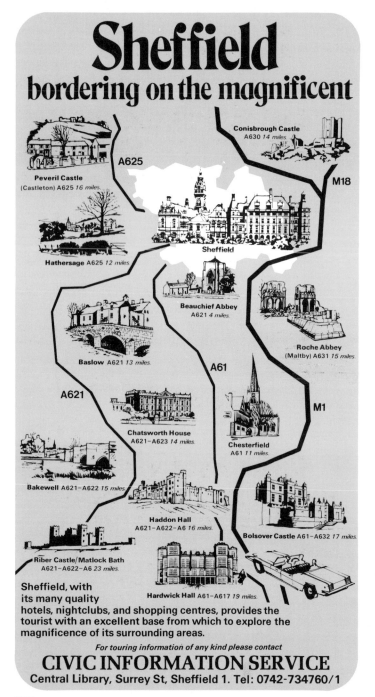

Sheffield
bordering on the magnificent

Conisbrough Castle
A630 *14 miles*

A625

M18

Peveril Castle
(Castleton) A625 *16 miles*

Sheffield

Hathersage A625 *12 miles*

Beauchief Abbey
A621 *4 miles*

Roche Abbey
(Maltby) A631 *15 miles*

Baslow A621 *13 miles*

A61

A621

Chatsworth House
A621–A623 *14 miles*

Chesterfield
A61 *11 miles*

M1

Bakewell A621–A622 *15 miles*

Haddon Hall
A621–A622–A6 *16 miles*

Bolsover Castle A61–A632 *17 miles*

Riber Castle/Matlock Bath
A621–A622–A6 *23 miles*

Hardwick Hall A61–A617 *19 miles*

Sheffield, with
its many quality
hotels, nightclubs, and shopping centres, provides the
tourist with an excellent base from which to explore the
magnificence of its surrounding areas.

For touring information of any kind please contact
CIVIC INFORMATION SERVICE
Central Library, Surrey St, Sheffield 1. Tel: 0742-734760/1

AA Road Service Centre (106) — Drakes Way
tel 21446 1¼m NE via Drakes Way A420 (H)

F *i*   **Tourist Information Centre** — Brunel
Centre *tel 26161*

Public buildings and places of interest

K(1) **Christ Church** This church, situated in
the old town, dates from the 19thC.

G(2) **Civic Offices** Thamesdown District
Council.

F(3) **Great Western Railway Museum and
Railway Village** Opened in 1962, the
museum contains the famous *City of
Truro, Lode Star* and *North Star* and
exhibits a wide range of nameplates,
models, illustrations, posters and
tickets. The Railway Village adjacent
to the locomotive work has survived
and is being restored.

O(4) **Museum and Art Gallery** Housed in the
19th-C Apsley House, the museum
contains collections of items of local
interest. The Art Gallery exhibits pictures
by 20th-C artists including Moore, Piper,
Sutherland, Grant, Bevan and Lowry.
There are also visiting exhibitions.

B(5) **Oasis Leisure Complex** An impressive
sports complex opened in 1975.

B(6) **Technical College** and new extension.

K(7) **Town Hall and Public Library**

K(8) **Wyvern Theatre and Arts Centre** Opened
in 1971 the Wyvern Theatre and Arts
Centre houses a fully-equipped theatre
and an auditorium seating over 600
people. The Arts Centre floor includes
meeting rooms and a Studio Theatre.

Hospitals

M   **Princess Margaret Hospital**, Okus Road
tel 36231

N   **Victoria Hospital**, Okus Road *tel 36231*

Sport and Recreation

H   **County Cricket Ground**, County Road
F   **Milton Road Swimming Baths**
B(5) **Oasis Leisure Centre** (see also public
buildings and places of interest)
H   **Swindon Town Football Club**, Shrivenham
Road
Blunsdon Greyhound and Speedway Stadium,
3½m N via Cricklade Road A345 (C)

Theatres and Cinemas

K   **ABC Cinema**, Regent Street *tel
22838*
O   **Arts Centre**, Devizes Road *tel
27211 ext 23*
K   **The Wyvern Theatre and Arts Centre**,
Theatre Square *tel 24481* (see also public
buildings and places of interest)

Department Stores

Debenhams Ltd, The Parade
Marks and Spencer Ltd, 85 Regent Street
Early closing day Wednesday

Markets

J   **Market Hall** (Monday to Saturday)

Advertisers

F   **Mercantile Credit**
F   **Godfrey Davis**

Great Western Railway Museum

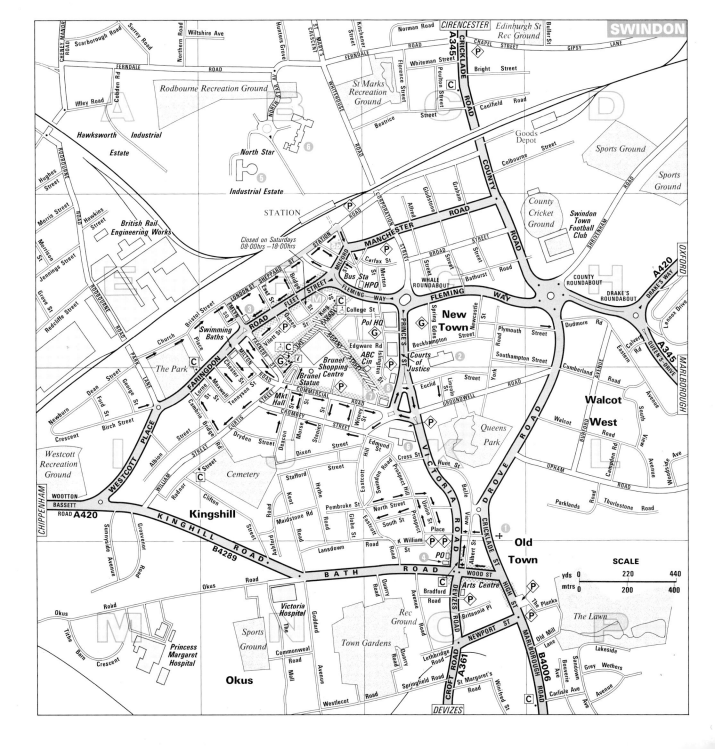

TORQUAY

L	**AA Road Service Centre** – Victoria Parade *tel 25903*
G i	**Tourist Information Centre** – Vaughan Parade *tel 27428*

Public buildings and places of interest

L(1)	**Aquarium,** Beacon Quay
H(2)	**Natural History Museum** Contains items on local archaeology, natural history and the folk life of Devon.
J(3)	**Torre Abbey and Gardens** An 18th-C house which contains the Corporation Art Gallery and interesting furniture. In the grounds are a 12th-C tithe barn and ruins of the abbey.
F(4)	**Town Hall and Library**

Kents Cavern Prehistoric stalactite and stalagmite caves of interest and natural beauty At Wellswood 1m NE via Babbacombe Road B3199 (H)

Hospitals

C	**Rosehill Children's Hospital,** Lower Warberry Road *tel 22570*

Torbay Hospital Lawes Bridge *tel 64567* 2m NW via Newton Road A380 (A)

Sport and Recreation

L	**Beacon Leisure & Entertainment Centre**
J	**Torquay Athletic Rugby Football Club,** Recreation Ground
J	**Torquay Cricket Club,** Recreation Ground
F	**Torquay Lawn Tennis Club,** Belgrave Road
B	**Torquay Tenpin Bowling,** Higher Union Street
L	**Royal Torbay Yacht Club,** Beacon Hill

Torquay United Association Football Club, Plainmoor 1¼m N via Bronshill Road (B)

Theatres and Cinemas

G	**ABC Cinema,** Castle Circus *tel 22004*
G	**Colony Cinema,** Union Street *tel 22146*
G	**Odeon Cinema,** Abbey Road *tel 22324*
K	**Pavilion Theatre** *tel 23251*
K	**Princess Theatre** *tel 27527*

Department Stores

Debenhams, 14 The Strand
Dingles of Torquay, Fleet Street
Early closing day Wednesday (higher part of town) and Saturday

Markets

G	**Market Hall,** Market Street

Advertisers

H	**Mercantile Credit**
B	**Godfrey Davis**
L	**THF** Imperial Hotel

Inner harbour

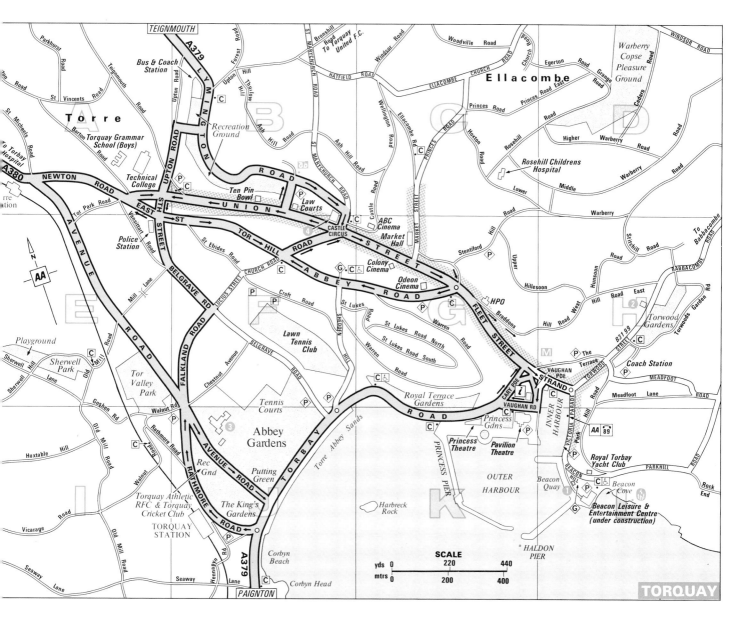

TORQUAY

213

WINCHESTER

Breakdown Service *tel Southampton 36811*

K [i] **Tourist Information Centre** — City Offices, Colebrook Street *tel 68166* weekdays, *65406* weekends

Public buildings and places of interest

K(1) **Abbey House and Gardens** The public gardens occupy the site of St Mary's Abbey, a Benedictine nunnery founded by Alfred the Great's wife in the latter part of the 19thC. The Abbey House, built about 1748 has been used since 1892 as the official residence of the Mayors of Winchester.

F(2) **Castle Hall** At present used as law courts, the 13th-C aisled Hall is all that remains of the castle. The reputed Round Table of King Arthur hangs on the west wall.

K(3) **Cathedral and Close** The second longest cathedral in Europe, it was begun in 1079 and finished in 1404. The many notable features include the splendid nave, the chantry chapels, carved 14th-C stalls, the 15th-C reredos, and a 12th-C black-marble Tournai font. The tombs of Izaak Walton and Jane Austen lie in the cathedral. In the Close are many old buildings, notably the Pilgrims' School with a 13th-C Hall, and the Tudor Cheyney Court.

G(4) **City Cross** Known locally as 'Butter Cross', this 15th-C High Cross was partially restored in 1865.

L(5) **City Mill (NT)** Built in 1774 this watermill is now occupied by the Youth Hostels' Association.

K(6) **City Museum** Contains displays relating to the archaeology and history of the city and central Hampshire.

K(7) **The Deanery,** Cathedral Close. A 13th-C and later house.

G(8) **Godbegot House** A picturesque, restored half-timbered building of Tudor date.

K(9) **Guildhall and Picture Gallery** Built in 1873, the Picture Gallery in the west wing of the Guildhall displays local prints, drawings and loan exhibitions.

C(10) **Hyde Abbey Gatehouse (AM)** The 15th-C gatehouse is all that remains of Hyde Abbey.

K(11) **King Alfred Statue** The bronze statue of Alfred the Great who held his court at Winchester, was erected in 1901.

G(12) **Old Guildhall** An 18th-C building with a projecting clock. Now in use as a bank.

F(13) **Plague Monument** Erected in memory of the plague of 1666, the monument dates from 1759.

F(14) **Royal Greenjackets Regimental Museum** Displays relating to the history of the regiment, including weapons, regimental silver, colours and banners.

J(15) **Royal Hampshire Regimental Museum,** Serle's House. The museum is housed in the reception hall on the ground floor of this 18th-C house.

H(16) **St John the Baptist Church** A 12th-C church with a 15th-C tower and old screenwork.

K(17) **St John's Hospital and Chapel** Founded in the 13th-C, the buildings are now mainly 18th- and 19th-C with some traces of the medieval building in the chapel.

F(18) **Westgate Museum** Small, civic museum housed above the Westgate.

K(19) **Winchester College** Founded in 1382 by William of Wykeham, this is one of England's oldest public schools. The Chapel and Tower, the Old School and the Fromond Chantry Chapel are all of interest.

K(20) **Wolvesey Castle** Remains of the mid-12th-C castle of Bishop Henry de Blois. Nearby stands the surviving wing of the present 17th-C Bishop's Palace, built by Wren with a late Tudor chapel.

St Cross Hospital 1¼m S via St Cross Road A333. Founded in 1136 by Bishop Henry de Blois, little remains of the original structure as most of the hospital was rebuilt by Cardinal Beaufort in the 15thC **(N)**.

Hospitals

I **Royal Hampshire County Hospital,** Romsey Road *tel 63535*

F **St Paul's Hospital,** St Paul's Hill *tel 3288*

Victoria Hospital, Alresford Road *tel 2048* 1¼m E via Magdalen Hill B3404 **(H)**

Sport and Recreation

I **Winchester City FC,** Airlie Road

C **Winchester Recreation Centre,** North Walls Recreation Ground — swimming, bowls, cricket, football, putting green, tennis

A **Winchester Tennis and Squash Club,** Bereweeke Road

Royal Winchester Golf Club, Sarum Road 1½m W via Romsey Road A3090 then Sarum Road **(I)**

Theatres and Cinemas

G **Studios 1, 2, and 3** North Walls *tel 2592*

Department Stores

The Co-operative, 8 High Street
Debenhams Ltd, 12/15 and 103/104 High Street
Marks and Spencer Ltd, 138 High Street
Early closing day Thursday

Markets

G **Friarsgate,** general (Wednesday)
G **Park Avenue,** antiques (Wednesday)
F **Stockbridge Road,** general (Wednesday/Saturday)
B **Worthy Lane,** cattle (Monday)

Advertisers

K **THF** Wessex Hotel

Godbegot House

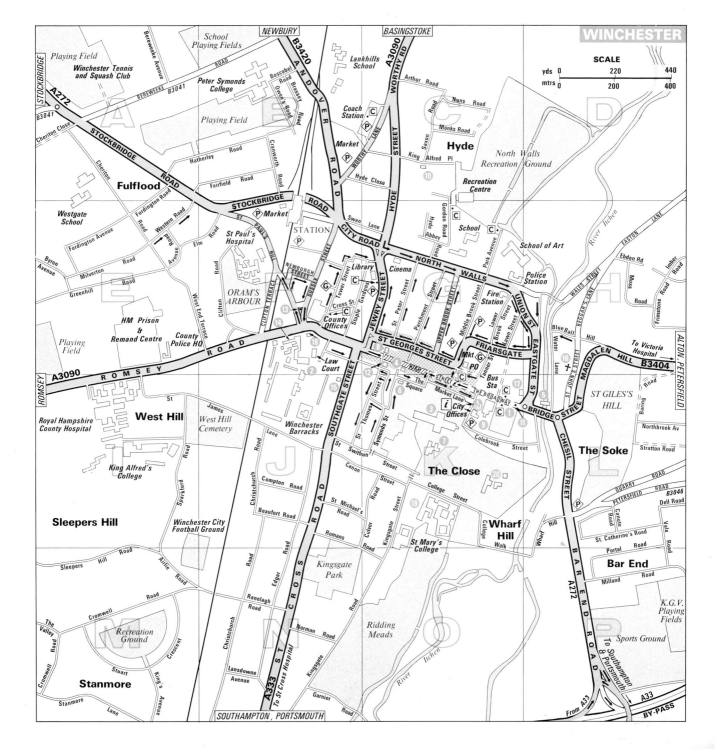

WINDSOR AND ETON

G [i] **Tourist Information Centre** — Windsor Central Station *tel 52010* (summer only)

Public buildings and places of interest

F(1) **Clewer Parish Church** Completed c1100, with the exception of the Chantry Chapel, which was added c1380 by Sir Bernard Brocas.

K(2) **East Berkshire College of Further Education**

C(3) **Eton College** This famous Public School, second oldest in the country, was founded in 1440 by Henry VI, a statue of whom stands in the cobbled School Yard. Buildings of particular interest are the chapel, an impressive example of Perpendicular architecture, and Lupton's Tower of c1517. The Library of 1729 includes the original of Gray's *Elegy Written in a Country Churchyard* and a copy of the Guttenberg Bible.

C(4) **Eton Parish Church** The present building dates from the mid 19thC and contains a handsome corona of Italian style in the chancel and parish registers dating back to 1594.

N(5) **Household Cavalry Museum,** Combermore Barracks. One of the finest military museums in Britain, with exhibits dating from the Monmouth Rebellion (1685) to the present day.

G(6) **King George V Memorial**

K(7) **Nell Gwynne's House** Dates from c1670.

G(8) **Old House Hotel** Dates from the late 17thC.

G(9) **Our Lady of Sorrows Church (RC)** This church in Italian Renaissance style is a perfect miniature of a Roman basilica.

G(10) **Queen Victoria Statue**

G(11) **Theatre Royal** This playhouse dates from 1793.

G(12) **The Cock Pit** A half-timbered building probably dating from 1420, now used as a restaurant. Inside are a knucklebone cockpit floor, and spurs and hood used in this sport, and outside are the parish stocks, whipping post and a 100-year-old pillar box, one of the three surviving originals.

G(13) **The Guildhall** A classical building of c1689 designed by Sir Thomas Fitz,

and completed by Sir Christopher Wren. It contains a museum of local historical and archaeological items, and a collection of Royal portraits.

H(14) **Windsor Castle** This famous Royal castle was built by William the Conqueror, and restored with large 19th-C additions for George IV by Wyatville. There are fine State Apartments and Queen Mary's Doll's House is of interest. St George's Chapel is a splendid fan-vaulted

Eton College

Perpendicular building containing Royal Tombs; in the choir are the stalls and brasses of the Garter Knights. The restored Albert Memorial Chapel was erected originally by Henry VII. The Home Park contains the Frogmore Mausoleum, with Queen Victoria's tomb.

G(15) **Windsor Parish Church**

Windsor Great Park Beautifully wooded and covering some 4,800 acres. The eastern fringe of the park contains the beautiful woodland Savill Gardens and nearby Valley Gardens is Virginia Water, one of the largest artificial lakes in England, reached by way of Englefield Green. 4m SE via Albert Road A308 (P)

Windsor Safari Park Once a royal hunting ground and now a drive-in zoo with lion and cheetah reserves and Dolphinarium. 3m SW via Winkfield Road B3022 (M)

Hospitals

O **King Edward VII Hospital,** St Leonards Road *tel 60441*

Sport and Recreation

H **Old Windsorians Rugby Football Club,** Home Park, Datchett Road

A **Royal Windsor Racecourse**

F **Swimming Pool,** Stovell Road

N **Windsor and Eton Football Club,** St Leonard's Road

H **Windsor Rovers Football Club,** Home Park

H **Windsor Rugby Football Club,** Home Park

H **Windsor Victorian Cricket Club,** Home Park

Theatres and Cinemas

G **ABC Cinema,** 59 Thames Street *tel 63888*

G(11) **Theatre Royal** *tel 61107* (see also public buildings and places of interest)

Department Stores

Caleys, 19 High Street

Daniel W J & Co Ltd, 120 Peascod Street

Early closing day Wednesday

Advertisers

K **Crest** Royal Adelaide Hotel

K **THF** Castle Hotel

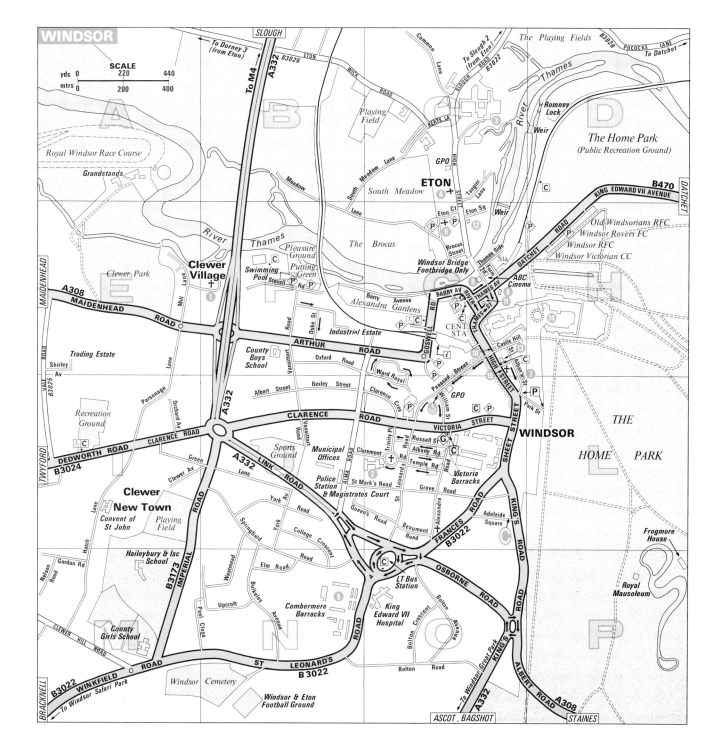

K   AA Service Centre — 19 The Gallery, Mander Square *tel 021-550 4858*

Public buildings and places of interest

K(1)   **Art Gallery** Contains a comprehensive collection including 18th- and 19th-C watercolours and oil paintings; modern prints, paintings and drawings; sculpture; Oriental art; and antiquities.

J(2)   **Civic Hall** A fine, modern building opened in 1938, containing a concert hall with seating capacity for over 1,750.

O(3) **St George's Church** This church was rebuilt in 1830.

O(4) **St John's Church** An 18th-C church, with fine 17th-C organ.

K(5) **St Peter's Church** A fine, mainly- 15th-C church, with a tall, panelled tower; an octagonal font; and notable carved pulpit. In the churchyard are the so-called 'Bargaining' stones and a very early carved cross-shaft.

J(6)   **Town Hall; Information Bureau**
Bantock House Museum Contains an important collection of English painted enamels and early Worcestershire porcelain; local japanned ware and cut steel work; pottery; local history; and English and foreign dolls. 1¼m SW in Bantock Park via Merridale Road (I).

Hospitals

K   **Chest Clinic**, Bell Street *tel 21180*
P   **Royal Hospital**, Cleveland Road *tel 51532*
I   **Wolverhampton and Midland Counties Eye Infirmary**, Compton Road *tel 26731*
E   **Women's Hospital**, Park Road West *tel 26731*

Sport and Recreation

O   **Ambassador Bowling Centre**, Birmingham Road
F   **Central Swimming Baths**, Bath Avenue
E   **West Park** (Boating, tennis etc). The annual Wolverhampton Fiesta is held here
F   **Wolverhampton Wanderer's Football Club**, Molineux Ground

Theatres and Cinemas

K   **ABC Cinema**, Garrick Street *tel 22917*
K   **Grand Theatre**, Lichfield Street *tel 25244*
J   **Odeon Cinema**, Skinner Street *tel 20364*

Department Stores

Beattie James Ltd, Victoria Street
Bedford Williams Ltd, 11 Mander Square
Marks and Spencer Ltd, 19 Dudley Street
Owen Owen Ltd, Mander Centre
Rackmans, Snow Hill

Markets

N   **Open Market** (Tuesday, Wednesday, Friday and Saturday)
J   **Retail Market Hall** (Daily)

Advertisers

J   **Mercantile Credit**

Bantock House

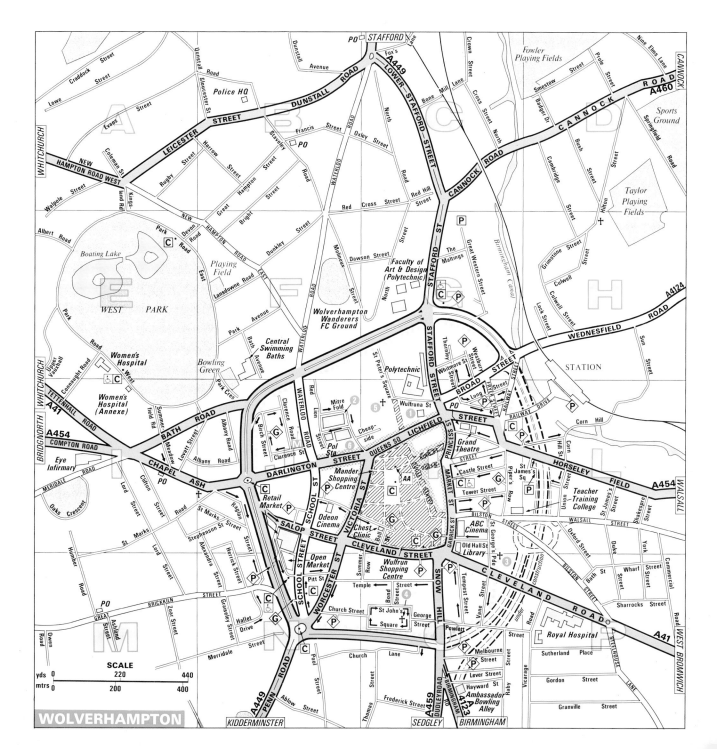

WOLVERHAMPTON

WORCESTER

B   **AA Road Service Centre (23)** — on A449 3m N of City Centre *tel 51070*

J(8)   **Tourist Information Centre** — Guildhall *tel 23471* (see also public buildings and places of interest)

Public buildings and places of interest

J(1)   **All Saints Church** A beautiful Georgian church of 1742, containing a rare chained bible of 1608.

F(2)   **Britannia House** An 18th-C building, now used as a school.

N(3)   **Cathedral** A 13th- to 15th-C building, preserving its original 11th-C crypt. Of special interest are the restored 14th-C tower; the choir stalls of 1379; Prince Arthur's Chantry: the effigy of King John — the earliest of its kind in England — and the Crypt Exhibition illustrating the history of the cathedral from monastic times.

F(4)   **City Museum, Art Gallery and Library** (Victoria Institute). Exhibits cover local history, archaeology, geology and natural history. Also collections of the Worcestershire Regiment and the Worcestershire Yeomanry Cavalry.

O(5)   **Commandery** Noted for its 15th-C Great Hall and interesting mural paintings. It was the headquarters of King Charles II at the Battle of Worcester in 1651.

O(6)   **Edgar Tower** A 14th-C gateway.

K(7)   **Greyfriars (NT)** A half-timbered house dating from c1480, with early fireplaces, panelling and other features of its period.

J(8)   **Guildhall and Tourist Information Centre** A notable restored 18th-C building in Georgian style, with wings added later. Paintings and armour on show.

K(9)   **King Charles House** A timber-framed house, from whence Charles II escaped from his enemies after the Battle of Worcester on 3 September 1651.

N(10)   **King's School** A foundation of 1541 housed in buildings dating from the 14thC.

O(11)   **Royal Porcelain Works Museum** Contains the world's finest collection of Worcester china. Tours of the factory can be arranged.

J(12)   **St Andrew's Church** A 12th- and 15th-C church of which only the tower and spire (245ft high) now remains.

K(13)   **St Swithun's Church** A fine Georgian church of 1736, features of which are the woodwork; the three-decker pulpit surmounted by a carved and gilded pelican, with the Mayor's chair built in beneath; wrought iron altar; and 17th-C organ.

F(14)   **Shire Hall** A classical style building of the Ionic order, with statue of Queen Victoria in the courtyard. The County Council meetings and courts are held here.

K(15)   **Tudor House** A 500 year-old timber-framed house, now a museum of local domestic life from Tudor to Victorian times.

Spetchley Park Fine gardens and park, with red and fallow deer, surrounding early 19th-C mansion. 3m E via London Road A44 and A422 (P)

Hospitals

L   **Ronkswood Hospital** *tel 356123*

L   **Shrub Hill Hospital** *tel 27122*, Maternity Unit *tel 22660*

B   **Worcester Eye Hospital**, Barbourne Road *tel 24017*

F   **Worcester Royal Infirmary**, Castle Street *tel 27122*

Sport and Recreation

F   **Sansome Walk Baths**

B   **Worcester City Football Ground**, St George's Lane North, Barbourne

J   **Worcester County Cricket Club**, County Ground, New Road

E   **Worcester Racecourse**, Pitchcroft

Worcester Citizens' Swimming Pool, Weir Lane, 1m S via Bromwich Road A449 (M)

Worcester Golf and Country Club, Boughton Park, St John's. 1m W via Bronsford Road A4103 (M)

Theatres and Cinemas

F   **Odeon Cinema**, Foregate Street *tel 24733*

F   **Swan Theatre**, The Moors *tel 27322*

Department Stores

Co-operative, Trinity House, St Nicholas Street

Debenhams, 69 High Street

Marks and Spencer Ltd, 39 High Street

Russell and Dorrell Ltd, 15 High Street

Early closing day Thursday

Markets

J   **Blackfriars Market** (Wednesday, Friday and Saturday)

I   **Fruit and Vegetable Market**, Hylton Road (Daily except Sunday)

K   **General Market**, Market Hall, The Shambles (Monday to Saturday, except Thursday afternoon)

J   **Livestock Market**, The Butts (Monday)

J   **Old 'Sheep' Market**, Angel Street (Saturday)

Advertisers

F   Mercantile Credit

K   THF Giffard Hotel

O   Godfrey Davis

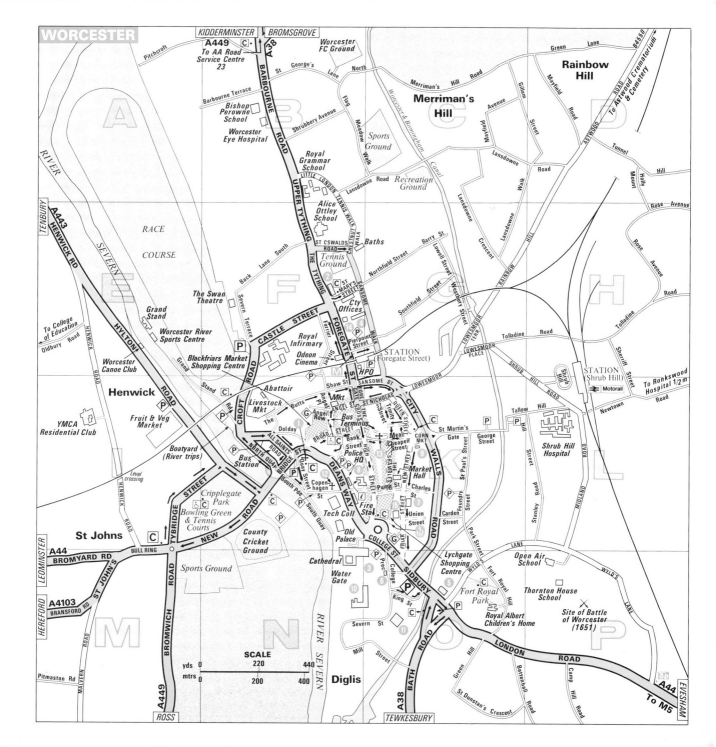

YORK

G   **AA Service Centre** — 6 Church Street
tel 27698

B(51)   **Tourist Information Centre** — De Grey
📋   Rooms, Exhibition Square *tel 21756*
(see also public buildings and places
of interest)

Public buildings and places of interest

F(1)   **All Saints' Church** A late-Norman
church, noted for its slender 120ft
spire and exceptional stained glass
of the 14th and 15thCs.

G(2)   **All Saints' Church,** Pavement. This
church has a fine octagonal lantern
tower and a 15th-C lectern with a
rare chained book.

B(3)   **Art Gallery** Contains interesting
collection of English and European
paintings from the 14th to 20thCs,
in particular the Lycett Green
collection of old masters.

F(4)   **Arts Centre** Formerly St John the
Evangelist church.

B(5)   **Assembly Rooms** An impressive colonnaded
ballroom of 1732-36.

H(6)   **Black Swan Inn** A 15th-C merchant's
house, now an inn, preserving an
interesting room with medieval painted
panels and Delft tile fireplace.

B(7)   **Bootham Bar** One of the medieval city
gates, built on the site of a former
Roman gate, which preserves its
portcullis.

B(8)   **Bootham School** The finest of the
Georgian houses in Bootham.

H(9)   **Borthwick Institute of Historical
Research** Part of the University of
York, housed in St Anthony's Hall, a
guild hall of the 15thC. There is an
exhibition of documents.

K(10)   **Castle Museums and Assize Courts**
The former Debtor's Prison of 1705 and
the Female Prison of 1780 have been
expertly converted to house one of the
most impressive folk museums in the
world. Adjacent are the Assize Courts
of 1777.

B(11)   **Central Library and City Information
Bureau**

G(12)   **Clifford's Tower** A 13th-C quatrefoil
keep, the largest single remnant of

York Castle. The mound, together with
Baile Hill, its twin across the river,
was constructed by William the
Conqueror.

L(13)   **Fishergate Bar** One of the smaller
city gates.

K(14)   **Fishergate Postern Tower** Built c1505
this tower originally stood on the
banks of the River Foss. It affords
good views of the Minster.

F(15)   **Guildhall** The mid-15th-C Commonhall,
completely restored after severe war
damage.

G(16)   **Herbert House** A picturesque half-
timbered Jacobean structure of 1557.

C(17)   **Holy Trinity Church,** Goodramgate. This
13th- to 15th-C church, has a saddle-
back tower and 18th-C box pews.

F(18)   **Holy Trinity Church,** Micklegate. A
fragment of a large Norman Priory
church, with ancient stocks in the
churchyard.

B(19)   **Hospitium** The 15th-C guest-house of
St Mary's Abbey, now a museum of Roman
antiquities.

G(20)   **Impressions Gallery of Photography,**
The Shambles. Displays of photographic
equipment and photographs.

F(21)   **Judges' Lodging** A fine Georgian house
of c1720 (not open).

B(22)   **King's Manor** A Tudor and later house,
with numerous royal connections. Now
part of York University.

F(23)   **Lendal Tower** A riverside tower rebuilt
in the 19thC.

F(24)   **Mansion House** The private residence of
the Lord Mayor, this fine Georgian
building of 1725-30 contains the city's
insignia, regalia and civic plate.

G(25)   **Merchant Adventurers' Hall** A superb
14th- to 15th-C timbered hall of the
town's wealthiest and most influential
medieval guild.

C(26)   **Merchant Taylors' Hall** A restored
medieval guild hall with a fine 14th-C
timbered roof.

F(27)   **Micklegate Bar** The most important of
the city gates, upon which the severed
heads of traitors were once displayed.

C(28)   **Minster** A magnificent structure in the
Early English to Perpendicular styles,

built between c1220 and c1470, famous
for the twin-towered west façade, its
wealth of medieval stained glass, the
octagonal chapter house and 15th-C
choir screen. In the undercroft, where
traces of earlier Roman and Norman
buildings can be seen, is a museum
illustrating the history of the Minster.

C(29)   **Minster Library** A large collection
of ancient books and manuscripts housed
in the 13th-C chapel of the former
Archbishop's Palace.

C(30)   **Monk Bar** The finest of the city's
gates, vaulted on three floors, and
with its portcullis still in working
order.

B(31)   **Multangular Tower,** Yorkshire Museum
Gardens. The west corner tower of the
Roman city, it was rebuilt c300. The
top section is medieval. Part of the
Roman wall extends north-east from
here to the Anglian tower of c600-700.

E(32)   **National Railway Museum** The largest
static collection of historic railway
exhibits in Britain, comprising some 25
locomotives, over 20 items of rolling-
stock and many smaller relics.

C(33)   **Old Starre Inn** The city's oldest pub,
in use as such from at least 1644. It
displays a rare beam, or gallow's sign.

H(34)   **Red Tower** Dating from 1490, it is the
only substantial brick-built section of
the wall.

G(35)   **Roman Baths Inn** A modern pub which ha
extensive remains of a Roman steam bath.

H(36)   **St Cuthbert's Church** After the Minster
this is York's oldest church, founded
in 687.

H(37)   **St Deny's Church** Noted for its richly-
carved Norman doorway, and 12th-C
glass, some of the oldest in York.

G(38)   **St Helen's Church** Dating from the
14thC, it is the civic church of York.
It contains 15th-C glass.

B(39)   **St Leonard's Hospital** Remains of an
11th-C and later building, founded
by Canons from York Minster.

H(40)   **St Margaret's Church** Although rebuilt
in 1852, this church retains a
magnificent Norman porch.

Continued on page 224

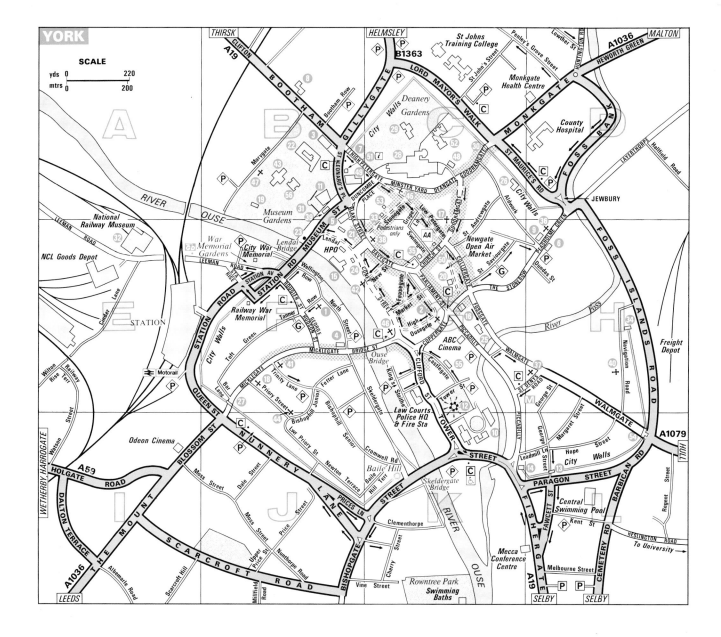

YORK

SCALE

yds 0 ——————— 220
mtrs 0 ——————— 200

THIRSK
A19 CLIFTON
BOOTHAM

HELMSLEY
B1363
LORD MAYOR'S WALK
GILLYGATE

St Johns Training College
Penley's Grove Street
Lowther St
HUNTINGTON RD
A1036 MALTON
HEWORTH GREEN

Monkgate Health Centre
MONKGATE

St John's Street
Deanery Gardens
City Walls

County Hospital
FOSS BANK

Laverthorpe
Hatfield Road

JEWBURY

St MAURICE'S RD
City Walls

RIVER OUSE

National Railway Museum
LEEMAN ROAD

NCL Goods Depot

Museum Gardens

Minster Yard
DEANGATE
GOODRAMGATE

Low Petergate
St Andrewgate
Aldwark
City Walls

FOSS ISLANDS ROAD

War Memorial Gardens
City War Memorial
Lendal Bridge
MUSEUM ST

HIGH PETERGATE
DUNCOMBE PLACE

Stonegate
Grape Ln
AA
Newgate Open Air Market
St Saviourgate

River FOSS

Freight Depot

LEEMAN ROAD
STATION RISE
STATION AV
STATION RD

Wellington Row
North Street

DAVYGATE
New St
COLLIERGATE

Dundas St

THE STONEBOW

Navigation Road

STATION

Railway War Memorial
GEORGE ST
HUDSON ST
Tanner Row

Feasegate
Market
High Ousegate

PARLIAMENT ST
PAVEMENT

PICCADILLY

Motorail

City Walls
Toft Green
Bar Lane

MICKLEGATE
BRIDGE ST
Ouse Bridge
COPPERGATE
Castlegate
TOWER ST

WALMGATE

George St
Margaret Street
Hope St
Regent Street
A1079 HULL

Odeon Cinema
BLOSSOM ST
A59 HOLGATE ROAD

MICKLEGATE
Trinity Lane
Priory Street
Bishophill Junior
Bishophill Senior
Fetter Lane
Skeldergate

ABC Cinema
King St
Clifford St

PICCADILLY
Leadmill Ln
George St
City Walls

WETHERBY HARROGATE
Watson St
Wilton Rise
Railway Terr
Holgate Hill
THE MOUNT
DALTON TERRACE
A1036

QUEEN ST
NUNNERY LANE
PRICES LN

Lwr Priory St
Cromwell Rd
Newton Terrace

Baile Hill
Skeldergate Bridge

Law Courts Police HQ & Fire Sta

PARAGON STREET
BARBICAN RD
FISHERGATE
A19 SELBY

Central Swimming Pool
Kent St

Melbourne Street

SELBY

Moss Street
Dale Street
Price Street
Upper Price St
Nunthorpe Road
Millfield Road
Scarcroft Hill
Albemarle Road

SCARCROFT ROAD

BISHOPGATE

Clementhorpe
Cherry Street
Vine Street

Rowntree Park Swimming Baths

RIVER OUSE

Mecca Conference Centre
FAWCETT ST
CEMETERY RD
HESLINGTON ROAD
To University

LEEDS A1036

F(41) St Martin-cum-Gregory's Church Now used as the Anglican Youth Centre, this church dates from the early 13thC.

F(42) St Martin-le-Grand's Church Mainly 15thC, but severely damaged during the war, it has been partly rebuilt in a modern style. The remainder is used as a shrine of remembrance.

B(43) St Mary's Abbey, Yorkshire Museum Gardens. Medieval remains of this important Benedictine monastery stand on the foundations of a Norman building founded c1080.

J(44) St Mary's Church, Bishophill Junior. An ancient church, with typical Saxon windows and herringbone work in the tower.

C(45) St Michael-le-Belfry's Church A fine Tudor church of c1536. Guy Fawkes was christened here.

G(46) St Michael's Church, Spurriegate. This ancient church has a beautiful interior with 12th-C arcades.

B(47) St Olave's Church The original church, founded in the 11thC, was used as a gun emplacement in the Civil War. The present building is mainly 18thC.

C(48) St William's College A fine building with timbered façade, dating from 1453. Behind is a picturesque Georgian quadrangle.

B(49) Theatre Royal Although extensively rebuilt in Victorian times, parts of the original building of 1740 survive.

G(50) The Shambles One of the finest preserved medieval streets in Europe.

B(51) Tourist Information Centre, De Grey Rooms A magnificent Regency building of the 1830's with facilities for meetings and conferences.

C(52) Treasurer's House (NT) A 17th-C house, with a fine collection of furniture and works of art.

C(53) Twelth Century House The restored remnant of a Norman dwelling house, situated behind Stonegate.

L(54) Walmgate Bar The only town gate in England to retain its barbican. Also preserved intact are the wooded doors and portcullis.

G(55) York Heritage Centre Formerly the church of St Mary, Castlegate, the centre displays the architectural development of York from past to present.

B(56) Yorkshire Museum, Botanical Gardens and Tempest Anderson Hall The neo-classical building of 1827 contains important archaeological, natural history, geological and Yorkshire pottery collections. Adjacent is the Tempest Anderson lecture hall of 1912. Both set in the beautiful gardens of the former abbey.

St Peter's School One of the earliest foundations in England, dating back to 718. ¾m NW via Clifton A19 (B)

University of York An attractive modern university, opened 1963, which is centred around an artificial lake. Incorporated within the buildings is the Elizabethan Heslington Hall. 1½m SE via Heslington Road (L)

York Tyburn Site of the gallows where John Palmer (alias Dick Turpin) was hanged in 1739. 1¼m SW via The Mount A1036 (I)

St Martin-le-Grand

Hospitals

D   County Hospital, Monkgate *tel 25314*

Sport and Recreation

K   Rowntree Park Swimming Baths, Terry Avenue (open air)

Fulford (York) Golf Club, Heslington Lane 2m S via Fishergate and Fulford Road A19 (L)

Heworth Golf Club, Muncaster House, Malton Road 1m NE via Heworth Green A1036 (D), then Burton Stone Lane

York City Football and Athletic Club, Bootham Crescent Stadium ¾m N via Bootham A19 (B) then Bootham Crescent

York Cricket Club, Clifton Park, Shipton Road 1¼m NW via Clifton A19 (B)

York Race Course 1½m SW via The Mount A1036 (I)

York Rugby League Football Club, Wigginton Road ¾m N via Gillygate and Clarence Street B1363 (C)

York Rugby Union Football Club, Clifton Park, Shipton Road 1¼m NW via Clifton A19 (B)

Theatres and Cinemas

G   ABC Cinema, Piccadilly *tel 24356*

F(4)   Arts Centre, Micklegate *tel 55490* (see also public buildings and places of interest)

I   Odeon Cinema, Blossom Street *tel 23040*

B(49) Theatre Royal, St Leonard's Place *tel 23568* (see also public buildings and places of interest)

Department Stores

Boyes W and Co Ltd, Ousebridge
Debenhams Ltd, 5 Coney Street
Leak and Thorpe, 19 Coney Street
Marks and Spencer Ltd, 9 Pavement
Early closing day Wednesday

Markets

G   Newgate — open air (Monday to Saturday)

Advertisers

G   Mercantile Credit
E   Godfrey Davis